THE ETHICS OF NATIONALISM

THE ETHICS OF NATIONALISM

MARGARET MOORE

OXFORD
UNIVERSITY PRESS

OXFORD

UNIVERSITY PRESS

Great Clarendon Street, Oxford OX2 6DP

Oxford University Press is a department of the University of Oxford.
It furthers the University's objective of excellence in research, scholarship,
and education by publishing worldwide in

Oxford New York

Athens Auckland Bangkok Bogotá Buenos Aires Cape Town
Chennai Dar es Salaam Delhi Florence Hong Kong Istanbul Karachi
Kolkata Kuala Lumpur Madrid Melbourne Mexico City Mumbai
Nairobi Paris São Paulo Singapore Taipei Tokyo Toronto Warsaw

and associated companies in Berlin Ibadan

Oxford is a registered trade mark of Oxford University Press
in the UK and in certain other countries

Published in the United States
by Oxford University Press Inc., New York

British Library Cataloguing in Publication Data

Data available

Library of Congress Cataloging in Publication Data

Moore, Margret, Ph. D.

The ethics of nationalism / Margret Moore.

p. cm.

Includes bibliographical references and index.

1. Nationalism—Moral and ethical aspects. 2. Self-determination, National—Moral
and ethical aspects. 3. Secession—Moral and ethical aspects. I. Title.

JC311 .M586 2001   172—dc21   00-066914
ISBN 0–19–829746–7

1 3 5 7 9 10 8 6 4 2

Typeset by Hope Services (Abingdon) Ltd.
Printed in Great Britain
on acid-free paper by
T. J. International Ltd
Padstow, Cornwall

ACKNOWLEDGEMENTS

I wish to thank a number of people and organizations who have helped me in the course of writing this book.

I began writing this book when I was a Visiting Scholar at Nuffield College, Oxford, in the Hilary Term, 1998. I thank David Miller for inviting me there, and for making my stay so enjoyable and productive. I am also grateful to the other visiting scholars, mainly Ted Carmines, Ariana Need, and Aage Sorensen, and the bright Ph.D. students and post-doctoral fellows I met there, who engaged me in helpful conversations about my project.

I have received written comments from a number of people on some or all of this text, which I found enormously helpful. For this, I am grateful to Rainer Bauböck, Avigail Eisenberg, Paul Groarke, Krishan Kumar, Patti Lenard, Ian Lustick, John McGarry, David Miller, Geneviève Nootens, Wayne Norman, Brendan O'Leary, Alan Patten, Jeff Spinner-Halev, and the four anonymous reviewers for Oxford University Press. Of course, the usual disclaimer applies.

A number of people have engaged with me on a number of points, usually in a paper-given venue, or at dinner or drinks afterward, and helped me to sharpen my argument. In addition to the people listed above, who sometimes did this—in addition to written comments—I would like to take this opportunity to thank Ronnie Beiner, Julie Bernier, Allen Buchanan, John Charvet, Jocelyne Couture, Denise Helly, Michael Keating, Will Kymlicka, Jacob Levy, Steven Lukes, Colin Macleod, Kai Nielsen, Daniel Philpott, Michel Seymour, Yael Tamir, Daniel Weinstock, Jonathan Wolff, and Bernie Yack.

On the financial side, I am grateful to the Social Sciences and Humanities Research Council of Canada for a research grant that helped defray the many expenses that are connected to research and book-writing of this kind.

Books require publishers and presses, and I am particularly fortunate to have dealt with Dominic Byatt from the very beginnings of this book to the end, who was understanding when the manuscript was delayed, and encouraged me first to write it and then to finish it. I am also grateful to Amanda Watkins, the Managing Editor in Politics for OUP, who helped negotiate the book through all its stages, and Mark Taylor, for carefully copy-editing and improving the text.

I have been to a number of conferences and presented papers relevant to this project, some of which are early drafts of chapters of this book. I received helpful comments and criticisms at two Annual Meetings of the American Political Science Association in San Francisco and Boston (1996 and 1998) respectively; the University of Wales Gregynog conference, September 1997; the conference on Minority Nationalism and the Changing State Order, at the University of Western Ontario, November, 1997; Nuffield College Political Philosophy workshop at Oxford in January, 1998; the London School of Economics Department of Government seminar in February, 1998; Conference on Mondialisation, Multiculturalisme et Citoyenneté, Université du Quebec à Montreal, March, 1998; the Nationality, Citizenship and Solidarity conference, Université de Montreal, May, 1998; the Annual Meeting of the Society for the Study of Social and Political Thought in Madison, Wisconsin in November, 1998; the University of Western Ontario secession conference, April, 1999; the Ethikon Society, which hosted a conference on Boundaries in Venice, July, 1999; the Carnegie Corporations' conference on boundaries and the changing state order September 30–October 1, 1999; and a talk at the University of Victoria, BC, February, 2000. I thank Howard Williams of the University of Wales at Aberystwyth; David Miller of Nuffield College, Oxford; John Charvet, the LSE; Denise Helly, the Université du Quebec à Montreal; Michel Seymour, Université de Montreal; Bernie Yack, University of Wisconsin at Madison; Michael Keating and Michael Milde, University of Western Ontario; Philip Valera of the Ethikon Institute; and Avigail Eisenberg, University of Victoria, for extending invitations to these various conferences and talks, and to the audiences at these talks for their insights and criticisms.

Earlier versions of some of the chapters were also published in other venues. I am grateful to the following journals and books for permission to use the material here. An early version of some of the ideas contained in this book were published as 'On National Self-Determination', *Political Studies* 45/5 (December 1997), 900–13. A version of some of the ideas contained in Chapters 2,3, and 4 were published as 'Liberal Nationalist Arguments, Ambivalent Conclusions', *The Monist* 82/3 (July, 1999), 469–90. This article was also reprinted in Nenad Miscevic, (ed.), *Nationalism and Ethnic Conflict* (Chicago, IL: Open Court Publishers, 2000). Part of Chapter 3 has been published in 'Beyond the Cultural Argument for Liberal Nationalism', *Critical Review of International Social and Political Philosophy*, 2/3 (Autumn 1999), 26–47. An early version of part of

Chapter 4 is published as 'Normative Justifications for Nationalism; Justice, Democracy and National Identity', *Nations & Nationalism* (January 2001). An early version of parts of Chapters 6 and 7 appeared as 'The Territorial Dimension of Self-Determination' in Margaret Moore (ed.), *National Self-Determination and Secession* (Oxford: Oxford University Press, 1998), 134–57. Part of Chapters 6 and 7 are published in 'The Ethics of Secession', *Canadian Journal of Law & Jurisprudence*, vol. 13, issue 2 (July 2000). Part of Chapter 8 has appeared in 'Cosmopolitanism, Globalization and Minority Nationalism', in Michael Keating and John McGarry, (ed.), *Minority Nationalism and the Changing International Order* (Oxford: Oxford University Press, forthcoming). I am grateful to these publishers for permission to use and incorporate this material in this book.

A much smaller number of people helped keep my personal life orderly and my children cared for, especially when I went away on research trips and conferences, or otherwise helped me find the time to work on this project. Of course my husband John did the most when I was away, but does not deserve thanks since they are his children too. My gratitude therefore extends to my sister Susan who looked after my children—in addition to her own three children—for an extended period when I went away for a research trip to Israel and Cyprus; and especially my mother, who looked after my children during many of the above named conferences. I am also grateful to Irena Baltuonidis for helping to prepare the bibliography and to Patti Lenard, both for research assistance, and for witty comments interspersed in her e-mails connected to this research help, which served as a welcome distraction.

Finally, I dedicate this book to the three men in my life: John, Séan, and Paul.

M.M.

March, 2000

CONTENTS

The impulsion towards nationalist sentiment in politics has ... exceedingly profound roots in the lifestyle of modern man. ... This situation cannot but make men into nationalists, and it is better to try and deal with the conditions which engender nationalism than to preach at its victims and beg them to refrain from feeling what, in their circumstances, it is only too natural to feel.

Ernest Gellner, *Nationalism*
(London: Weidenfeld and Nicholson, 1997), 102–3

CHAPTER 1

The Ethics of Nationalism

There are two distinct, but related, kinds of problems associated with nationalism: the first is state break-up; the second is control of the state by the majority nation.

State-breaking is one of the most destabilizing consequences of a successful nationalist movement. The issue of the justifiability of state-breaking, or secession, has become very pressing. In the post-Second World War period until 1989, superpowers were committed to upholding existing state boundaries. While decolonization was permitted, the borders of states were treated, in international law and practice, as permanent—non-negotiable—features of the international state system. But, with the collapse of communism, national divisions have tended to rear their heads, and the multinational states of Yugoslavia, the Soviet Union, Czechoslovakia, and Ethiopia have disintegrated along national lines. The process may not be completed, since many of the successor states are as multinational as the states they left behind; and there are other serious secessionist movements in many parts of the globe—from Quebec to Kashmir, Scotland to Chechnya.

In his 1991 book, *Secession: The Morality of Political Divorce from Fort Sumter to Lithuania and Quebec*, Allen Buchanan begins by pointing out that the issue of the morality of secession has received very little consideration from a normative standpoint. He then expresses the hope that his book will help to initiate a debate on the subject. Since then, writers in political philosophy, normative theory, sociology, comparative politics, and other fields have taken up the challenge and there are now a number of diverse philosophical perspectives on this subject.

This book examines most of the philosophical work on the ethics of secession, arguing that they wrongly abstract from the fact that most secessionist movements are based on groups that have a strong national identification, and are fuelled by nationalism. Most of the theories of justified secession proceed by *applying* established liberal arguments (justice theories) or well-established liberal values (autonomy) to the issue of secession. This book argues that a theory of secession should be concerned primarily with the legitimacy of nationalist claims and with the potential problems attached to conferring political rights on nations. It doesn't make sense to derive a theory of secession by applying liberal principles or theories to the issue: a theory of secession should consider directly the various normative claims that nationalists make, and the dynamics of national mobilization and national conflict.

Similarly, prior to 1989, liberal debate about political and institutional arrangements in the state was confined largely to theories of the just distribution of the goods of social interaction—money, power, status, and so on—but did not consider issues of group identity, membership in the state, or cultural biases of the state. Since that time, a number of minority cultural or other disadvantaged groups within the state have argued that the policies of the liberal-democratic state have the effect of disadvantaging them. Women, gays and lesbians, minority religious, racial and ethnic groups, and disabled people have pointed out the numerous ways in which the construction of the public sphere has marginalized them, and they have made claims on the state for the public affirmation of their identity. They have argued that, in many cases, the construction of the public sphere, which claims to be treating everyone as an equal, in fact is based on the majority culture. This movement, which is discussed in Chapter 5 under the rubric of multiculturalism, implicitly questions the homogeneity of the traditional state and the vaunted equality of its citizens, but also makes demands on the state for the recognition of their difference from the norm.

Minority nations, in multination states, have also criticized state policies on the grounds that they implicitly privilege the majority national group on the territory. They have resisted majority control over certain aspects of state policy, and have made claims for state protection of their culture or for recognition of their distinct identity. This usually means that they want their language to be used in official capacities and their children to be educated in their language and about their culture. They typically demand their own political institutions, to enable them to control their own affairs. This is true not only of several national minorities in Europe—the Basque region, Catalonia, Wales, Scotland—but also for the indigenous peoples in the

Americas—who now self-identify as 'First Nations'—who typically seek limited forms of political self-government within the state context. These groups too have served notice that they are not satisfied with equal rights and equal citizenship but seek rights to public recognition of their identity in the public sphere. For this reason, it is important that we examine the kinds of nation-building policies that the state is justified in pursuing, and the relationship between national identity, culture, and the state that is appropriate and justifiable.

This book is concerned to develop a normative theory of nationalism. It evaluates the various different arguments for giving importance to national identity, and for claiming rights to territory, in order to develop a theory about the justifiability of, and limits to, the claims that nations make on their own behalf. It then applies these normative arguments to the issues of nation-building and national self-determination.

This introductory chapter defines 'nationalism' and its related terms, and examines the various accounts of the origin and persistence of national identities, and their relevance to developing an ethics of nationalism. In this context, it distinguishes between three types of constructivist arguments, and argues that only one type of constructivism seems adequate in explaining how national identities originated and maintained themselves. This type of constructivism, properly understood, suggests the importance of providing a normative theory of nationalism, rather than simply dismissing it as a product of élite manipulation, or as easily transformed through altering the logic of the discursive practice.

What is Nationalism?

Before one can develop a normative theory of nationalism, it is necessary to be clear about what nationalism is, and a whole host of related phenomena: the idea of a nation, of course, and national identity. One problem in the study of nationalism concerns the contested definitions of its two key components: nationalism and nations.

A common line of argument, running through the works of social scientists interested in nationalism, is that 'nationalism' is not an 'ism' like other 'isms'. We should not assume that there is a core idea to 'nationalism' in the way that there may be to 'liberalism' or 'socialism'. Part of the difficulty is the contextual and protean nature of nationalism. It is very responsive to circumstances and can adopt many different forms. In John Hutchinson and Anthony Smith's view, nationalism takes so many different forms—'religious, conservative, liberal, fascist, communist, cultural, political, protectionist, integrationist, separatist, irredentist, diaspora, pan'—that the most that a theorist can do is to study a few aspects or examples of nationalism.[1]

Another reason for thinking that nationalism should not be identified with a few fundamental principles or beliefs is that the term often incorporates cultural, political, psychological, and social phenomena. The term 'nationalism', Smith argues, can refer to the process of forming nations or nation-states, the process of state-directed nation-building, the consciousness of belonging to a nation, or having a national identity, as well as political movements to achieve the goals attributed to the nation.[2] The range and diversity of phenomena encompassed by the term 'nationalism' makes it imperative for students of nationalism to define the term carefully. One of the potential problems attached to theorizing about nationalism is this lack of clarity about what the object of study is.

Some theorists, however, do treat nationalism like other 'isms' and identify it with a few fundamental principles or beliefs. Thus, Ernest Gellner argues that 'nationalism is primarily a *political principle*, which holds that the political and national unit should be congruent.'[3] This has the advantage of conceptual clarity, indeed simplicity; but it also entails that every nationalist movement seeks separation or independence.

In fact, there are many movements which we might think of as nationalist, and which bear many similarities, in terms of their discourse and concerns, with nationalism, but which do not demand independent statehood. These movements espouse doctrines of freedom in the sense of freedom from external control and popular sovereignty, but these groups are content with other forms of recognition, within the existing multinational state. Gellner's definition has the unfortunate effect of obscuring from view the range of policies and prescriptions that nationalists might endorse and the extent to which these policies and prescriptions are similar.

Both positions are flawed *as* definitions of nationalism. Smith's description of the range of phenomenon incorporated in the term 'nationalism' does not define it in any helpful way, but does emphasize the importance of conceptual clarity in the discussion. Gellner's strat-

---

[1] John Hutchinson and Anthony D. Smith, *Nationalism* (Oxford: Oxford University Press, 1994), 3.

[2] Anthony D. Smith, *National Identity* (Harmondsworth: Penguin, 1991), 72.

[3] Ernest Gellner, *Nations and Nationalism* (Ithaca, NY: Cornell University Press, 1983), 1, my emphasis.

egy of identifying the principles that are 'fundamental' to nationalism is very problematic: because of the protean and malleable nature of nationalism, it is misleading to associate it with a particular set of demands or particular principles.[4] It makes more sense to adopt an intermediate approach—to recognize the amorphous character of the phenomenon, but also to attempt to identify nationalism instead with a range of normative argumentation that emphasizes the moral significance of the national community, its existence in the past and into the future, and typically seeks some form of political protection to safeguard the future existence of the nation.

We should understand nationalism, then, as a normative argument that confers moral value on national membership, and on the past and future existence of the nation, and identifies the nation with a particular homeland or part of the globe. This pattern of argument is normative in the sense that it is intended, by nationalists, to offer a reason that is not merely self-interested. Nationalists often appeal to the good of the nation, and this presupposes a conception about *legitimate* political action.[5]

One advantage of viewing nationalism as a normative theory about the value of national membership and national communities is that it can account for the key policies or demands of nationalists. On this conception, the demand for national self-determination is an important plank in many nationalist movements although not, *contra* Gellner, a fundamental principle of nationalism. Nationalists may, and often do, seek complete independence or state sovereignty. However, in some cases, where the costs of independence are too high, or the benefits of independence too precarious, nationalists may seek other forms of institutional recognition.

What Is A Nation?

Although it is very difficult to enumerate a list of characteristics that is shared by all examples of what we would normally regard as national communities, mainly because every list has at least one exception to it, there is general agreement on certain clarifications of the

[4] Rogers Brubaker, 'Myths and Misconceptions in the Study of Nationalism', in Margaret Moore (ed.), *National Self-Determination and Secession* (Oxford: Clarendon Press, 1998), 233–65.
[5] Wayne Norman, 'Prelude to a Liberal Morality of Nationalism', in Samantha Brennan, Tracy Isaacs, and Michael Milde (eds.), *A Question of Values: New Canadian Perspectives in Ethics and Political Philosophy* (Atlanta, GA: Rodopi, 1997), 12–13.

concept of the 'nation'. There is a well-established distinction between nations, states, and ethnic groups. Obviously, these three concepts—state, nation, and ethnic group—are closely interrelated, since ethnic groups have the potential to become nationally mobilized; many nations aspire to be politically self-governing—aspire to be states—and states like to characterize their body politic as being a 'nation', for this implies that they have a common political identity.

The distinction between nations and ethnic groups is recognized even by those who argue that many nations have ethnic groups at their core—that they were founded around one particular ethnic group—and that many ethnic groups have the potential to become nations.[6] Ethnic groups, like nations, are social groups, characterized by myths of common descent, some common culture and mutual recognition, and complex rituals regarding boundary-maintenance—but they are not co-extensive with nations because they lack the political self-consciousness that is usually associated with national communities. What is distinctive about nations is the way in which they frame their aspirations or understand themselves in terms of a certain kind of social solidarity. Their collective identity involves a rhetoric about indivisibility, sovereignty or an aspiration to sovereignty, political legitimacy, common descent or common culture, and special relations to a certain territory. This is not a definition or a perfect list of an ideal type of nation, but a common pattern of the kind of claim that is indicative of the collective identity that we call nationhood.[7]

It is also important, as Walker Connor has argued, to recognize that nations are not co-extensive with states.[8] His distinction is repeated here, mainly because this confusion still pervades the literature especially in international relations, and is embedded in terms such as 'United Nations'. Some states have more than one recognized nation—they are viewed as a 'compact' between two founding 'nation', as is Canada for example—and some nations, such as the Kurdish and Palestinian nations, do not have their own states, although many of their members aspire to this.

Yael Tamir has argued that we should distinguish between communities whose distinguishing features are independent of the percep-

---

[6] Anthony D. Smith, *The Ethnic Origins of Nations* (Oxford: Basil Blackwell, 1983), 9–18. Smith distinguishes nations from ethnic groups even while acknowledging that many nations have an 'ethnic core'.

[7] See Craig Calhoun, *Nationalism*, (Buckingham: Open University Press, 1997), 4–7.

[8] Walker Connor, 'Terminological Chaos (A Nation Is a Nation, Is a State, Is an Ethnic Group, Is a . . .)', in *Ethnonationalism. The Quest for Understanding* (Princeton, NJ: Princeton University Press, 1994), 90–117.

tions and feelings of the agent, and those that are not.[9] If we follow this distinction, it is apparent that the category 'nation', like 'friends' and 'lovers', falls into the second group. It is contingent on its members' sustaining a certain image of it based on their perceptions and feelings—although of course there are a number of conditions which lead to the construction of an image of a nation, such as shared religion, language, law, geographical isolation, colonial policies, bureaucratic decisions, and the like.

Most theorists agree that this subjective component is a necessary condition for shared nationality. Ernst Renan, the most famous exponent of a psychological or subjective definition of nationhood, emphasizes that two elements constitute the 'spiritual principle' that he says is nationhood: 'The one is the possession of a rich heritage of memories; and the other is actual agreement, the desire to live together, and the will to continue to make the most of the joint inheritance.'[10] Renan's complex treatment of nationhood reflects both the importance of the subjective component—the identification with a historic territory or homeland, and with co-nationals; and also an objective element—memories of the various ties of shared language or religion or culture or public life that help to make members identify with one another as a community.

Similarly, Otto Bauer's list of the characteristics that national communities must have to qualify as nations suggests that the subjective component is a necessary condition for shared nationality, but that this is also informed by certain objective shared elements. He defines a 'nation' as a group of people bound together through a sense of common destiny into a 'community of character', and in his description of the constituent elements—such as language, history or territory—of such 'communities of characters', Bauer emphasizes that these elements could be constituted in different ways.[11]

David Miller lists five elements that together constitute a nation: it is, he writes 'a community (1) constituted by shared beliefs and mutual commitments, (2) extended in history, (3) active in character, (4) connected to a particular territory, and (5) marked off from other communities by its distinct public culture'.[12] This definition also suggests that the subjective identification is crucial.

[9] Yael Tamir, 'The Enigma of Nationalism', *World Politics*, 47 (April 1995), 418–40.
[10] Ernst Renan, 'What is a Nation?', in Alfred Zimmern (ed.), *Modern Political Doctrines* (London: Oxford University Press, 1939), 186–205, at 202–3.
[11] Otto Bauer, 'The Nation', in Gopal Balakrishnan (ed.), *Mapping the Nation* (London and New York, NY: Verso, 1996), 39–77, but particularly at 41–4.
[12] David Miller, *On Nationality* (Oxford: Oxford University Press, 1995), 27.

It makes sense to list, as Bauer and Miller do, some of the objective features that nations typically have, as long as one recognizes that these features or 'objective' markers—such as language, or religion, or shared history, or shared public life—are important mainly because they tend to foster the one necessary, and possibly even sufficient, condition for being a nation, namely, national identity. As Bauer recognizes, which 'objective' features are important in shaping the identity will be different for different nations.

Some may object that this emphasis on subjective identification with co-members engaged or aspiring to be engaged in a common political project, and with a particular homeland of the group—and the vagueness of the 'objective' requirement—makes it possible for 'nations' to develop among people with no shared history and no shared public culture. This is a theoretical possibility, but it is not a serious problem. Even the most ardent defender of the modernist theory of national identities, and the manufactured nature of national communities (Gellner) concedes that they do not emerge 'out of thin air' but require some pre-existing material to work with.[13] It is important to distinguish, on the one hand, between the idea that they are entirely false, that they involve completely duping or manipulating the masses and, on the other hand, the idea that such identities are not fixed but fluid, that their identification and invocation are variable in the sense that they are constituted and maintained through social processes which could have been something other than they are. This book rejects the view that they are entirely false and the product of élite manipulation. At the same time, it recognizes the socially constructed and potentially variable nature of nations and national identities.

Even within the confines of this definition of nationhood, there can be widespread disagreement about who meets the criteria for nationhood. There may be agreement on what qualifies a group in being considered a nation, but disagreement over whether a particular group shares the right kind of political self-consciousness or the right kind of attachment to a territory. This debate emerged in Canada in 1996, when the (separatist) Quebec Premier described Canada as 'not a real country', by which he seemed to mean that Canadians did not have the right kinds of feelings of identification to qualify for nationhood.[14] The debate was

[13] Ernest Gellner, *Thought and Change* (London: Weidenfeld and Nicholson, 1964), 168.

[14] In his swearing-in speech as Premier of Quebec and at the ensuing news conference, Premier Bouchard said, 'We are a people, we are a nation, and as a nation we have a fundamental right to keep and maintain our territory. Canada is divisible because Canada is not a real country. There are two people, two nations, and two territories. And this one is ours.' *The Globe & Mail*, 29 January, 1996, A3.

effectively stopped when the Prime Minister quipped that this would be hard to explain to a Canadian Second World War veteran.[15]

National Identities and Constructivism

Personal identities are generally thought to be grounded in genetic (DNA) continuity.[16] There are, of course, interesting philosophical questions about the nature of personal identities and the relationship between physical (DNA) continuity and subjective identity.[17] Nevertheless, the physical continuity of the person, and the capacity of the person to identify with her physical being, as having both a past and stretching into the future, provides an important basis for the ordinary assumption that personal identities are unproblematic. They also help to explain the sense in which personal identity in the OED sense of 'the condition of being the same as a person or thing described or claimed' has a primordial character.

National identities, on the other hand, are social identities, constructed from the social categories that unite and divide people. Although they have various rules of inclusion and exclusion (boundary-maintenance), they are also more fluid, especially in comparison with personal identities. That national identities are socially constructed and hence more fluid than personal identities is generally accepted by almost all scholars of nationalism. In fact, the so-called primordialist-constructivist debate—in the history and sociology of nationalism—was completely sterile in large part because there were very few academic exponents of 'primordialism'.[18]

The almost universally-held view[19] that national identities are socially constructed does not give us much prescriptive guidance on

[15] Doug Ward, 'Parts of Quebec could stay in Canada, PM says', *Vancouver Sun*, 30 January, 1996, A1/A2.

[16] For an interesting discussion of this, see David D. Laitin, *Identity in Formation; The Russian-Speaking Populations in the Near Abroad* (Ithaca, NY: Cornell University Press, 1998), 14–15.

[17] See here Derek Parfit, *Reasons and Persons* (Oxford: Oxford University Press, 1986).

[18] Anthony Smith does not endorse primordialism—only the view that nations frequently have a premodern ethnic component, which is reshaped in modern times. This is hardly the view that national identities are primordial in the sense of immutable. Clifford Geertz is also often held up as an example of 'primordialism', but in fact this is unclear. He could be interpreted as only claiming that it is the agent's *belief* in their primordial attachments that drives conflict, but not that these attachments are in fact primordial in the sense of immutable. See Clifford Geertz, 'Primordial and Civic Ties' in Hutchinson and Smith, *Nationalism*, 28–34.

[19] There are of course primordialist assumptions in much lazy journalism, which tends to reflect the way people think about their attachments and identities but does not critically examine these beliefs.

how these identities should be regarded by the state, or treated from a normative standpoint. This is partly because there are a number of different characterizations of what 'social construction' entails, with different implications for the normative status of national communities and national forms of identity.[20] It is on these questions that there is room for genuine debate.

One common line of argument, associated with the work of Gellner, Anderson, Hobsbawm, and others, is that national identity is linked with broad historical forces. National forms of identity become prominent in the modern period as a result of industrialization, and the social and bureaucratic changes that accompany industrialization—or precede it, in the case of states aspiring to be industrialized. In Gellner's formulation of the argument, the modern economy is crucially dependent on standardized modes of communication and cultural practices, and people's life chances are shaped by the language in which they communicate, as well as other cultural forms of interaction. This is in contrast to the premodern period when cultural or linguistic differences were politically irrelevant. Benedict Anderson's *Imagined Communities*[21] builds on this basic idea by suggesting that the boundaries of national identity have been shaped by the vernacular reading communities which were created through print capitalism.

This rendering of the claim that national identities are socially constructed does not suggest that these identities are easy to deconstruct or that they should be treated less seriously. They help to explain in broad historical terms why people have divided themselves into different groups, and they also identify the very real advantages in terms of life-chances, of being a majority group in a state, and the almost inescapable logic, in the modern context, of identifying oneself in this way. But this explanation, in terms of broad social and historical processes which have impacted on all groups, does not suggest that these identities should be ignored or treated as irrelevant—quite the contrary: Charles Taylor, for example, has argued that the inextricable interdependence of nationalism with modern notions of popular will and popular sovereignty suggests that, once we understand the modern context of nationalist consciousness, we will have a strong appre-

---

[20] For an interesting discussion of the different types of social construction, on which the following discussion draws, see James Fearon and David Laitin, 'Violence and the Social Construction of Ethnic Identities', unpublished manuscript, 22 January, 1999 version.

[21] Benedict Anderson, *Imagined Communities: Reflections on the Origin and Spread of Nationalism* (London and New York, NY: Verso, 1993).

ciation for the prominence of nationalism and the centrality of national forms of identity.[22]

Another, less plausible rendering of constructivism is the idea that nations are the product of 'discursive formations'.[23] The development of discursive formations at the level of a symbolic or cultural system can set one group in opposition to another because what drives the identity construction is the internal logic of the group's discourse. It is of course possible to identify certain discourses—about land, community, or sovereignty—as important to a national group. Indeed, this is one of the things that distinguishes a national group from a mere ethnic group. On this form of constructivism, there is very little reason to give any institutional recognition to national identities. National identities, after all, are simply created out of a logic of language, with the clear implication that altering the discourse will have the effect of changing the identity.

The problem with this understanding of social construction is that it begs the question of why this discourse has emerged and how this discourse is maintained. If the discourse has no basis in anything beyond the discourse, why can't this discourse be reinterpreted? It is not satisfactory here to appeal to the logic inherent in the discourse, for this doesn't explain how that logic emerged or what maintains it— especially if one has a reasonably complex view of the varied natures of discourses. Because this approach cannot explain why this discourse so powerfully constrains individuals' actions, it seems to presuppose a view that discourse theorists formally reject, namely, that discourses (cultures?) are internally bounded and strongly shape their members' behaviour.[24]

A third type of constructivist approach views construction as the product of individual actions, usually action by élites. Crude

---

[22] Charles Taylor, 'Nationalism and Modernity', in Ronald Beiner (ed.), *Theorizing Nationalism* (Albany, NY: SUNY, 1999), 219–45. In his introductory essay, Beiner writes: 'I don't think one can get as much normative mileage out of this idea of identity as Taylor thinks one can. No one can deny that struggles over identity are central to modern politics. But the sheer possession of a given identity confers no normative authority on the kind of politics that goes with that identity.' Ronald Beiner, 'Nationalism's Challenge to Political Philosophy', in *Theorizing Nationalism*, 1–25, at 6. I agree with Beiner's assessment, which is why, in Part One, I assess the various normative arguments that are made for the recognition of national identities. But I also think that it is a mistaken move to dismiss national identities on the grounds that they are 'socially constructed', a term which is often used loosely, and which characterizes many different kinds of relations of national identities to the society in which these forms of identity take hold.

[23] Calhoun, *Nationalism*, 3. The idea of nationalism as based on a 'discursive formation' is based on Michel Foucault, *Power/Knowledge: Selected Interviews and Other Writings, 1972–77* (New York, NY: Pantheon, 1977).

[24] This point is from Fearon and Laitin, 'Violence and the Social Construction of Ethnic Identities'.

élite-manipulation models view national identity as the product of actions by political or economic élites, who foster national identities for their own (self-interested) ends. More sophisticated élite-manipulation theories describe élites as encoding violence or antagonism as ethnic or national which could be described in other ways—as criminal or class violence, say—for their own ends.

This interpretation of constructivism, like the discourse model, suggests that there is no normative merit in recognizing national identities. After all, these forms of identity are simply created by élites for their own self-interested ends, as a way to mobilize people for the élites' political purposes. The prescription that follows from this view of the constructed nature of national identities is to adopt measures to curb the role of élites. Nationalism has no moral value: it is merely a means for élites to preserve or enhance their own power and status in the society.

The élite-manipulation model is flawed in an important way, however. It fails to explain why people so readily embrace this kind of identity—or this interpretation of violence or events. The élite-manipulation interpretation of constructivism does not explain why this is a successful strategy, and why other attempts at identity-construction—class identity, say, or Yugoslav identity—fail. In a liberal-democratic society, where there is free access to alternative views, the assumptions underlying this form of constructivism are extremely problematic. Indeed, it is important to note that this kind of argument is also a standard argument against democratic government—namely, Plato's argument that the masses are easily duped and so cannot steer the ship of state—and indeed against the liberal ideal of the rational autonomous self-directed person, able to make decisions over his/her own life. Even in relatively closed societies, where the state controls all media outlets, and the élite-manipulation model has more credibility, such as in Slobodan Milosevic's Serbia, there still remains the question why other—class or communist—identities failed to attract sufficient support, and why national forms of identity were successful.

The most plausible form of constructivism, then, and the one adopted in this book, views national identities as the product of broad social and economic changes that render these social categories as both politically important, and ones with which people identify. One implication of this view is that, if history had been different, Serbs and Croats needn't have thought of themselves as Serbs and Croats; they could have believed that they were all Serbs or all Croats or all-Yugoslavs. Many different kinds of identities were (historically) a possibility, but failed, for various reasons, to be compelling; and of course it is possible that new forms of national identities will have increasing salience.

The fact that nations are socially constructed does not suggest that they are less real or are to be regarded with suspicion. Some people focus on the fact that they are 'imagined' communities to suggest that they may have no basis in 'reality'. Here, it is important to distinguish between 'imagined' communities and 'imaginary' ones.[25] Indeed, it is an unfortunate consequence of Anderson's brilliantly catchy title that almost everyone thinks they understand what the book is about from reading only the title. Anderson uses the term 'imagined community' in order to emphasize the central role played by the *image* of the nation in creating a national community. The image is important because it is impossible for all its members to engage in face-to-face contact with each other at all times. Therefore members must refer to their perception of the image of the nation. Of course, on this definition, many, if not most, communities, except the very smallest, are imagined in the same way. Religious communities are imagined; my university is imagined; even my extended family is imagined.[26] But they may all be important, and legitimate, bases of identification.

The modernist interpretation of identity construction is, of course, consistent with attributing some role to individual agency and even individual constructivism. Susan Woodward's account of the descent into violence in the Balkans emphasizes the role of élite manipulation, but is consistent with a modernist explanation of national identities— to explain why groups are divided in this way.[27] It is not clear from her analysis that the crucial work of the élites was in constructing the two identities: it seems more accurate to describe élites as creating a context in which minorities felt insecure, and this (a) made it strategically important for individuals on the ground, who felt threatened by possible minority status, especially given certain (self-fulfilling) assumptions about the behaviour of members of the other group, to identify with extremists in their own group, and to consolidate their other, weaker identities into a uni-dimensional identity; and (b) made escalation into violence more likely.

---

[25] I owe this distinction, and following critique of Anderson's use of the term 'imagined communities' to Tamir, 'The Enigma of Nationalism', 423.

[26] These examples are all from Tamir, 'The Enigma of Nationalism', 421.

[27] Susan Woodward, *Balkan Tragedy; chaos and dissolution after the Cold War* (Washington, DC: The Brookings Institution, 1995).

While the élite-manipulation and discursive models of identity-construction fail to account for the fundamental questions of the origin and maintenance of this form of identity (or discourse), they may have an important role to play in contributing to more or less peaceful (or violent) resolutions of conflict. The role of élite-manipulation and inflammatory discourse in encouraging violence and insecurity is one of the reasons why a normative analysis of nationalism is necessary—or, more precisely, a normative analysis of the kinds of policies that a liberal democratic nationalism could endorse—as well as empirical research into the causes of this violence.[28] However, it does not suggest that the identities themselves are problematic. Obviously, the fact that there is a group-based identity is a necessary condition for group violence, but in no way *explains* it, because there are many national identities which operate in peaceful contexts.

The fact that national identities are deeply bound up with modernity—either processes of industrialization and bureaucratization, as on Gellner's account, or modern democratic notions of popular sovereignty and democratic governance, as on Taylor's account—does not, itself, constitute a *normative* argument for recognizing these identities. But it does suggest that an account of the constructed nature of these identities gives us no reason to dismiss or ignore them, and indeed, suggests the likelihood that they will persist.

Construction, Deconstruction, and State Action

This account of the constructed nature of national identities has several implications for an ethics of nationalism. This account does not conceive of national identities as infinitely malleable, but as having a social, historical, cultural, or institutional basis. These identities have been formed over time around these bases. At the same time, national identities are not reducible to these social and historic differences: they are *political* identities, connected to the political community with which one identifies, and cultural difference is not a crucial or even necessary element. In this respect, many nationalists, such as Herder, were quite wrong to think of the celebration of difference as an important aspect of national identity.

---

[28] Fearon and Laitin argue for more empirical work on the causes of violence as such, distinct from the creation of national or ethnic identities, in 'Violence and the Social Construction of Ethnic Identities'.

The relationship between the cultural and political elements in national identities has been expressed by Bhikhu Parekh in terms of a distinction between two types of national identities. On the one hand, according to this distinction, there are national identities that base the identity of a particular political community on the traits, habits, customs, and social practices of the society; and, on the other, discussions of national identity that focus on the structure or organizing principles of a community.[29] This book does not adopt Parekh's formulation of two types of national identities, which falsely dichotomizes the relationship between the two, but argues that it is more accurate to describe national identities as existing along a continuum, with some versions emphasizing the habits or customs or character of the group, and others emphasizing only the institutional structure and constitutive principles.

The discussion of identity adopted throughout this book mainly refers to identity in the second sense. It is concerned with the identification that people have with a particular political community, by which I mean a territorially concentrated group of people who aspire to or accept a common mode of conducting their collective affairs. It is concerned with the institutional, structural, and constitutive principles of such a community, but not with the habits or customs or character traits that are supposed to be common to all members, and which distinguish it from others—although this emphasis on what is unique or specific to a community can be used, and often is used, to strengthen national solidarity and is frequently appealed to in nation-building projects.

Both elements are present to some extent in all national communities, since identification with the group usually has social—by which is meant linguistic or cultural—historical and/or institutional bases; but is not reducible to these social or historic differences. Many nationalists have tended to concentrate or emphasize its social component—such as the language and customs of the group—and have ignored the institutional and historic basis of these types of identifications.

The recognition of these two elements in national identities is important, because they suggest the extent of and limits to their malleability. The French and American models of nationhood, which presuppose a political entity making uniform rules to incorporate individuals into the republic, do not provide a general model for dealing with most minority national identities. Assimilation or integration

[29] Bhikhu Parekh, 'Discourses on National Identity', *Political Studies,* 42 (1994), 492–504, at 501–2.

has been generally effective in immigrant societies such as the United States, Canada, and Australia, where groups of people left their various 'homelands' to become part of a different political project. Immigrant groups did not have the demographic basis to reproduce their own culture *en masse* and the political identities in question—the Canadian, Australian, and American identities—were genuinely available to them, in the sense that the host society did not exclude them from the political project and the political project was compatible with their cultural or ethnic identity.

The experience of France is also not generalizable to other minority national groups. In the case of France, ethnic groups were incorporated or integrated into France prior to the Age of Nationalism, and assimilation was largely effective. There has been some attempt to revive these minority nationalisms, but minority nations typically lack much shared (institutionally separate) history—since Normandy, Brittany, Aquitaine, Languedoc and Burgundy were all incorporated into France prior to 1500.[30] They lack an institutional basis, as well as social differentiation. The nationalisms are accordingly very weak. The French formula cannot be applied to other areas, where separate institutional or bureaucratic structures were in place by the time of mass democratic participation and the politicization of national and cultural differences by the bureaucratic modern state. In these cases, assimilationist measures are typically not only strongly resisted, but are counter-productive.

This suggests that national identities should be understood as constructed socially but not easily deconstructed, or infinitely manipulable. Of course, it is true that national identities can, over time, be altered. They are constructed over time, and these identities are continually shaped by social and political processes. As little as forty years ago, Britain was thought to be a homogeneous society, with strong class politics, but little in the way of national politics. Now, however, the conglomerate 'British' national identity seems to be eroding and is challenged by Scottish, Welsh, and to a lesser extent—and mainly in reaction to the other two nationalisms—English national identities. Identities can change, in response to the social context. In the case of Britain, one could have predicted the lines along which these nationalisms could emerge. Scotland, for example, has had a long, separate history, and, since 1707, has had separate government departments, a separate legal system, has been geographically differentiated (has bor-

---

[30] Details in Hugh Seton-Watson, *Nations and States; an Enquiry into the Origins of Nations and the Politics of Nationalism* (London: Methuen, 1977), 42–6.

ders), and, more recently, has had some international (sporting and EU) recognition. It is hardly surprising, given this separate history and tradition and institutional embodiment, that Scottish nationalism has asserted itself, and is even stronger than Welsh nationalism, which has not had its own institutional structure since the fifteenth century. This analysis suggests that it does not follow from the observation that these identities should be understood as constructed socially that they are therefore infinitely malleable.

In fact, from the micro (individual) perspective, there are only a limited number of identities genuinely available to one. Individuals cannot adopt national identities like they can adopt hats, moving between them as it suits, but are constrained by various factors. As David Laitin has shown in the context of Russian-speakers in Russia's 'Near Abroad', in many cases people have no choice but to adopt a particular identity, given the options open to them by the host society, or state, and given the family that they come from, the language they speak, the geographical area in which they are born, and much else.

Similar evidence is also available from Colley's careful historical examination of the development of British identity. In her study, *Britons: Forging the Nation 1707–1837*, Colley asks why the Welsh, the English, and the Scots could feel that they being Welsh, English, and Scottish was consistent with *also* being British, and the Irish could not. Her answer is that the Irish were effectively excluded from developing a British national identity because Protestantism was absolutely central to Britishness, particularly in the eighteenth and nineteenth centuries. On this analysis, the Irish national identity was a relational one, defined, at least in part, in opposition to a British identity. This oppositional relation was due to the fact that the British identity was not genuinely available to Irish Catholics.[31] This account recognizes both the social or cultural basis of the identity, and also how that history shapes the development of the identity, and can lead to the mobilization of a national group. In many cases, the cultural or ethnic component of the identity emerges when we consider the extent to which other national identities are often unavailable to some people, given who they are—their religion, or language, or ethnic group.

How is this relevant to an ethics of nationalism? First, the constructed, and relational, character of these identities should be recognized, particularly in the design of political institutions. This has

---

[31] Linda Colley, *Britons: Forging the Nation 1707–1837* (London: Pimlico, 1992), 11–54; 322–3.

relevance for the type of nation-building policies that it is appropriate for states to pursue. It means, as will be argued in Chapter 5, that we should be reluctant to erect institutionally distinct categories and groups, unless it is necessary, either to achieve political peace, or justice between rival nationally mobilized groups. We should be reluctant because institutional differentiation can help to strengthen identities, or even to 'create' them where they otherwise wouldn't exist. First, appropriate recognition of non-national identity groups—sexual orientation, cultural, religious, ethnic, gender identities—can typically be done at the state-level, through policies of inclusion and accommodation. Second, political and institutional recognition as distinct and potentially antagonistic identity groups can have the effect of transforming them into political communities. This is particularly true of cultural, religious, or ethnic groups, which are often territorially concentrated. These kinds of identities can become the axes along which national groups mobilize as distinct, aspirant political communities.

It does not follow from this emphasis on the constructed nature of national identities, however, that state action designed to deconstruct mobilized national groups will be easy.[32] Indeed, I will argue in Chapter 5 that assimilationist policies are highly unlikely to be successful, precisely because of the politicized nature of these identities. State neutrality is problematic, because it is unlikely to be viewed by the minority in these terms (as neutral). The evidence suggests that state action, designed to eradicate a particular national identity, will often be viewed by the target group as an attempt by one national group—the national group(s) which is privileged by the state—to foist their identity on all peoples, and will therefore be counterproductive.[33] This is so because the modern state is not and cannot be neutral with respect to national membership: state policies, and state boundaries, are necessarily implicated in the recognition (or non-recognition) and reproduction of national groups. That context helps to explain why there are important considerations of fairness involved in the state's treatment of its national groups, and why state action, which is designed to ignore or abstract from and thereby deconstruct a particular national identity, often fails.

---

[32]   Laitin, *Identity in Formation*, 9–11, 13–14.
[33]   There is strong empirical evidence of the extent to which the formation and consolidation of national identities occur through reaction to the various policies of inclusion and exclusion of dominant groups. See Laitin, *Identity in Formation*, 13, 275–99.

Structure of the Book

This book is about the normative limits of nationalism. It assesses the justificatory arguments for the institutional recognition of national identity. It is concerned with the normative merits, and the limits of, national assertion from an ethical perspective that is broadly sympathetic to liberal-democratic values.

There are a burgeoning number of treatments devoted to the normative significance of national identity or national membership, mainly from the perspective of whether liberalism can accommodate nationalist lines of identification. Much of this literature is concerned with the possibility of a defensible liberal nationalism. This has been the subject of several important books,[34] all of which argue that conceptions of state neutrality and formal equality of citizens, which were a commonplace in liberal political philosophy, are inadequate in dealing with issues of national identity. The dominant theme of Part One of the book is that it is important to consider the various arguments that have been put forward in defence of nationalism, and to try to suggest the ethical limitations of nationalism.

Chapters 2, 3, and 4 identify three types of arguments that are frequently used to justify giving institutional recognition to national identity. These are the 'intrinsic value argument' (Chapter 2), the 'culture argument' (Chapter 3) and 'instrumental arguments' (Chapter 4). These arguments are used to justify both national self-determination and nation-building projects. The two central nationalist projects—nation-building and national self-determination—are, in practice, frequently in tension with one another. Chapter 5 suggests some guidelines for determining when one is more appropriate than the other, and draws on the analysis in the previous three chapters to address the issue of the appropriate and legitimate policy that states can follow in giving preference to a particular national or cultural group.

Part Two assesses the second political project associated with nationalism: national self-determination. Chapters 6 and 7 assess the various arguments put forward by national groups for jurisdictional authority over particular pieces of territory. Chapter 6 is concerned with just-cause theories of secession and the related view that the appropriate area of jurisdictional authority in which secession should

---

[34] Yael Tamir, *Liberal Nationalism* (Princeton, NJ: Princeton University Press, 1993); Will Kymlicka, *Multicultural Citizenship* (Oxford: Oxford University Press, 1995); David Miller, *On Nationality* (Oxford: Oxford University Press, 1995); Charles Taylor, *Multiculturalism and the Politics of Recognition*, edited by Amy Gutmann (Princeton, NJ: Princeton University Press, 1992).

take place is that of previous administrative boundaries. Chapter 7 examines choice theories of secession, which are designed to give importance to the wishes or desires of the people living in the state, not the justice of their claims, and the various normative arguments that have typically been put forward for rights to particular pieces of territory. These two issues are related because any appeal to the choices of people within a unit, say, in a referendum on the issue, presupposes an answer to the problem of how to determine the jurisdictional unit in which a referendum is to be held.

The issue of rights to territory is also important because one basis of the distinction between immigrant groups and national groups is that the latter have territory and the former do not. Whether a group has territory is therefore crucially important, not only to this conceptual distinction, but it also affects, on at least one influential argument, the kind of rights and entitlements that attach to the groups.[35] This book argues that there is an important basis for this distinction, but it also argues that rights to territory tend to be second-order kinds of rights, and that the most important argument for institutional recognition flows from national identity. It also suggests that context is important in determining appropriate remedies for unfair treatment. The fact that a group is territorially concentrated on a particular piece of land opens up more opportunities for remedying the situation, and different types of remedies than are available to scattered, or dispersed populations.

The normative analysis of both national identity or national membership arguments (Part One) and jurisdictional authority over territory (Part Two) has important implications for state practice. Some of this is already discussed in terms of the ethics of nation-building (Chapter 5). Chapters 6 and 7 are concerned with the ethics of secession. An important theme in Chapters 6, 7, and 8 is that state break-up should not be evaluated by applying liberal principles or ideals, but should be regarded as an example of national assertion. I therefore suggest that a theory of justified secession should be placed within the context of a normative theory of nationalism, and suggest, in Chapter 8, the kind of procedural right that should be institutionalized in domestic constitutions or in international law.

The analysis of normative arguments in Part One provides guidelines for thinking about national claims, and these are relevant especially in the hard cases where different national groups overlap on the same territory. The underlying appeal to a conception of justice among

---

[35] Kymlicka, *Multicultural Citizenship*, particularly chapter two.

national groups suggests the need to think imaginatively about the ways in which rival claims to institutional recognition can be accommodated fairly. Some of these more complex institutional arrangements are discussed in the concluding chapter (Chapter 8).

PART ONE

MEMBERSHIP

CHAPTER 2

The Intrinsic Argument (or, Are Nations Moral Communities?)

This chapter, and the next two, are concerned with various moral arguments about *membership* in a national community. They focus on the bonds of attachment that co-nationals feel toward those who share the same national identity, and the moral importance that should be placed on that. This chapter is concerned specifically with the claim that the bonds of attachment that co-nationals feel have intrinsic moral value. The following chapter is concerned with the basis of this attachment, and arguments in terms of well-being and autonomy that have been made. Chapter 4 is concerned with the (instrumentally) positive role that shared national identity plays in facilitating the goods of social justice and democratic governance.

The justificatory argument that nations are intrinsically valuable is developed at length by David Miller in *On Nationality* and Thomas Hurka in an article entitled 'The Justification of National Partiality'.[1] This is an important argument because it rests on a particular view of moral reasoning, and suggests that claims about national identity and national attachments cannot simply be theorized within the confines of liberal theory, but that these communities themselves are ethically valuable, and should be entitled to the kind of regard and consideration that a moral community normally warrants.

This chapter proceeds to outline, and summarize, this argument, and suggests that its proponents make several important and valid

---

[1] David Miller, *On Nationality* (Oxford: Oxford University Press, 1995); Thomas Hurka, 'The Justification of National Partiality' in Robert McKim and Jeff McMahan (eds.), *The Morality of Nationalism* (New York, NY: Oxford University Press, 1997), 139–57.

points. It argues that the conception of morality underlying this view is a plausible and attractive one, without at the same time denying the importance of the impartial perspective. The empirical claims that are highlighted in this argument—the fact that people feel attached to these communities, people have bonds of memberships with fellow nationals—gives us the basis of a very good argument for recognizing national identity, especially when it is combined with the recognition that states are not neutral with respect to national membership. This chapter develops an argument based on fairness, which is implicit in this line of argument.

Three objections to the view that nations are intrinsically valuable are then considered. The first problem concerns the description of obligations that flow from membership in a national community. The second problem concerns the place of false beliefs on this conception. The third, and most serious problem with this argument is that it fails to distinguish nations from other intrinsically valuable communities. The chapter concludes that the 'intrinsic value' line of argument helps to draw attention to the normative dimension of nationalist claims, and provides some rough guidelines for assessing rival claims, but it needs to be supplemented by other arguments to justify the conclusion that nationalists seek, namely, political rights for nations.

Nations as Moral Communities: An Outline of the 'Intrinsic Value' Argument

The intrinsic argument for national identity has been developed in response to a debate about legitimate forms of partiality. What is the basis of the demand that co-nationals give priority to their nation over others or priority to the interests of co-nationals over non-nationals? What could justify this departure from the universalist standards of morality?[2]

A common objection to nationalist lines of argument is that nationalism is undesirable and indefensible because its core idea—that we should give preference to fellow nationals and to our own national traditions and institutions—is incompatible with the moral point of view.[3] Central to the moral point of view is the conception that actions are to be governed by principles that give equal consideration to all

[2] This question is asked by Jeff McMahan, 'The Limits of National Partiality', in McKim and McMahan (eds.) *The Morality of Nationalism*, 107–38, at 109.
[3] Paul Gomberg, 'Patriotism Is Like Racism', *Ethics*, 101/1 (October 1990), 144–50.

people who are affected by an action.[4] Because nationalism advocates a form of partiality, its critics contend that it is like racism: both, its critics allege, treat the in-group—the national group/the racial group—with a different set of criteria than the interests of outsiders, and do not weight the interests of all equally.[5]

David Miller pursues his defence of the intrinsic value of national communities through an analysis of the debate between ethical universalists and ethical particularists. Because his analysis is situated within this debate, he does not address the issue of the intrinsic value of national communities directly, but is mainly concerned with rebutting the claim that nationalism is unsatisfactory or illegitimate because it is non-universal. He argues, convincingly, that being non-universal is not equivalent to being unethical, because there is a legitimate and persuasive view of ethics, which suggests that our communal attachments and relationships themselves give rise to ethical obligations. On this view, humans have obligations to other human beings as such, but these obligations also have to be weighed against competing particularist obligations, which flow from the person's relationships and commitments. Moral action, on this view, involves the person (the moral agent) in weighing a number of factors and obligations, including obligations deriving from relationships, in deciding what is the right thing to do. Miller writes:

[W]e are tied in to many different relationships, families, work groups, voluntary associations, religious and other such communities, nations—each of which makes demands on us, and there is no single overarching perspective from which we can order or rank these demands. In case of conflict . . . I simply have to weigh [the] . . . respective claims, reflecting both on the nature of my relationship to the two individuals and on the benefits that each would get from the help I can give.   (David Miller, *On Nationality*, 53.)

This is an attractive vision of ethical reasoning, for it does seem to capture the process of reasoning that many of us go through in weighing moral considerations.

Miller's conception that we have associative obligations—obligations derived from membership in particular communities—is consistent with common-sense morality and most ethical theories. Most ethical theories view us as having particularist obligations, some of which cannot be assimilated to the idea of a moral agent entering into

---

[4] This formulation is suggested by Gomberg, 'Patriotism Is Like Racism', 144.

[5] Giving special priority to co-nationals does not necessarily imply a departure from universalism, of course. It is possible to defend special ties or more limited forms of ethical action from a universalist standpoint. See Robert Goodin, 'What Is So Special about our Fellow Countrymen?' *Ethics*, 98 (1988), 3–86.

a contract (or promise) with someone else, and so giving rise to special obligations. The family is the clearest example of an *unchosen* associative relationship, which is generally thought to give rise to obligations. Despite some liberals' emphasis on the importance of equality and neutrality in the moral point of view, most liberals do think that we have duties to people simply in virtue of our relationship to them.[6] The question, then, can be reformulated as follows: is national partiality an unacceptable form of partiality—and so like racism— or is it an entirely legitimate and acceptable form of partiality—and so like the family?

The argument that nations are moral communities, and therefore legitimate, proceeds in two steps. The first move in this argument is to suggest that national attachments and relationships are important to individual self-identity. These relationships matter to individuals, and, in fact, define individual identity in a way that is particularly strong.

It is not at all clear that the fact that people have a particular identity, in itself, constitutes an argument for recognizing it, politically or institutionally, at least not without additional arguments. I supply some of these additional arguments, however, and claim that there are important normative implications involved in the claim that national attachments matter to people. I discuss this through exploring the analogies, and disanalogies, between national and religious commitments. The second issue that arises in the attempt to argue that nations have intrinsic ethical value concerns the kinds of arguments that can ground this kind of moral claim.

In Hurka's formulation of this argument, nations and nationality are intrinsically valuable because co-nationals are creating a good in common. This is developed through an analogy with the goods created in a good marriage. People in a good marriage create goods internal to the marriage. These goods need not be grand ones nor unique to that couple: they are benefits produced jointly, such as companionship and love, but they are, nevertheless, objectively good. Hurka then argues that Canadian national identity is valuable because Canadians are rightly proud of the various goods that they have created in common: they have maintained political institutions and through them the rule of law in Canada, which ensures liberty and security for all Canadian citizens. Other goods, such as universal health care, have also been produced through the relationship. Hurka extends his argument to Quebec. All the people of Quebec, he argues, are justly proud

---

[6] See Will Kymlicka, *Contemporary Political Philosophy* (Oxford: Clarendon Press, 1990), 21–5 for the importance of special relationships in moral thinking.

of the goods they have created: many of these are the same liberal-democratic goods that are produced in Canada as a whole, and replicated in many other places, such as a flourishing democracy and the rule of law. Others are more specific to Quebec: they have managed to keep their language and culture alive. Hurka's point is that these are objectively good and have been produced by Quebeckers in their relations with each other.

Miller's formulation of the intrinsic value argument is somewhat different. He emphasizes, as we have seen, first, that national identity is an important element of personal identity, and second, that it is a relationship involving mutual benefit and trust, sentiments of affinity and solidarity. Miller does not offer an objective list of the kinds of goods produced by nations, or internal to the bonds of attachments felt by co-nationals. Instead, he takes it as given that such collective forms of identity are valuable, because important to people, and that the different national communities embody different goods.[7]

At this point, Miller confronts the problem of critical moral justification. It is widely thought that there are difficulties attached to justifying a particular ethical good or objective value. Specifically, the critical principle that is supposed to play a foundational role—whether they are Platonic forms or Aristotelian wholes and their ends, or Lockean natural law or Thomistic human nature or utilitarian general happiness—is essentially contested.

Miller's response to this problem consists of two parts. On the one hand, he seems to suggest that we believe that nations are ethically valuable communities and that this is an important moral judgment. As Nielsen has argued, in a similar fashion, there is a non-derivative value attached to social identities and control over our own lives. This is one of our 'bedrock moral judgments'. Against those, such as Brighouse, who demand a further justificatory argument for the view that nations, which furnish our social identity, are valuable, Nielsen claims:

We have no more reason to treat social self-identification as an unacceptable value because we cannot prove that it is intrinsically good than we can have

---

[7] In this respect, Hurka's formulation seems superior. It is not vulnerable to the criticism that Simon Caney advances against Miller's version of the argument in 'Nationality, Distributive Justice and the Use of Force', *Journal of Applied Philosophy*, 16/2 (1999), 123–38, at 125. Caney argues that, unless the value of nationhood is tied to objective goods, it will be too undiscriminating. The problem arises because in many cases people have repugnant cultural identities—the examples he provides are of the snob and the racist—and it is counterintuitive to claim that these imply special duties—to favour your own race, for example.

for saying that pleasure is not good or pain is not bad because we cannot prove they are intrinsic goods and bad respectively. (Kai Nielsen, 'Secession: The Case of Quebec', *Journal of Applied Philosophy*, 10 (1993), 29–43.)

The second line of argument in response to the problem of critical moral justification involves an appeal to the public culture of the community. This appeal functions rather like reflective equilibrium in Rawls's theory: to situate the bedrock moral judgements that we have within the context of an open debate that itself performs a justificatory function. Miller argues that the concept of public culture ensures that the obligations that national identification carries with it are not defined subjectively, by each individual. As Miller argues, the concept of the public culture is objective in relation to the individual—the individual could be wrong about what is required of him or her, for example—and it performs a justificatory function as long as an ideal condition obtains, namely, that the culture is arrived at through a process of open critical debate and reflection.[8] Miller describes the 'ideal condition' in this way: 'national identities and the public cultures that help to compose them are shaped by process of rational reflection to which members of the community can contribute on an equal footing'.[9] This suggests that the concept of public culture is intended to serve a critical, justificatory role to ground both the obligations that attach to individuals as members of national com munities and the goods internal to those communities. It does this because the public culture is conceived of as an open debate in which certain principles and obligations emerge as reasonable and, in a plausible sense, foundational.

This chapter will treat the argument that these two theorists have developed together, despite the fact that there are sharp differences in focus and emphasis. Hurka, for example, focuses on the fact that there is an obligation to fellow nationals if they are all engaged in a common relationship that produces ethically valuable goods. Miller argues that the relationship and attachments that define nationality are themselves intrinsically valuable, but that the obligations that follow from this flow from a shared public culture which results from deliberation over time about what it means to belong to that nation. In spite of these differences, however, they both share the view that nations are intrinsically valuable moral communities, and much of the discussion in both works focuses on the bonds of solidarity and the goods of trust and membership that co-nationals share.

---

[8] Miller, *On Nationality*, 69.   [9] Miller, *On Nationality*, 70.

In what follows, I will suggest that this argument can be spelled out in ways so that it is primarily an argument from fairness. However, despite its strength—outlined in the section below—this line of defence leaves some important questions unanswered and gives rise to some serious criticisms. Specifically, it leaves unclear the nature (or scope) of our obligations to fellow nationals. It is also open to the objection that nations require a belief in myths and falsehoods, and this raises questions about whether they are genuine moral communities. The most serious problem with this line of argument, however, is that it fails to distinguish nations from other intrinsically valuable moral communities, or help us to adjudicate claims between nations.

An Argument from Fairness

This section elaborates on the claim that national identities are important to people, that they care about them, to suggest that this provides the basis of an important normative argument centred on the issue of fairness.

Of course, by itself, the empirical claim that national identities matter to people does not justify strong rights or protections. However, there is an important normative dimension to this claim. These implications are usually explored through a discussion of the analogy between national and religious commitments. Much recent work in contemporary liberal political philosophy has been concerned with those considerations that are publicly admissible and can count as a *reason* in public discussion and adjudication. The appropriate due given to religious arguments has been central to this debate about the scope of liberal public reason. Historically, liberals have been averse to religious arguments and religious sentiments. They have argued that religious appeals grounded in God's will are an inappropriate justificatory basis for liberal public policy. At the same time, however, liberals have advocated religious toleration, and have deemed religious beliefs as 'reasonable' in light of the 'burdens of judgment'. Even more, (Rawlsian) liberals have recognized the deep importance of religion in people's lives: they have recognized that religious commitments can be 'constitutive' of particular personal identities and so should be subject to protection by a fair and neutral liberal state.[10]

---

[10] This point is from Andrew Levine, 'Just Nationalism: The Future of an Illusion', in Jocelyne Courture, Kai Nielsen, and Michel Seymour (eds.), *Rethinking Nationalism, Canadian Journal of Philosophy Supplementary Volume* 22 (1996), 345–63, at 351.

At this point, it should be clear how the reference to the deep and constitutive importance of people's national identity could operate within a liberal framework. The state should not attempt to repress national commitments, just as it should not repress religious faith, but should be fair to competing national claims. This is a compelling argument, as far as it goes. If national identity *matters* to people, if people are nationally mobilized and this identification is important to them and they care about it, then, why should they have to give this up, as long, of course, as their national affiliation isn't hurting anyone else? If liberalism means anything, it means that individuals should be free, as far as possible, to make choices about what is important to them, in their own life. The empirical fact that people tend to care about their identities is significant for liberal public policy, because it suggests that liberals, whatever they might think of national identities and national membership, should treat these identities fairly and certainly not require individuals to give up these identities.

When this empirical claim is put in the context of the public policies of liberal-democratic states, it is apparent that this discourse about identities and liberal public reason is too narrow to accommodate claims arising from national identity. To begin with, contemporary liberal-democratic states are not neutral on issues of relevance to nationalists: they do not adjudicate impartially between rival claims, but, in fact, are both historically and conceptually complicit in privileging a particular national identity or identities. Since this is so, we cannot treat a nationalist reason as just one more reason to be considered by the neutral liberal state, since political and institutional recognition—by the state—of a particular language, culture, and history is crucial to the reproduction of many national groups, and the lack of such institutional recognition is a serious handicap for national groups—especially since they are operating in the face of some other group's political and institutional recognition. In many cases, the claims of members of a national group to institutional recognition of their identity is a claim to equal or fair treatment because these claims arise in the context of some (other) group having such recognition.

Moreover, treating claims arising from national identity as admissible reasons in the context of liberal public reason tends to suggest that reasons based on national identities are similar to reasons from the purely self-interested standpoint. This is extremely problematic, however. It misrepresents national claims, and does so in a way that suggests that they should be treated less seriously. If national claims were based merely on some kind of emotional identification with a particular group, it is not clear that we should take them seriously. As

Dworkin once argued in the course of a debate with Lord Devlin concerning the degree to which morality should be enforced by the state, we cannot base a moral position on an emotional reaction. While emotions are insufficient to justify a moral position, and so cannot produce moral reasons, moral reasons frequently *do* produce an emotional reaction. It is necessary therefore to demonstrate that there is a normative argument or moral reason that justifies the position.[11]

It is relevant, therefore, that nationalist arguments *are* primarily normative, not self-interested. Nationalists see their arguments as arguments about what *should* be done, about what is *legitimate* state action. They often appeal to the good of the nation, as part of a claim about legitimate political action. They think that this sort of claim counts as a moral reason in favour of a particular policy. Wayne Norman has argued convincingly that nationalists do not merely 'debate the merit of policies in terms of their impact on justice and individual well-being. Nationalists ... appeal to considerations or sentiments that cannot be directly reduced to these terms. In addition to the question of justice or material benefits of a policy, they care about what it does to the nation's soul, so to speak. Is it consistent with the nation's identity?'[12] In other words, nationalist reasons are presented as moral reasons for or against particular courses of action. Nationalist forms of justification *compete* with other forms of justification based on issues of justice or economic efficiency. They present a competing argument about the kinds of considerations that should count as relevant to legitimate public action.

Moreover, nationalists are right to see their arguments as primarily normative. Because the operations of governments are bounded by the borders of the state, most normative arguments about acceptable state action are arguments about the good of the community and assume that the person making these arguments cares about the community. Indeed, if one knew that the person didn't care about the community, one might question whether his/her recommendations should be taken seriously. These kinds of arguments about the good of a community with which one identifies or happens to belong are not

[11] Ronald Dworkin, 'Lord Devlin and the Enforcement of Morals', in Richard Wasserstrom (ed.), *Morality and the Law* (Belmont: Wadsworth Publishing Company, 1971), 63. See also Geneviève Nootens, 'Liberal Restrictions on Public Arguments', in Couture, Nielsen, and Seymour (eds.), *Rethinking Nationalism*, 255–7. Thanks to Geneviève for first bringing my attention to this point during a conversation in Montreal.

[12] Wayne Norman, 'Prelude to a Liberal Morality of Nationalism', in S. Brennan, T. Isaacs, and M. Milde (eds.), *A Question of Values: New Canadian Perspectives in Ethics and Political Philosophy* (Atlanta, GA: Rodopi 1997), 12–13.

normally viewed as self-interested, because the thrust of the argument is the good of the community as a whole, not what is good for that person. It is difficult to see why it should be viewed as other than an ethical position in the case of the national community.

The ethical dimension of this concern for the community does not apply only to politically embodied nations, however. Indeed this argument has important implications for nations that do not yet have, but perhaps aspire to, institutional embodiment. To see this, consider another significant *dis*analogy between religious arguments and nationalist arguments. Neutrality with respect to religious commitments is possible, as long as religious beliefs are confined to private life and protected as part of a person's long-term project and plan of life, but not as a valid public reason for restricting abortion, say, in the circumstances of 'reasonable pluralism' about good ways of life.[13] But nationalist arguments cannot be privatized in the same way. This is so, not only because, as argued above, the state is and has been complicit in privileging a particular language and culture and identity, and so cannot be viewed as neutral, but because national identities themselves cannot be regarded as purely private conceptions of the good. It is implicit in nationalist forms of justification that nationalist arguments are intended as public reasons, competing with other legitimate reasons concerning the merits of certain policies. Indeed, nationalist identities are *primarily* political identities: they are concerned with the political community with which one identifies, and are normally characterized by the aspiration for some kind of political or institutional recognition of this community.

The empirical claim—that national identities are important to people—when put in the context of contemporary liberal-democratic states, is an important component of an argument about fairness. It underlines the fact that government decisions advantage some groups and disadvantage others, and that those people who are disadvantaged may *care* about their national identity just as much as those people who take for granted the fact that the state expresses their particular political (and cultural and linguistic) identity. This suggests that this empirical claim is a crucial component of an argument about fairness. It raises the question: if identities matter to people, then, how can the state justifiably privilege a particular national identity at the expense of

---

[13] The contrast between religious and national identities is not perfect, however. Religous identities are not in fact confined to private life, and often involve communal practices. And quite often, liberal states are not perfectly neutral with respect to religious identities. The contrast, while not perfect, is still relevant: liberal states are in some respects not perfectly neutral towards religion, but inevitably non-neutral towards national identities.

all others? Isn't it unfair of the state to recognize one national identity and to marginalize others?

This is the normative argument implicit in the claim that national identities matter to people. This argument is not always clearly brought out by proponents of liberal nationalism, but many theorists do combine this empirical claim about the importance of national communities to individual self-identity with some recognition of the non-neutral character of the state.[14] This is not the only argument implicit in the intrinsic defence of nations. This defence also relies on a certain quite persuasive conception of moral reasoning; and a kind of foundational argument to ground this kind of claim. However, this is a compelling line of argument for the normative importance of national communities.

How Can We Be Obligated to Fellow Nationals?

One of the problems with the argument that national attachments are intrinsically valuable is that it leaves unclear the precise kind and scope of our obligations. Specifically, it does not explain either the nature of our obligations—whether they are voluntary or not—or the scope of the obligations we owe to fellow nationals.

The first problem—that of unclarity regarding the scope of our obligations—is not very serious. In Hurka's formulation, the obligations that co-nationals have to fellow nationals and to the nation would seem to be limited to supporting relationships that produce objectively valuable goods. Hurka does not want to condone a form of nationalism that is objectively despicable, or racist, or devoid of value. Recall the question posed earlier: is nationalism a form of partiality more like racism (and so to be condemned) or more like the family (and so legitimate)? Hurka's answer to this question is: it depends. If, like the family, it produces various objectively valuable goods, then it carries with it certain obligations to uphold this relationship. But if, like racism, the form of nationalism is exclusive and hierarchical and oppressive—there are no goods internal to the relationship—then, there are no obligations arising from the association.

On the face of it, this is quite different from Miller's argument. Miller does not make the obligations that arise from national attachments dependent on a conception of objective value. Indeed, at times Miller seems to suggest that that formulation would render the

[14] Miller, *On Nationality*, 20, 33–5.

obligations not genuinely associative ones, but, rather, obligations derived from the objective value in question—justice or some conception of the good. However, Miller also seems to take it for granted that there will be goods internal to a national community of equal members, who share the same identity and have forged bonds of mutual attachment. In other words, his description of nationhood carries with it certain objective goods like mutual trust and reciprocity.

Since the goods are internal to the relationship or the attachment, and hence dynamic—not something to be distributed—it makes sense for Miller to describe the obligations as determined by the members themselves in an open debate, in which each has an equal say. This appeal to the public culture of the community leaves the obligations owed indeterminate in the sense that they cannot be derived logically, and hence will vary from community to community.[15] It is hard to see this as a serious problem, however, since it is in the nature of the case that a self-determining, self-governing political community—or one that aspires to be self-determining and self-governing—would decide for itself, in an open debate, the kinds of obligations that they owe to each other.

The second problem with the discussion of obligations, at least in Miller's and Hurka's work, is that it leaves unclear the precise nature of the obligations, whether voluntary or not. I think this problem stems from conflating two quite different kinds of national communities.[16] We need to distinguish between, on the one hand, nations conceived as political communities, engaged in a system of co-operation and subject to a common set of laws and institutions, and, on the other, nations which are not yet, but perhaps aspire to be, political communities, such as the Kurdish nation.

In the case of a nation conceived of as a political community, the obligations that are owed to it stem not merely from associative ties, but from being a participant in and recipient of the benefits of political co-operation. This can be justified in a variety of ways: as based on a

---

[15] Miller recognizes that, in the absence of a political forum, the obligations remain merely traditional in nature, whereas once you have a politically organized nation, the content of those obligations become democratically debated and subject to critical reflection. With the state in place, some of these obligations are embodied in the formal obligations of citizenship so that everyone knows fairly concretely what is required of her/him by way of social contribution; and everyone can have reasonable confidence that others will be made to do their bit as well. This provides a normative case for nations having states, but it doesn't deal with the issue of what national obligations might amount to in the absence of states.

[16] Miller does distinguish between these two conceptions in *On Nationality*, 59, and claims only to be concerned with the independent ethical weight to be attached to nationhood, but his examples conflate the two.

conception of reciprocity or fair play; as voluntarily incurred or con-
sented to through participation in democratic political institutions; or
as derived from a general moral obligation to support just institutions.[17] In this section, I want to argue that part of the force of the
argument that we have (non-renounceable) obligations to the nation
derives from the kinds of practices and institutions that characterize
politically embodied nations.

In cases where the state embraces a nation—or, to put it another
way, where a nation also forms a political community—the mutual
obligations that co-nationals owe to one another are enforced by the
state and citizens benefit from the goods that the state helps to secure.
The example most frequently cited in Hurka's article does not distinguish between these two different conceptions of a nation. In his
example, Canadians together have produced a good (the rule of law)
through political action and thereby have an obligation to support the
good (the rule of law). But this example—supposedly of the way in
which the moral bonds of *nationality* furnish obligations—seems
closely bound up with the basis of *political* obligation, and specifically,
the moral duty to uphold just institutions and practices. This is
because state action is absolutely crucial to securing the good in question.

This conflation between the two different meanings of the term
'nation' is also at work in Miller's example of Britons having together
produced a good—the National Health Service. They are obligated to
support it, in part it would seem, because these public policies and the
moral arguments that support it emerge through democratic debate.
As Miller puts it, we should support the National Health Service for
the reasons that were given when the National Health Service was first
introduced (into Britain) and which are still given when the subject is
debated from time to time.[18] In this case, it is not clear that the obligation is a genuine associative one—dependent on the bonds of attachment that co-nationals feel for one another—but seems to be derived
from an argument that presupposes the legitimacy of democratic decision-making at the state level.

---

[17] I am not endorsing any of these justificatory arguments in particular. The idea that we
consent to political authority, and so acquire an obligation to obey by engaging in a democratic practice is particularly problematic, since it grounds the moral requirement to obey
in individual autonomy, while ignoring the obvious fact that the democratic 'choices' we
face are hardly an open option. The idea that we have a general obligation to uphold just
institutions, combined with Jeremy Waldron's distinction between those who are insiders
and those who are outsiders with respect to certain institutions and practices, seems more
promising. Jeremy Waldron, 'Special Ties and Natural Duties', *Philosophy & Public Affairs*
22/1, (Winter 1993), 3–30.
[18] Miller, *On Nationality*, 70.

In cases where a nation is not yet politically embodied, it is difficult to see these obligations as binding in exactly the same way. This is not only for the reason given above—that it is unclear what, say, Welshmen owe to one another given that there is as yet no Welsh state—but also because the subjective element is constitutive of national identities or attachments, and this suggests that the obligations that a national identity may carry with it are potentially renounceable. Both Miller and Hurka emphasize the fact that people do in fact *care* about the nation to which they belong; that it is a significant part of their identity. Hurka argues that nations produce goods that are objectively, intrinsically valuable. But he is at pains to point out that their objective value is not objective in some sense unrelated to the well-being of the people who are creating the good in common. The goods created are not necessarily special or distinctive in the world; rather, they are goods *for* the people who are creating them through their relationship. In Miller's case, he emphasizes that the subjective component (of national identity) is an important, indeed necessary condition for nationhood. While it is of course true, as Miller emphasizes, that national identity is not completely chosen, it is also the case that an important element of nationality is a sense of '*shared* belief and *mutual* commitment'.[19] If the Welsh person feels no sense of Welsh identity, no feelings toward fellow Welsh women and men, but instead identifies with Britain, then, it is hard to conceive of what sense that person should be thought of as Welsh, and how that person could then have any special obligations towards others.[20]

Now, if this is right, it seems that it is very important to distinguish between nations that are also states—that have political institutions and have implemented various just rules of law and democratic prac-

[19] Miller, *On Nationality*, 27. The italics are mine.

[20] It might be objected here that people can have obligations that are not acknowledged. Suppose, for example, that I am a Ruritanian, and that the actions of other Ruritanians ensure that I am not discriminated against, and also ensures the survival of the language and culture of the community that I participate in. While you might object that I am free riding on their actions, and that a principle of reciprocity or fair play suggests that I do have (unacknowledged) obligations, it seems to me that this is too strict. I think that this is a version of a free rider problem, and the possibility of free riders is part of the reason why nations aspire to have political or institutional recognition. But I don't think that, in the absence of states, this can constitute even a normative argument for imposing obligations. For while I might myself benefit from the continued existence of this culture—because it is difficult to learn another language, or another culture—I might think it would be better, all things considered, if Ruritanianism disappeared. Would I be wrong, for example, to ensure that my children learned German, say, on the grounds that they would then have more opportunities. I don't think such a person can be faulted. Unless we suppose that there is something intrinsically valuable about the Ruritanian identity, that is not carried by some other kinds of identity, then I don't think this move is available to us.

tices—from nations that merely aspire to some form of self-government or perhaps statehood, but do not have the political or institutional mechanisms to implement a scheme of justice or democratic governance. This distinction has important practical implications: it suggests that the American who does not identify with America is an alienated American, who still owes obligations to his (politically embodied) nation; but that the Kurd who does not identify with Kurdistan, and who does not want to think of himself as Kurdish—he has become assimilated into the Turkish way of life and has adopted a Turkish identity—does *not* owe any obligations to his fellow Kurdish nationals or to the Kurdish homeland.[21]

Miller and Hurka avoid this distinction between the two kinds of nations, and the implications that this has for the nature of obligations owed to fellow nationals. At crucial points in their argument, they conflate the two different senses of the term 'nation', and so are able to suggest both that national identity is, in part at least, subjective; and that these obligations attach to all co-nationals.

At this point some might object that my emendation has profoundly pro-statist implications. It suggests that the obligation that individuals have to support just *states* is, to some extent at least, non-voluntary; while the obligation to support one's *nation*—conceived of in non-political terms—is voluntary, at least in the sense that it is capable of being renounced.

Certainly, my interpretation of the differential obligations owed to the different kinds of nations, and specifically, about the nature of the obligation that arises from associative ties, suggests a limit to nationalist claims. Indeed, this is suggested by the conception of nation in Chapter 1, according to which nationhood must be, in part at least, subjectively defined.

This subjective definition of nationhood is necessary if we want to avoid the problem of contested definitions of what 'really' constitutes a nation. Identification of a national group by others—by people outside the group—is often used to *deny* particular national identities. Thus, Turkey has frequently referred to the Kurdish population in the southeast corner of Turkey, not as Kurds, but as 'mountain Turks'. In this way, Turkey denies their distinctive national identity, and so can ignore the political claims to self-determination, which flow from this.

---

[21] The example of the alienated American is used by Harry Brighouse to question Miller's theory. Harry Brighouse, 'Against Nationalism', in Couture, Nielsen, and Seymour, *Rethinking Nationalism*, 375–405, at 385. I think, however, that it makes more sense to distinguish between the two conceptions of the nation, as is done here, than to reject the theory wholesale.

Greek nationalists deny that Macedonians are a distinctive national group: they claim that the Macedonians in northern Greece are really Greeks; and Bulgarian nationalists claims that Macedonians in the former Yugoslavia are really Bulgarians. If we want to avoid people denying the national identity of others, or attributing a particular national identity to the person that is not the one that the person herself accepts, then we have to conceive of the obligations that flow from nationality as potentially renounceable. To put this another way: if part of the normative claim that nations make is dependent on the fact that people feel strongly about them, then, people's obligations must be conceived as at least partly dependent on their identities and feelings and preferences.

This, of course, is not the view that many nationalists have of the matter. Many nationalists conceive of *the nation* itself as the highest good, which all members of the nation ought to strive for. In Parnell's famous words, inscribed on his statue in Dublin,

> No man has a right to fix the boundary to the march of a nation.
> No man has a right to say to his country,
> Thus far shalt thou go and no further
>
> Inscribed on the foot of the statue of Charles Stewart Parnell,
> in O'Connell Street in Dublin.

The implications of this are clear: first, and primarily, that the nation has a historical destiny which no one individual can deny; second, and implicit in this view, is the idea that you can have obligations to the nation, whether or not you think of yourself as belonging to the nation. This was directed in part at the Protestants who formed a majority in the north-eastern part of the island of Ireland and who did not think of themselves as Irish, and their Conservative allies in Britain. It informs one of two arguments frequently given by Irish republicans against the partition of the island.[22] But not only is this view of obligations hard to argue for, as I said earlier, without invoking the unacceptable idea of a national historical mission, but it leads us straight into the politics of denial, whereby the national identity of the other—a British national identity, felt by Protestants—is rejected as invalid and indeed, treacherous.

[22] The other is a historical argument about the democratic will of the community. The claim is that in the 1918 Westminster general election, the first conducted in the United Kingdom of Great Britain and Ireland under universal suffrage, the two major parties which supported Irish independence, and opposed partition won three-quarters of Ireland's parliamentary seats. See John McGarry and Brendan O'Leary, *Explaining Northern Ireland* (Oxford: Blackwell, 1995), 25.

In response to the claim that there are definite statist implications in this formulation of the type of obligations that are owed to nations, it is important to emphasize that the issue of the nature of the obligations—whether the identities on which they are based are renounceable or not—does not tell us much about which kind of obligation should trump the other in the case of conflict. This is an extremely important question that arises whenever a minority national community seeks greater self-government or independence from a just liberal-democratic state. In many cases—Catalonia in Spain, Quebec in Canada, Scotland and Wales in the United Kingdom—the interesting question of obligation is not this one we have been considering, namely, the necessary conditions for acquiring the obligation, but which obligation should take precedence when they conflict. This is the question that arguably indicates whether there is a statist bias in this argument. Nothing argued here bears on this question. Indeed, while this chapter has envisaged a person who owes obligations to support just institutions and practices, it has not yet defined justice at all. In later chapters, it will be clear that a just society is one that not only respects rights of individuals to their basic freedoms and rights, including their right to democratic governance, but also embodies a conception of justice among national communities.

Myths, Lies, and Civic Education

In the section above, on the obligations that people have to fellow members of their nation, it was clear that Miller specifies that this must be determined by an open debate among all members of the national community. This conception of a public culture is meant to address a second challenge to the intrinsic value argument. This is the concern that national identities cannot be legitimate elements of one's personal identity, and that nations cannot be ethical communities, because they are based on beliefs about shared history or shared culture that we know, in fact, to be false.

This criticism is probably one of the most common ones levelled against nationalism. Nations are not face-to-face communities in which each person has direct personal knowledge of the other, but are 'imagined' in Benedict Anderson's sense that they are communities of shared beliefs which are transmitted by cultural means. This has led many to worry that they may indeed be wholly spurious inventions.

This concern about the 'invented' and therefore spurious nature of nations and national identities has been supported by a number of writers in the history and sociology of nationalism who have pointed to serious discrepancies between the beliefs that undergird the nation and factual evidence about the actual history of the group. We know, for example, that in the nineteenth century, many spoken dialects were transformed into the status of a language, with a dictionary, a grammar, and so on; and that this process tended to emphasize differences between that language and other related languages. For example, many theorists in the nineteenth century, when they considered the various 'peoples' of Europe, were inclined to view Slavs as one people, with no idea that various distinct nations would emerge, each speaking distinct, though related, languages. Examination of the process that led to this suggests that the current divisions, and current identities, were by no means inevitable. To some extent, it is safe to say that a particular language was 'created' or 'invented', although, as even the most extreme proponents of the 'created' school of thought have admitted (Gellner), this process did require 'some pre-existing differentiating marks to work on'.[23] As Hobsbawm says, referring to the nationalist belief in the deep and enduring nature (and naturalness) of the nation: 'nationalism requires too much belief in what is patently not so'.[24] Gellner sums up the evidence on the constructed nature of national communities in a pithy remark: 'It is nationalism which engenders nations, and not the other way round'.[25]

This analysis also underlies criticisms by both Marxists and liberals that nationalism is an indefensible form of identity. Marxists have typically viewed nationalism as an invention of the bourgeoisie, designed to deflect the proletariat from understanding their true interests.[26] Similarly, liberals tend to dismiss nationalism as an irrational communal identity, and conceive of the person instead in terms of his/her essential interests in personal autonomy, and, following from this, the resources to further his/her plan of life. '[N]ationalisms', Andrew Levine has alleged, reflecting this line of criticism, 'are deliberately contrived and promoted. They are the work of political entrepreneurs

[23] Ernest Gellner, *Thought and Change* (London: Wiedenfeld and Nicholson, 1964), 168.

[24] Eric J. Hobsbawm, *Nations and Nationalism Since 1780* (Cambridge: Cambridge University Press, 1990), 12.

[25] Ernest Gellner, *Nations and Nationalism* (Ithaca, NY: Cornell University Press, 1983), 55.

[26] However, as Walker Connor has emphasized, Marxists have frequently made use of nationalism. See Walker Connor, *The National Question in Marxist Leninist Theory and Strategy* (Princeton, NJ: Princeton University Press, 1984). Erica Benner, *Really Existing Nationalisms; A Post-Communist View from Marx and Engels* (Oxford: Clarendon Press, 1995) argues that Marx and Engels had a more sophisticated view than this one commonly attributed to them.

who mold popular longings for communal forms appropriate to modern life in nationalist directions'.[27]

Despite its popularity, this general line of argument, at least in its strongest form, is not very convincing. In the first place, it is a very strong requirement for treating an identity seriously that it be universally true or embedded in the nature of human beings. Most identities—ethnic identities, racial identities, sexual identities, even gender identities—are more fluid than the bearers of these identities experience them as. They experience them as relatively stable features of themselves, as part of their very identity, even when they also recognize that they were formed through interaction with other people and through social relations—in the jargon, socially constructed.

Second, it is unclear what normative significance we should attach to the knowledge that historians and sociologists of nations have revealed their contingent nature, as part political project, part response to the processes of industrialization and modernization. Many of the institutions that we view as legitimate—the family, the liberal-democratic state—have similarly murky origins. An investigation of the origins of the family, for example, may reveal it in a less than heroic light: as formed from biological necessity, or sexual conquests, or unequal power relations. But this is not thought to be necessarily relevant to the legitimacy of the family as an institution, as long as the family can be grounded on another, morally acceptable basis, such as love, consent, or equality.[28]

The liberal-democratic state may also have contingent and less than illustrious origins: in power politics, coercion, and the functional imperatives of a modern bureaucratic regime. But this is not thought to affect its legitimacy. Rawls, in *A Theory of Justice*, does not think that the origins of the liberal-democratic state are relevant to the question of its justificatory basis. The question he asks is whether there are *principles* underlying the liberal democratic state that can serve to justify it. If this question is applied to the nation—which is a community of equal members, sharing a belief in a common history or culture or shared future, and relevantly self-governing—there is no doubt that it can be grounded on principles which are themselves justifiable, and which are also fundamental to moral conceptions that liberals and democrats are committed to.

However, critics of nationalism do not merely claim that nations are socially constructed, or functional in conditions of modernity, but that

---

[27] Andrew Levine, 'Just Nationalism: The Future of an Illusion', in Couture, Nielsen, and Seymour (eds.), *Rethinking Nationalism*, 345–63, at 361.

[28] I owe this point to Daniel Weinstock, although he can't remember ever saying it.

they involved deliberate manipulation of large groups of people by those holding positions of power. This, I take it, underlies the Marxist criticism of nationalism that it serves the interests of the bourgeoisie; and of Levine's concern that these are deliberately contrived by political élites to further their own interests. This charge does go some way toward delegitimating national identities. Like Plato's Noble Lie, which is propagated by the Guardian class in order to ensure both the harmony of the society and the contentment of different groups with their class position, nationalism is conceived as employed by capitalist or political leaders simply to serve their ends.

The problem with this interpretation of nationalism is that there is very little evidence for it. First, and directed toward both Levine and the crude Marxist argument that nationalism is an ideology designed to serve the interests of the ruling (economic or political) class, it must be said here, that nationalism has a mixed history, sometimes acting as a progressive force, sometimes acting in the service of entrenched interests. It is not at all clear either that élites supported it originally, or that subsequently it has principally served élite interests.[29]

Second, the very idea that nationalism is the product of political manipulation begs the question: why can people be mobilized along national lines, rather than along class lines, when the two compete? The idea that it is pure political project, pure manipulation by élites, fails to come to grips with the reasons for its success—rather than that of other forms of identity, which presumably can also be manipulated. More seriously, for liberal-democrats anyway, this line of criticism fails to treat people with respect, as agents capable of making decisions over their own destiny. Perhaps, in a society in which all sources of information are controlled by the state, the élite-manipulation argument makes sense, but in a society with relatively open avenues of communication, and open political debates—that is, liberal-democratic societies—it is hard to describe nationalism in this way and maintain the basic assumptions about the autonomy and rationality and reasonableness of all agents, which is central to both liberalism and democratic theory.

There is, however, an important difference between the origins of liberalism or the origins of the family, say, and that of the nation. Whatever the political or economic circumstances that originally gave rise to liberalism, liberals today are not required to endorse this past, but only to accept the underlying principles of liberalism. But national

---

[29] This mixed history is well documented in Liah Greenfeld's *Nationalism. Five Roads to Modernity* (Cambridge, MA: Harvard University Press, 1992).

identities have a more complex relationship to the past. Belief in a certain history, certain bonds of attachment to co-nationals and a special relationship to a certain territory is part of what it means to be a nationalist.

At this point, it is important to distinguish between two separate issues. One is the appropriate response to the beliefs that people have. As we saw earlier, in our discussion of the analogy between religion and nationalism, liberals can accept the importance of religious beliefs in people's lives, and treat them with due respect, without sharing the religious person's particular story of Creation or belief in God. Similarly, we do not need to endorse the particular version of history that a nationalist believes and accepts. Liberal justice does not require that we accept or endorse every ideology or sentiment or conception of the good that people feel or believe. Liberals need only acknowledge that many people find religious beliefs or nationalist sentiments central to their plans of life or personal identity. As Mill argues, we are free to reason with or persuade or entreat people with whom we disagree,[30] and this liberal stricture should apply also to disagreements about interpretations given to historical events.[31]

Some have argued, however, that, for a strong unambiguous identification with the nation—its people and the land—to occur, it is necessary to engage in a nation-building civic education that depicts the nation's history in an idealized light. This is a quite different issue, because it involves the question of appropriate public policy or state action. This is the view of William Galston, in *Liberal Purposes*. He argues that, in order to ensure that the individual has a willingness to fight on behalf of one's country, to obey the law, and evince loyalty to the society and its members, they must have a patriotic civic education:

If children are to be brought to accept these commitments as valid and binding, the method must be a pedagogy that is far more rhetorical than rational .... Civic education ... requires a nobler, moralizing history: a pantheon of heroes who confer legitimacy on central institutions and are worthy of emulation. It is unrealistic to believe that more than a few adult citizens of liberal societies will ever move beyond the kind of civic commitment engendered by such pedagogy. (William Galston, *Liberal Purposes; goods, virtues and diversity in the liberal state* (Cambridge: Cambridge University Press, 1991), 243–4.)

---

[30] John Stuart Mill, 'On Liberty', in *Utilitarianism, On Liberty, Considerations on Representative Government* (London: J.M. Dent, 1993), 78.

[31] There are limits to the kinds of disagreements that are permissible in liberal states. I do not want to suggest that disagreement about whether the Holocaust took place is legitimate.

If it is true that nationalism requires the deliberate obfuscation of history, it would be a serious problem for a liberal nationalist. It would suggest that liberalism cannot be reconciled with nationalism, because nationalism falls afoul of the liberal publicity condition—the liberal requirement that the institutions and practices of the society be debated in public and subject to critical public reason.

While many nationalists have sought to interpret nationalist requirements in this way, and have engaged in precisely the sort of sentimental, moralizing history that Galston advocates, it is far from clear that this is a prerequisite for developing patriotic bonds of attachment. In his book *Creating Citizens*, Eamonn Callan positions his view on patriotic civic education against those of Galston. He argues that teaching a 'noble, moralizing history' is in violation of the liberal emphasis on critical analysis and critical engagement. He argues that we can encourage the development of bonds of attachment to the community if we examine its past with the question, 'What is the best in this tradition?' at the centre.[32]

This resolves the tension between the liberal requirement of transparency and the emphasis on critical reason, while, at the same time, justifying the state in imparting history in a manner designed to encourage the development of bonds of attachment to the community. It suggests that people can be taught to be proud of their political community, and its traditions, without abridging their critical reason.

Callan's proposal also suggests an important limit to justifiable nation-building for the liberal nationalist: the educational institutions of the state should not be used to inculcate desirable emotional responses in the citizens at the expense of openness or critical scrutiny.[33] Rather, attachment to the community can be encouraged only through the teaching of a history that involves both critical engagement with and emotional generosity in interpreting the events of the past.

[32] Eamonn Callan, *Creating Citizens. Political Education and Liberal Democracy* (Oxford: Clarendon Press, 1993), 87–121.

[33] Part of Galston's challenge to the liberal is to suggest that liberals cannot dispense entirely with the emotional side. They do need to encourage some emotional responses or desires like 'the sense of justice' or the desire to be a critical, self-examining person. I think Galston is right about this, but that he goes too far in dispensing with critical reason.

What's So Special About Nations?[34]

The most serious problem with the argument that nations are morally valuable communities is that it is not very helpful in adjudicating between claims—usually over territory—by rival national communities, or to resolve disputes that arise when nation-building projects compete with policies designed to recognize other particularist identities, based on a different, intrinsically valuable, community.

Both versions of the intrinsic value argument fail to distinguish nations from other intrinsically valuable communities that produce objectively valuable goods. The authors who advance this argument tend to take the question of how to justify particularist attachments as the basic problem. Their argument proceeds by noting that memberships and attachments in general have ethical significance—analogous to membership in and attachment to a family. Because the basic problematic is the defensibility of non-universalist ethics, this argument does not help us adjudicate between the different rights and obligations that attach to different non-universalist communities. So, while this argument is a useful corrective to a purely impartialist ethics, and points to the intrinsic value of these bonds of membership and relations of trust, it does not get us very far: specifically, it fails to distinguish nations from other intrinsically valuable communities or, in Hurka's formulation, communities that produce objectively valuable goods.

Gay communities, for example, have a claim to be intrinsically valuable. Like co-nationals, members of the gay community have relations of mutual trust and their networks of relations provide a context in which its members can feel secure and gain self-respect. They can enjoy love and tolerance and pleasure and a sense of belonging. Within the gay community, people can enjoy the goods of participation and community; and many gays argue that there is a quite specific, and profoundly ethical duty that gays have to other gays—the duty of rescue.[35] In practice, of course, the celebration of sexual and ethnic identities may take place at the expense of national identities, as Miller, particularly, is at pains to note;[36] and yet, the intrinsic value argument

[34] This title is borrowed from Allen Buchanan's article, 'What's So Special about Nations?' in Couture, Nielsen, and Seymour (eds.), *Rethinking Nationalism*, 283–309, which, in turn, bears some similarity to the title of Robert Goodin's article, 'What's So Special about our Fellow Country-men?'

[35] See Brian Walker, 'Social Movements as Nationalisms or, On the Very Idea of a Queer Nation', in Couture, Nielsen, and Seymour, *Rethinking Nationalism*, 505–47, especially at 526–7.

[36] Miller, *On Nationality*, 133–9.

is unable to prioritize these claims, or give us much guidance on how to weigh them when they compete.

This argument is similar in some respects to the one advanced by Allen Buchanan in his essay, 'What's So Special About Nations?' There, Buchanan argues that it is morally arbitrary to privilege national identity against other forms of identity that might compete with it. This is a serious challenge to the liberal nationalist project, not only because it presses on the difficult issue of what is special about nations, but also because it suggests that it is not possible to develop a liberal form of nationalism. Buchanan writes:

To confer special rights of self-government on nations . . . is an insult to the equal status of every citizen whose primary identity and allegiance is other than national and to all who have no single primary identity or allegiance. In a word, singling out nations for self-government is a form of *discrimination* and like all discrimination violates the principle of equal respect for persons. (Allen Buchanan, 'What's So Special About Nations?', 295.)

On this view, any state that articulates the values of a particular nation, or any claim that national groups are entitled to a right to self-government, is in violation of the liberal principle of equal respect for persons—because some people are not nationalist, or care less about the nation than some other community.

One problem with Buchanan's argument is that it ignores the political and non-neutral context in which nationalists make their case. The Scottish nationalist who is seeking self-government for Scotland is not demanding *special* rights for Scotland, but only that the United Kingdom, which tends to privilege a British national identity, or associate Britishness with Englishness, be organized to give equal recognition to the Scottish national identity.[37]

It also ignores the political aspirations that tend to characterize national identities, and not other kinds of identities. There are many different kinds of identities, based on different associations, and each has different goals and seeks different goods. Members of a religious group, for example, may seek to associate so that they can worship in common. Members of the gay community share similar pursuits and a similar lifestyle and have a common identity based, in part, on bonds that develop from being discriminated against by the heterosexual majority. Accordingly, they tend to seek special protections against discrimination and their own space in civil society where gays are able to enjoy their own lifestyle. Members of a national community share an identity as members of a common *political* community and seek

---

[37] I am grateful to Alan Patten for this example.

recognition of their aspirations to be collectively, politically self-governing. The right to self-government which nationalists demand can be explained in terms of the kind of association and identity that it is; and it is odd to think, as Buchanan seems to do, that granting self-government rights to nations devalues other (non-political) identities. There are simply different identities that require different kinds of expression, and it is a fallacy to think that treating them equally means treating them the same way.

However, in cases where one's particularized identity conflicts with a nation-building project, it must be admitted that the intrinsic value argument is quite unhelpful in establishing criteria to deal with the conflict. In order to be a well-functioning national community, there has to be some form of a common public life, a common framework of laws and a forum in which debates can take place. This is likely to be hampered by the celebration of certain particularized identities. For example, it would seem necessary to have some common language(s) in which public debate can take place and through which the community can be self-determining. But if each particular ethnic group demands the preservation of its own language, it is evident that this might, if carried too far, hamper the development of a common public language in which a national debate can take place. The intrinsic value argument gives us no guidance in developing an appropriate public policy that respects both intrinsically valuable communities, since it simply confers value on both kinds of communities, and both kinds of identities.

Not only does the intrinsic value argument fail to distinguish *between* particularist attachments, it offers very limited guidance in assessing conflicts between different intrinsically valuable national communities. In other words, this argument has difficulty coping with the very likely situation that national groups will be commingled on the same territory and there will be conflicting claims between national minority groups and national majority groups, on the same territory.

For example, if Quebecois' national aspirations are justified on the grounds that national identity and bonds of attachment are *intrinsically* valuable, then, it must also be true that aboriginal nations *within* Quebec, who have a different national identity, and create a different good in common, are entitled to the same rights, because *their* national identity is also *intrinsically* valuable. This obvious point is often overlooked, because the intrinsic value argument tends to proceed in abstraction from the questions of conflict *between* different national communities, and also in abstraction from the question of territory.

There is no normative argument regarding territory to help resolve this question. Indeed, there is very little discussion of how these issues can be resolved in cases of conflict, namely, where different people feel differently about their communal attachments—with some valuing the gay community above the national community, say—or when different people are attached to different national communities, and the two overlap on the same territory.

Conclusion

This chapter examined the argument that nations are moral communities. On this argument, nations are communities characterized by bonds of solidarity and mutual trust; and objective goods are produced through this relation.[38]

The conception of morality underlying this view is a plausible and attractive one, and does not preclude obligations that are more universalist in scope. Moreover, the fact that people feel attached to these communities, and have bonds of solidarity with co-nationals is a good argument for recognizing their identity, especially when this is combined with the recognition that states are not neutral with respect to national membership. In other words, there is a very strong, incipient argument centred on fairness implicit in this conception.

This chapter then analysed three different objections to the intrinsic value argument. First, it examined the nature and scope of obligations that flow from membership in this community and suggested that the current formulations of this argument are wrong to suggest that there is no difference in kind between the obligations that are owed to nations that already are political communities, and the obligations owed to nations that do not yet form a political community. This objection is directed at Hurka's and Miller's particular versions of this argument, but does not constitute a fundamental objection to this argument.

Next, the chapter examined the objection that nations are socially constructed, the product of élite manipulation, and require a belief in falsehoods and myths, and cannot therefore be genuine moral communities. Of these criticisms, the problem of belief in myths is the most serious one for a defensible nationalism. This chapter argued, following Callan, that civic education in the interests of nation-building must be limited by the need for a genuine, open, critical debate.

---

[38] The emphasis on objective goods is more a feature of Hurka's argument than Miller's.

The third, and most serious problem with the intrinsic argument is that it offers only limited guidance in cases where there is conflict between the claims of nations and other intrinsically valuable communities including other nations. It provides a useful corrective to a purely impartialist ethic, but it needs to be supplemented by other arguments that will justify particular nation-building policies or help to establish criteria to adjudicate between rival national claims.

While the intrinsic argument *by itself* doesn't resolve these problems, it is an important argument because at least it tells us about the nature of what is being lost in certain trade-offs. It suggests, for example, that the national community with which a person may identify is not of mere instrumental value, and this may be important in providing direction in public policy choices. Moreover, as was suggested in the argument about fairness, this argument has strong egalitarian implications. This may have relevance in a policy-guiding sort of way when, for example, there is a choice between certain kinds of multi-national federal or consociational institutional arrangements—which can accommodate different national identities—and an exclusive nation-state model—which may marginalize one of the groups on the territory. However, to make the argument more precisely, much more would need to be said about the political dimension of national communities and the various considerations that might justify particular policies based on arguments about national identification.

CHAPTER 3

Beyond the Cultural Argument

This chapter assesses the merits and limitations of a prominent argument for liberal nationalism, which I call the cultural argument. This is probably the most common argument to justify both state protection of national cultures and national self-determination. The latter follows because rights to self-determination are, it is argued, the best way to protect national cultures.

This argument has been put forward by Yael Tamir, David Miller, Will Kymlicka, Neil MacCormick, and Avishai Margalit and Joseph Raz,[1] although in somewhat different versions. Version (a) of this argument is most concerned with explaining why certain kinds of protections for national identity are normatively acceptable from a liberal standpoint; even more, it aims to explain why liberals should be concerned about the viability of national communities. To do this, the authors suggest that culture and autonomy are internally related, such that a rich understanding of the basic conditions for exercising autonomy will include a rich and flourishing culture. This argument is most closely associated with Kymlicka's argument for group rights, but has also been put forward, with slight variations, by Miller and Tamir. Version (b) of this argument focuses on the importance of culture for individual self-respect and well-being. This chapter argues that this version of the argument is more successful. It is put forward by MacCormick and by Margalit and Raz. To some extent, treating these as two quite distinct versions or arguments is artificial, because

[1] Will Kymlicka, *Liberalism, Community and Culture* (Oxford: Oxford University Press, 1989) and *Multicultural Citizenship* (Oxford: Oxford University Press, 1995); Neil MacCormick, *Legal Right and Social Democracy* (Oxford: Oxford University Press, 1982); Avishai Margalit and Joseph Raz, 'On National Self-Determination', in Joseph Raz (ed.), *Ethics in the Public Domain* (Oxford: Oxford Clarendon Press, 1994); David Miller, *On Nationality* (Oxford University Press, 1995); Yael Tamir, *Liberal Nationalism* (Princeton, NJ: Princeton University Press, 1993).

many of the theorists discussed put forward elements from both versions. They are, however, analytically distinct, and it is helpful to separate them, in order to make it clear that a criticism of one variation does not necessarily affect the integrity of the other line of argument.

The chapter argues that version (a) of this argument, which focuses on autonomy, is problematic, first because it confers rights only on those groups or cultures that respect autonomy, and this is both counter-intuitive and unfair. Moreover, both versions—although particularly the first—misunderstand the relationship between nationality and culture. It is important to distinguish between a culture, at least as that is ordinarily understood, and national identity. National identities are connected to identifying with a political community, and are primarily about jurisdictional authority, not the policies or practices that a political community might implement. The chapter then argues that a certain understanding, or modified version (b), of the cultural argument is successful, and discusses the implications of this analysis.

Version A of the Cultural Argument Explained

The most prominent version of the cultural argument focuses on the internal relationship between culture and autonomy, and so demonstrates why liberals have a reason to care about the viability of culture. The first step in this argument is to identify liberalism with the value of individual autonomy. Yael Tamir, for example, defines liberalism in terms of respect for personal autonomy, reflection, and choice.[2] Kymlicka echoes this conception of liberalism: 'I . . . defend a certain vision of liberalism—grounded in a commitment to freedom of choice and (one form of) personal autonomy'.[3] This conception of liberalism is in contrast to some writers who identify toleration as the fundamental liberal value and so arrive at a different political conception of the appropriate relationship between the state and diverse cultural practices.[4]

The next step in the argument is to examine the conditions under which individuals can be said to be autonomous. The important move in this argument is the claim that culture provides the context from which individual choices about how to live one's life can be made. According to Miller, 'A common culture . . . gives its bearers . . . a

---

[2] Tamir, *Liberal Nationalism*, 6.   [3] Kymlicka, *Multicultural Citizenship*, 7.
[4] Chandran Kukathas, 'Cultural Toleration', in Will Kymlicka and Ian Shapiro (eds.), *Nomos 39: Ethnicity and Group Rights* (New York, NY: New York University Press, 1997).

background against which meaningful choices can be made.'[5] Kymlicka follows the same line: '[I]ndividual choice is dependent on the presence of a societal culture, defined by language and history . . .'[6] Not only does the culture provide the options from which the individual chooses but it infuses them with meaning. This is important to the argument: the autonomous ideal of a self-choosing, self-forming being presupposes some conception of value according to which the life is constituted, and this conception of value is provided by a national or societal culture.

At this second stage of the argument, most of the writers stress the importance of a coherent conception of value: they speak of a 'societal culture' (Kymlicka)[7], or an 'integrating culture' (Nielsen)[8] or a 'national community' (Miller). The integrating or societal nature of the cultural option is necessary to locate the various options within a coherent overall conception of what is good, or what is valuable.

The third step in the argument is the claim that, since a rich and flourishing culture is an essential condition of the exercise of autonomy, liberals have a good reason to adopt measures that would protect culture. At this point, the argument has only shown that the existence of (some) flourishing cultural structure is necessary to the exercise of autonomy but not a particular culture.

Proponents of this argument then go on to claim that the particular cultures to which people are attached should be protected because they provide the context in which autonomy is exercised. Drawing on the 'legitimate interest' that people have in ensuring 'access to a societal culture' and the 'deep bond [that most people have] to their own culture', Kymlicka argues in favour of polyethnic rights for ethnic groups and self-government rights for national minorities.[9] Similarly, Miller argues that 'everyone has an interest in not having their inherited culture damaged or altered against their will', and that sometimes 'the only way to prevent this is to use the power of the state to protect aspects that are judged to be important.'[10] Tamir also argues in favour of using state power 'aimed at protecting the cultural, religious, and linguistic identity of minorities.'[11]

---

[5] Miller, *On Nationality*, 85–6.   [6] Kymlicka, *Multicultural Citizenship*, 8.
[7] Kymlicka, *Multicultural Citizenship*, 82–3.
[8] Kai Nielsen, 'Liberal Nationalism and Secession', in Margaret Moore (ed.), *National Self-Determination and Secession* (Oxford: Oxford University Press, 1998).
[9] Kymlicka, *Multicultural Citizenship*, 107.
[10] Miller, *On Nationality*, 86–7.   [11] Tamir, *Liberal Nationalism*, 76.

Version A and the Link between Autonomy and Culture

This section focuses on version (a) of the cultural argument, which emphasizes an important link between culture and the exercise of autonomy. It assesses the criticism that the culture argument is problematic because it only gives rights to those cultures that value autonomy. It argues that this criticism is valid and that this version of the cultural argument should therefore be rejected.

Before we approach this argument, it is important to remember that an important advantage of this argument is that it suggests that there is no contradiction between liberal autonomy and unchosen membership in a nation. Contrary to those who argue that liberalism is an oxymoron—that liberalism is universalist in scope and cannot be reconciled with particularist attachments, or that the liberal emphasis on the value of individual autonomy is in sharp contrast to the unchosen character of membership in many national communities—this argument suggests that, in fact, there is a close internal connection between autonomy and cultural/national identity. If liberalism is based on autonomy, liberals cannot simply and crudely identify freedom with preference-satisfaction: they must be concerned to ensure that the appropriate conditions for the exercise of autonomy are also met. The national or encompassing culture provides the options and gives a sense of the meaning or value of these options from which the individual chooses and so forms his/her life. On this view, the opposition between autonomy and national/cultural identity is a superficial one: in fact, a rich and flourishing culture is an essential condition of the exercise of autonomy.

Now, while this argument is very strong in meeting one kind of challenge to the liberal-national project—the challenge that it is antithetical to liberalism—this focus on autonomy is also an important element in what is also the main weakness of this argument. Because culture is valuable in so far as it contributes to the exercise of autonomy, rights to the protection of culture are justified only in the cases of those groups, or those cultures, that value autonomy.

The problem that is identified by this line of criticism is that it seems unfair to limit cultural protection only to groups that protect autonomy. This is counter-intuitive because, while the argument ostensibly is designed to give recognition to a particular culture by the state, what this argument in fact ends up showing is that cultural recognition is unjustified in many cases. It justifies cultural recognition only when the culture is a liberal one. This seems unfair, because the proponents of this argument have also pointed out, in the course of making this argument, the extent to which many people care about their culture, and how people need their culture for making sense of their life, and giving it structure and meaning. If there are many people who care about their cultures—including cultures that might value things other than autonomy—and if their cultures give meaning to their life, and afford it an integrating structure, then, this, in itself, should suggest a serious problem with this argument. It suggests that what is required is a more universal type of argument, which extends to all cultures that are important to people.

The 'Snooker Ball' View of Culture

In spite of the obvious attractions for liberal-nationalists of an argument that links the value of autonomy to national or cultural protections, this argument is too problematic to be accepted. Specifically, the conclusion of the cultural argument—that we should endorse a *general* right to self-government—does not follow. In cases like Canada and the US where two groups share the same language, say, and have broadly similar cultural values, then, on this argument, it does seem to be the case that the option to assimilate is a real one. It is genuinely available to the individual to become a member of an alternative cultural community. While most (English-speaking) Canadians prefer not to be Americans, it would be hard to argue that the adoption of American culture would be so difficult and disorienting that it does not constitute a genuine option. It would also be difficult to claim that the American cultural structure was not sufficiently rich—compared to the Canadian one—that it could not provide a full range of goods from which to choose. In this case, it seems that the preferences of the Canadians are not respected; but it would be hard to describe these people as rendered *unautonomous* by their assimilation into an American culture—unless one argued, implausibly, that all collective decisions that didn't respect first preferences rendered one unautonomous. In this kind of case, it seems to me that the cultural argument would have difficulty giving self-government rights on the grounds that this is essential to autonomy, or essential to human flourishing.

This reveals a deeper, or more fundamental problem with the cultural argument for liberal nationalism. Specifically, it raises questions about the basic assumption of this argument that there is a close identification of nation with cultural community. It assumes a 'snooker ball' view of nationality, according to which nationality is a knock-on effect from culture and language. The desire to base nationality on objective cultural characteristics is understandable, but it is almost certainly false. Indeed, it is often remarked by anthropologists, sociologists, and political scientists who study national conflicts that national and ethnic identities require some 'cultural marker', some mechanism for mutual recognition of members—and so implicitly a method for recognizing outsiders—but that these do not necessarily correlate with sharp linguistic or cultural differences.[12] Of course, in some cases, national identities do correspond to cultural differences, but, even in this case, it is not clear that the identities are *based* on the different cultures. Rather, the political or institutional structures that correspond to national identities, or the various mechanisms of boundary-maintenance that groups employ, can be used to *reinforce* cultural homogeneity and so increase the extent to which the members of the group are different from outsiders. Whatever the precise relationship, the important point is that linguistic and cultural differences are not central to national identities because national identities can be mobilized along other lines.

This insight, while initially counter-intuitive, at least for people who like to ground distinct identities, and especially conflicts about identities, in some 'deeper', more objective characteristic, is confirmed when we think about some of the most violent conflicts between competing national or ethnic groups. If we compare Northern Ireland, Burundi, Rwanda, and the former Yugoslavia with Canada, Switzerland, Belgium, what is striking about the first group is that, the level of violence involved in the conflicts tends to be greater and the members of the antagonistic communities speak the same language and have broadly similar cultural values; whereas, in the latter group, relations between the communities are generally peaceful and the members of the communities speak different languages and exhibit deeper cultural differences. In other words, cultural differences do not correspond with the violence or intensity of the conflict.

This cultural similarity is often recognized by members of the antagonistic groups themselves. For example, in Northern Ireland, where there are two distinct and mutually antagonistic national communities on the same territory, the conflict between the two groups is not about some objective cultural difference. Despite a common

[12] Walker Connor, *Ethnonationalism. The Quest for Understanding* (Princeton, NJ: Princeton University Press, 1994), 32–6; Donald L. Horowitz, *Ethnic Groups in Conflict* (Berkeley, CA: University of California Press, 1985), 36–54; Thomas Hylland Eriksen, *Ethnicity and Nationalism: Anthropological Perspectives* (London: Pluto Press, 1993), 38–46.

misconception, it is not religious in nature. The groups are not arguing over the details of doctrinal interpretation. Religious leaders—priests, nuns, ministers—are not targets for violence, as they were in the Reformation period, when conflict was genuinely religious.[13]

Nor is the argument about sharp *cultural* differences. A 1968 survey of cultural similarity in Northern Ireland revealed that 67 per cent of Protestants thought Northern Irishmen of the opposite religion were about the 'same as themselves', while only 29 per cent thought the same about Englishmen. Similarly, 81 per cent of Catholics regarded Ulster Protestants as about the 'same as themselves' but only 44 per cent thought this about southern Catholics.[14] Similar results have been found by Rosemary Harris, an anthropologist studying a rural community in Northern Ireland, who argued that, despite social segregation, there was a 'considerable area within which Catholics and Protestants shared a common culture'.[15]

Analysts of the conflicts in the former Yugoslavia, especially those who adhere to the élite-manipulation school of conflict analysis, almost universally emphasize the cultural similarities between the different groups.[16] Analysts begin the puzzle of explaining what happened in the former Yugoslavia by noting that, prior to the conflict, Serbs, Croats, and Muslims shared a common life, language, physical appearance, a lot of history. The Muslims were among the most secularized Muslims anywhere in the world. One of the primary divisions was between urban and rural communities, which meant, in effect, that an urban Serb would have more in common with her urban Croat neighbour than with rural Serbs. In short, the groups themselves were culturally very similar; and cultural variation was as great *across* groups as within them.

There is a revealing dialogue between Michael Ignatieff and a Serb gunner in Croatia in 1995, which Ignatieff recounts, with some puzzlement, in an article, 'Nationalism and the Narcissism of Minor Differences'. Ignatieff tells the gunner that he can't tell Serbs and

[13] John McGarry and Brendan O'Leary, *Explaining Northern Ireland* (Oxford: Blackwell, 1995), 171–213.

[14] Richard Rose, *Governing Without Consensus: An Irish Perspective* (London: Faber, 1971), 218.

[15] Rosemary Harris, *Prejudice and Tolerance in Ulster* (Manchester: Manchester University Press, 1972), 131.

[16] Michael Ignatieff, 'Nationalism and the Narcisissm of Minor Differences', *Queen's Quarterly*, 102/1 (1995), 13–25, at 13; Paul Mojzes, *Yugoslavian Inferno* (New York, NY: Continuum Press, 1995), xvi; Noel Malcolm, *Bosnia: A Short History* (New York, NY: New York University Press, 1994), 282; Christopher Bennett, *Yugoslavia's Bloody Collapse: Causes, Course and Consequences* (New York, NY: New York University Press, 1995), 247.

Croats apart. At first, the gunner tells him that Croats and Serbs have nothing in common. Everything about them is different. Then, a few minutes later, he changes his mind and says that they are all the same: 'Look, here's how it is. Those Croats, they think they're better than us. Think they're fancy Europeans and everything. I'll tell you something. We're all just Balkan rubbish.'[17] Ignatieff uses the example to illustrate how the gunner's personal knowledge of these people, as friends and neighbours prior to the outbreak of the violence—'we're just the same'—conflicts with the political and ideological message of Serb leaders that Serbs and Croats are culturally distinct, antagonistic communities.

There is no cause to deny that the Serbian leaders attempted to escalate the violence and divisions between the communities for their own ends. Nevertheless, if national divisions are not necessarily based on different cultures, then, it is wrong to infer from the cultural similarity of groups that there are no genuine national differences between them.

Kymlicka, in *Multicultural Citizenship*, rightly argues that, during the Quiet Revolution of the 1960s, French Quebec changed dramatically from a religious and rural society to a secular and urban one. He emphasizes that he does not assume a fossilized conception of culture, but that cultures change naturally as a result of the choices of their members. Kymlicka thus concludes that we must 'distinguish the existence of a culture from its "character" at any given moment'.[18] However, this distinction between the existence and the character of a culture could be clearer. It might be better to distinguish, on the one hand, between the persistent identity borne by a shared sense of nationality and, on the other, the unremitting cultural change by which any persistent identity must be marked. A clearer formulation that captures the relationship between a shared sense of nationality and changing culture is that between culture and national *identity*.

Version B of the Cultural Argument

The second version of the cultural argument works rather differently from the version outlined above. What does the work in this version of the cultural argument is the claim that cultures are important to individual self-identity or individual self-respect. Margalit and Raz

---

[17] Ignatieff, 'Nationalism and the Narcisissm', 13–14.
[18] Kymicka, *Multicultural Citizenship*, 104.

begin their argument by characterizing the groups that, they contend, have a right to self-determination. Among the most important features of these groups are: they have a common character and common culture, which encompasses many important aspects of life; membership in the groups is an important identifying feature for each person; and the groups are large and anonymous, and mutual recognition is secured by possession of the group's general culture and other aspects.[19]

There are several steps in this argument. First, and most importantly, the groups are conceived as important to the self-respect of their members. In Margalit and Raz's view, the encompassing groups—extensionally equivalent to national groups—provide 'an anchor for their [members'] self-identification and secure belonging'.[20] Similarly, MacCormick argues that 'a sense of belonging to some nation is an element in [many people's] . . . fabric of identity'.[21] Individuals' well-being is crucially dependent on the integrity and flourishing of the encompassing group with which s/he identifies, or belongs. Margalit and Raz write: 'People's sense of their own identity is bound up with their sense of belonging to encompassing groups, and . . . their self-respect is affected by the esteem in which these groups are held.'[22]

At this point in the argument, it has been shown only that individuals' well-being is bound up in important ways with the flourishing of their group. The next step in the argument is to move from the importance to individuals of a flourishing 'encompassing group' to the claim that they should have political rights to self-government. They argue that political sovereignty is important to the flourishing of encompassing groups, mainly because the groups themselves are in the best position to judge their own interests. This mirrors Mill's argument in *On Liberty*, in which he argues that each individual is the most interested in his/her own well-being and so should be entrusted with rights to protect him/her from interference in making decisions over his/her own life. This is not, of course, a conclusive argument, but it does offer good reasons for a presumption in favour of national self-determination.

This argument helps to explain both the ethical importance of nations, and why political rights are important to such groups. However, this line of argument, at least as it has been advanced so far, does not address the hard questions raised by any theory of national

[19] Margalit and Raz, 'On National Self-Determination', 129–32.
[20] Margalit and Raz, 'On National Self-Determination', 133.
[21] MacCormick, *Legal Right and Social Democracy*, 174.
[22] Margalit and Raz, 'On National Self-Determination', 134.

self-determination. To see this, consider the parallel between J. S. Mill's idea that individuals should have sovereignty over 'that portion of a person's life and conduct which affects only himself'[23] and Margalit and Raz's idea that 'members of a group are best placed to judge' the interests of their group.[24] If Mill's distinction between self- and other-regarding behaviour in individuals is problematic, this is doubly so for nations which aspire to self-government over (diverse) territory. In the case of nations, the 'self' may be disputed, because the concept of nations is comprised of different elements, such as a sense of membership or feeling of attachment; and attachment to a territory, or 'homeland' for the national group. These two elements give rise to two different conceptions of the nation: the former is based on feelings of membership or subjective identity; the latter is based on a territory and is inclusive of all groups resident in that territory. Unfortunately, not all people who reside within the territory will self-identify, or are recognized by others, as part of the nation—usually because the nation in question has strong ethnic or cultural components. This is not a decisive criticism of this line of argument; rather, it merely points out that the proponents of this line of argument have not (yet) developed it to address many of the hard questions that arise in cases of national self-determination.

Second, and most importantly for the argument of this chapter, this version of the cultural argument seems to assume that the groups in question—the encompassing groups or national groups—are bound together by a shared culture, and that this cultural component is what makes these groups so important for individual identity and self-definition. As argued in the section above, the conflation of national groups with cultural communities is problematic. However, this does not challenge the additional point made by proponents of this argument, namely, that individuals identify with national groups and that these groups are important to individual self-respect. Version (b) of the cultural argument could be modified to reflect a more accurate conceptualization of the relationship between cultural groups and national communities.

[23] J. S. Mill, 'On Liberty', in *On Liberty, Utilitarianism, On Representative Government* (London: J.M. Dent, 1993), 69–185, at 80.
[24] Margalit and Raz, 'On National Self-Determination', 141.

The Empirical Assumption about Attachment to a Particular Culture

There is an important empirical claim at the centre of version (b) of the cultural argument, and implicit in version (a), to explain the transition from the importance of culture in general to the importance of culture in particular. This is the claim that people are attached to, or identify with, their own particular national group. This section discusses this empirical claim, first, as it arises in a prominent criticism of version (a) of the cultural argument, particularly as it is put forward by Kymlicka, and then, as an important component of an argument for the recognition of national identity.

One prominent criticism of the cultural argument focuses on the transition from the importance of culture to the exercise of individual autonomy/individual well-being, to the liberal-nationalist conclusion that particular cultures should be protected. Against this argument is the obvious point that people can be autonomous or can flourish in many different cultures. A Flemish nationalist may care passionately about the continued existence of the Flemish language and culture, but it would be hard to argue that his/her children would be un-autonomous or unable to flourish if they became assimilated into the French culture. Some culture is clearly essential to provide options, and give meaning to these options, but one would have to be an extreme bigot to claim that the autonomy or well-being of individuals could only be provided by the Flemish culture. However, while this criticism does contain a kernel of truth, it does not ultimately succeed.

To see this, consider Allen Buchanan's version of this criticism. In his example, he considers the case of an indigenous culture faced with a modern technological culture. He notes the possibility that members of a traditional culture 'can leave the sinking ship' of one culture and board another, more seaworthy vessel.[25] He suggests that those people who seek to try to preserve their culture by demanding political self-government or political rights within a state are:

like people who refuse to be rescued from their sinking lifeboat because it is *their* craft and because any other vessel seemed alien and untrustworthy to them. Indeed, they demand that we provide them with timbers and pumps (special group rights, greater autonomy, and/or other resources) to shore up what we have every reason to believe is a doomed vessel.   (Allen Buchanan, 'The Morality of Secession', 357.)

[25] Allen Buchanan, 'The Morality of Secession', in Will Kymlicka (ed.), *The Rights of Minority Cultures* (Oxford: Oxford University Press, 1995), 357.

The implication of Buchanan's argument is that while liberal-nationalists have argued that some cultural structure is necessary as a context to make choices, as a good from which people choose, they have not, however, shown that it is permissible to defend a particular culture which is unviable in the cultural marketplace of ideas.

It might be admitted, even by Buchanan, that in some cases, a presumption in favour of protecting the existing culture is warranted and rights to protect particular cultures, justified. For example, in many of the aboriginal communities in North America and elsewhere, with which Kymlicka is concerned, the original aboriginal culture has been eroded but it has not been fully replaced by any alternative cultural structure. The residential school system in Canada, for example, which was designed to facilitate assimilation of the native groups into 'white' Canadian culture did strip them of their knowledge of their original culture—language, religion, way of life—without integrating them successfully into an alternative culture: the resulting high rates of suicide, drug, and alcohol abuse in these communities are well documented.[26]

In a case such as this—where the culture was not going to be replaced by another—it might be conceded that there is a good reason to defend the culture already in existence. Perhaps, in Buchanan's terms, this is analogous to refusing to allow the person to mend his or her own lifeboat and instead, offering them another which is incapable of holding them up. So, in this situation only, cultural nationalist measures would be justified. However, it is important to note that it is very difficult to know *in advance* whether assimilationist policies—including here simply the refusal to give public protection to the minority culture—will lead to successful adoption of an alternative culture or whether it will lead to dislocation and *anomie*.

Moreover, Buchanan's analogy between the member of the minority culture who feels attached to his or her culture and the person who is offered another lifeboat but insists on his/her own completely trivializes what is at stake in the first case. In the case of lifeboats, the two are more or less the same, as long as both will shore one up. The attachment to one's own lifeboat seems to be an 'endowment effect', that is, the well-known irrational attachment to things one already has, which a more rational understanding of value would overcome. Moving from one culture to another, however, is a quite different thing, and the difficulty and dislocation involved in doing so should

---

[26] Andrew Armitage, *Comparing the Policy of Aboriginal Assimilation; Australia, Canada, New Zealand* (Vancouver: University of British Columbia Press, 1995), 236–40.

not be underestimated. The option of working and living (assimilating) in a French culture is of course open to the Flemish, but this is not a simple matter of opting for one over the other: the adoption of a whole new language and culture and way of life is possible, but may be costly and disorienting. Buchanan's objection, in other words, depends on an ambiguity in the idea of having another culture available, and while one lifeboat might be available to the person, a new culture (language, value-system) is not easily available, but can only be adopted at great cost.

This brings us to the empirical claim that justifies the transition from the importance of culture in general to the importance of a particular culture. The claim is that there is strong empirical support for the view that individuals have strong bonds to their own culture, and that this is particularly so for national minorities, ensconced on their own homelands. John Stuart Mill, writing in 1861, could look back to a quite recent past and write: 'Experience proves it possible for one nationality to merge and be absorbed in another: and when it was originally an inferior and backward portion of the human race the absorption is greatly to its advantage.'[27] Walker Connor, writing in the late twentieth century, has argued that nationalism has become such a powerful source of identity that he can think of no case in the twentieth century where territorially concentrated national minorities, on their own territory, have voluntarily assimilated. Indeed, he claims that assimilationist measures directed at minorities tend to backfire, and almost always lead to a consolidation of the minority identity.[28] There are many examples of groups—for example, Crimean Tatars, Kurds—that have struggled to resist assimilation, often at great cost to themselves.[29]

An argument based on this empirical claim doesn't show why it matters objectively for a culture to survive across generations. This argument does not demonstrate the value of a diversity of nations, or of national identities, for their own sake. The cultures matter only because they matter to people, because they are importantly related to the well-being or autonomy of people. This suggests that there are important limits on the extent and type of justifiable nation-building, specifically, an argument based on treating minority identities fairly

[27] John Stuart Mill, 'On Representative Government', in *Utilitarianism, On Liberty, Considerations on Representative Government* (London: J.M.Dent, 1993), 395.

[28] Walker Connor, *Ethnonationalism*, 51–5.

[29] John McGarry, '"Demographic Engineering": The State-Directed Movement of Ethnic Groups as a Technique of Conflict-Regulation', *Ethnic & Racial Studies*, 21/4 (July 1998), 613–38; Connor, *Ethnonationalism*, 38–9.

means that nationalist demands should only be respected if they them-selves do not violate fairness—for example, by denying minority rights within their region. It also suggests the importance of ascertain-ing, empirically, the extent to which people actually *care* about this group-based identity.

Nevertheless, as was suggested in the previous chapter, a modified version of this empirical claim, when combined with a recognition of the non-neutral character of most states, provides a strong normative argument for recognizing national identities. It explains why we should support or recognize national identities that people are attached to.

Identities and Fair Treatment

The empirical claim implicit in the cultural argument, namely, that people are attached to their particular culture—read: have a particular national identity—is an important element in two (good) arguments for the recognition of these kinds of identities. The first concerns the *practical* difficulties attached to policies of non-recognition; the sec-ond, related argument is centred on the issue of fairness, and on the state's role in treating these identities fairly, and with equal respect.

By itself, the empirical claim that national identities matter to people does not justify strong rights or protections. In fact, part of the above argument has merely suggested the practical difficulties, alluded to in the above section 'Snooker Ball', of eradicating national identities. Once mobilized, national identities are often relatively stable: even when acculturation occurs and the Northern Irish Catholic, say, has lost his/her language (Gaelic) and now speaks English, and has become thor-oughly secular and no longer attends church, even then, the identities can be very strong. This is especially so when there is a strong historical or institutional basis for these identities, or when these identities have been formed *in relation to*—in rejection of—another identity. As Walker Connor has argued, citing strong empirical evidence, in these cases, all that is required for the identity to persist is some marker to tell the groups apart—and this might be such a small thing that it comes down to the person's last name. To achieve the complete eradication of all signs of a distinct identity, is not logically impossible, but it is extremely diffi-cult, especially for a group that is living on its own territory and which has the demographic strength to survive as a distinct community.

There is also a second, more strongly normative dimension to this empirical claim, which has been discussed in the previous chapter in relation to the disanalogies between national and religious claims. That chapter pointed out that the empirical fact that people have a particular national identity—that they feel attached to their national communities, and identify with co-nationals and a particular home-land—cannot simply be incorporated into liberal public policy as one consideration in the weighing of interests by the neutral liberal state. The modern (liberal-democratic) state is not neutral on these matters; rather, all its decisions advantage some groups, and disadvantage others. Yet, those people who are disadvantaged may *care* about their national group, their national identity, just as much as those people who can take for granted the fact that the state expresses their particu-lar political or cultural or linguistic identities.

There are important considerations of fair treatment and equal respect implicit in the claim that national identities are important to people. Put in the context of the contemporary state, it suggests that the state should recognize and attempt to accommodate the different national identities of the people in its territory through creating appropriate (nationally-fair) political and institutional structures. This is the only way to treat these identities fairly: the other mechanism for neutral or fair treatment, which has been attempted with diverse reli-gious groups, is the privatization of these identities and concerns, and this is not an option in the case of an identity which, at its core, is polit-ical. National identities, after all, are about the political community to which one belongs or identifies with.

The importance of national identities, combined with the non-neutrality of the state, also helps to illuminate the earlier observation concerning the practical difficulties of eradicating national identities. Minority groups are often acutely aware, not only of their minority status, but the extent to which state policy is implicated in giving pref-erence to a certain, usually majority, group on the territory. State poli-cies and practices which ignore the national identity of one group on the territory are unlikely to be viewed by the minority group as a legit-imate attempt by the state to deconstruct their superficial, socially constructed identity. It is likely to be viewed by people who identify with the group as threatening to their very survival as a group, and as perpetrated by a state, which is frequently identified with the majority national group on the territory. These policies of non-recognition—what I later call 'the politics of denial'—often serve to strengthen the national identity of the threatened group, since their own identity is often formed in relation to another identity. It explains why it is counter-productive, at least from the point of view of the goal of assimilation or integration.

Three Objections Considered

There are three serious, but ultimately not convincing, criticisms of arguments centred on the importance of recognizing a particular national identity, which will be addressed in turn. First, some might claim that this way of putting the argument—and especially the focus on those people who happen to identify with a particular national community—tends to be biased in favour of only one group of people. In any large group, there will be some people who identify with something (the identifiers), people who don't identify with it (non-identifiers), people who no longer identify with it (ex-identifiers), and so on. It is hard to see why we should give importance only to those people who happen to be identifiers.[30]

This objection operates on the assumption that all these various forms of identity—non-identifiers, ex-identifiers, and so on—are equivalent in some way, and this is precisely what I wish to dispute. In the context of a secure national identity, which has political and institutional recognition within recognized borders, and can therefore be taken for granted, we might imagine a whole range of attitudes toward a Danish national identity, say, or a French one. However, in situations where groups are making claims to national recognition in the context of the denial or minority status of their identity, this attitude is highly unlikely. In this situation, there may be individual differences in intensity, or in strategy, or in viewpoints, but the polarizing effect of making these kinds of claims ensures that national groups are encompassing social groups. One has to make some kind of stand on membership in the group, even when national membership was not a salient issue prior to contestation. In other words, when national groups operate in the context of contested claims, political communities tend to become polarized. This is certainly true of seriously divided societies, such as Northern Ireland and Israel/Palestine, though this polarization also extends to peaceful societies.[31] This suggests, firstly, that

---

[30] I owe this objection to Steven Lukes, who posed this challenge to me at a CSPT conference on 'Citizenship and Cosmopolitanism' in Madison, Wisconsin, November, 1998.

[31] The 1995 Quebec referendum on sovereignty revealed and exacerbated cleavages in Quebec. The 'No' vote on the part of anglophones and allophones is estimated to be in the 90% plus range, thus revealing the limited ethnic appeal of the (civic) Quebec project. It also led to bitterness on the part of some majority francophone sovereigntist nationalists. For example, then-Quebec Premier Parizeau claimed, on the eve of the referendum defeat, that the defeat was attributed to 'money and the ethnic vote'. The reference to 'money' was widely understood in the rest of Canada as referring to English-speaking Quebeckers and the 'ethnic vote' was thought to be referring to immigrants. Parizeau also spoke of a 'we' winning again and gaining 'revenge'. The 'we' seemed clearly to be a majority francophone

the description of individual differences in a group ignores the actual dynamics of national conflict. Second, while it is true that, even in this polarizing context, there are important individual differences concerning the extent to which national recognition matters, or the kind of recognition deemed acceptable, it is important to keep in mind that the context of these claims is that of a non-neutral political state that is already, and indeed necessarily, identified through its language, laws, symbols, and policies, with a particular national community. It is misleading, therefore, to suggest that identifiers, non-identifiers, and so on are all on the same level, for the political structure is itself biased, and this criticism ignores the central argument concerning fairness.

There is a second line of criticism, which has been advanced forcefully by Alan Patten. This criticism focuses on the implicit claim in this argument, and in MacCormick's and Margalit and Raz's arguments, that we shouldn't require people to give up their culture—on my version, their identity—because of the dislocation and disorientation that this would cause. This criticism takes issue with the view that leaving one's culture/way of life is problematic because disorienting. This raises the question: why do we not regard it as similarly dislocating, similarly disorienting, for people to give up an economic way-of-life? The transition from one technology to another, such as is involved with the computer revolution or the introduction of automobiles, may involve just as much change for the person as cultural changes, especially if their educational investment is now rendered obsolete and their way of life is wholly transformed. And yet, while we think that the state has an obligation to re-train workers, we don't think that they should be wholly protected from this kind of change.

The analysis presented here is capable of responding to this line of criticism. There is a crucial disanalogy between state policy with respect to economic matters and state policy with respect to national identities. The liberal-democratic state is certainly biased in favour of a capitalist marketplace, but is not normally seen as biased in favour of a particular agent of capitalism. If it were, this would certainly raise questions about the legitimacy and justifiability of state policy with respect to the economy. But state policy with respect to national identities is crucially different, for the state is seen (and rightly seen) by minority national groups as the instrument of a particular (usually the majority) national community on its territory. Indeed, the only way that the state could be interpreted as neutral between national identi-

'we'. See the translation of Premier Parizeau's speech delivered on referendum night (October 30), 'We won't wait another 15 years', *Globe & Mail*, November 1, 1995.

ties is precisely through the kinds of institutional recognition of minority national identity that most minority nations seek.

Third, it might be claimed that, in areas where different national identities come into conflict, as in the cases I've been discussing—Northern Ireland and the former Yugoslavia—it would be better if the people did not have distinct and mutually antagonistic national identities, and this raises questions about whether the appropriate policy is recognition and accommodation. At some level, of course, this criticism is right: if this diagnosis of the conflict is correct—namely, that they are national conflicts—then, it follows that, if there were no national divisions, there would be no conflict. The argument advanced here is not analogous to an eco-diversity argument; it doesn't value diversity-of-identities for their own sake; so it follows that it would have been better if the groups shared the same national identity—that they all thought they were Irish, say, in Northern Ireland, or they all thought they were Yugoslav, in the former Yugoslavia. But this does not lead us to the view that these identities, in themselves, are undesirable and should be eradicated—on the contrary, as the previous chapter argued, they are intrinsically valuable. In addition to the practical difficulty of implementing policies designed to foster assimilation, there is the issue of fairness. The state has a responsibility to treat the groups within its territory fairly, and for a national identity, a political identity, this can only be done through some kind of recognition of the existence of these identities, and an attempt to accommodate them politically. This suggests that the right solution to conflicts, such as those in Northern Ireland and the former Yugoslavia, is not to 'transform' people but to create the political and institutional structures to accommodate and recognize the identities that they have.

In certain situations of competing and irreconcilable national sovereignty claims—that is, precisely the situation in these two conflict-zones—the problem is that the structure of claims and the dynamics between the groups makes conflict almost inevitable. It is necessary, therefore, to think more imaginatively about how to accommodate and reconcile these various different national identities and at the same time, to give importance to the degree of interdependence that the groups evince, especially in cases where the different groups overlap on the same territory. Here practice has moved in advance of theory—for example, the parties to the Northern Ireland conflict have gone some way towards developing shared sovereignty arrangements in recent talks and treaties aimed at arriving at a peaceful solution to the conflict there. Complex institutional mechanisms to accommodate minority nationalisms have not been generally developed, however, partly because of a general reluctance to treat national identities as worthy of recognition, and partly because of majoritarian biases towards those identities that correspond to an already existing state.

The Distinction between Nation and Culture

This section argues that an identity-based view of national identity is superior to the culture-based view in conceptualizing some important issues facing national and cultural groups. While identities may be constructed from the available cultural, historical, or institutional material, and so in that sense culture may be important to national identities, nevertheless, it is important to distinguish between the two. This can be seen most clearly in terms of Buchanan's own example of the indigenous group faced with a modern technological society. In his example, Buchanan suggests that the members of the unviable, indigenous culture who are demanding self-government rights are like the members of a sinking lifeboat demanding timbers and pumps to keep their own lifeboat (culture) afloat.

The distinction between identity and cultures enables us to see that both the demand and the dynamics are quite different from Buchanan's interpretation. It is true that most parents want their children to be taught the culture of the parents—if the values and history of the group are important to the parents, then parents naturally will want to teach this to their children. But parents also want their children to do well in the world. Of course, there may be different conceptions of what doing well means, but I would think it fairly unusual for parents to want to teach their children a wholly unviable way of life based on buffalo hunting, say, in the context of very little wild plains and buffalo being an endangered species. In fact, it is doubtful if Buchanan's interpretation of the group's motives for wanting self-government rights—to teach the children a wholly unviable, traditional way of life—is correct.

A more plausible interpretation is that the indigenous group wants to preserve their identity as Cree or Sioux or whatever. Once again, it is important to emphasize the distinction between national identity and cultural differences. The native member of an indigenous culture who requests political or institutional support for his or her cultural 'lifeboat' may be prepared to appropriate elements of other cultures, in order to modernize, but what they don't want to give up is their identity as native. To extend the analogy of the sinking lifeboat in a somewhat different direction, one can imagine that it would be particularly problematic (dislocating) to be required to adopt the *identity* of the group that rammed and stole your boat in the first place, thus causing it to sink. Analogously, in the case of Northern Ireland, it would be particularly problematic to adopt the identity of the group that oppressed members of your group, and dispossessed your fore-mothers and forefathers of their land; or, in the case of the former Yugoslavia, to adopt the identity of the group that engaged in large-scale slaughter against your people. None of this means that you blame the current people; but only that this identity is one that would be difficult for you to adopt, because your own identity is at least partly developed in relation to it.

The preservation of national identity, then, is quite consistent with appropriating elements from other cultures in order to adapt to a new technological context. After all, identities can persist even while cultures are changing, even rapidly, just as in Kymlicka's example of the transformation of Quebec culture during the Quiet Revolution. But in order for the culture to be accepted as one's own—in order for the appropriation from other cultures to be viewed as non-threatening to the identity of the group, rather than viewed as an attempt at assimilation—groups would have to see the change as one *internal* to the group, as one that in some sense they have made. This means that they must feel that they have some collective control over their own future. This was the case in Quebec during the Quiet Revolution. Although Quebec is part of Canada, it is a fairly strong, rich province, with a wide area of jurisdiction in one of the most decentralized federations in the world.

This suggests that some collective control over a group's own destiny is absolutely central to the capacity to appropriate elements from other cultures and ways of life without feeling that this, in any way, impinges on or is threatening to one's identity. As long as the group with which you identify is in control of these changes, in some sense, then the changes and adaptations that are made are ones that the group has adopted and so are completely non-threatening to the existence (identity) of the group. But if you lack this control, if the changes are forced on you from outside, as in the attempt to forcibly assimilate native children into 'white' society through the residential school system, then, the old culture can be effectively forgotten—because not taught—while the new white culture is perceived as 'foreign' or 'alien', and inconsistent with native identity. The result, of course, was that native children were left with very few cultural resources, having been deprived of one culture and unable to adopt another. The result of this experiment was anomie and despair on the part of a whole generation.

There is no need to justify political rights on the basis that these protect some objective cultural feature that is 'special' to nations: it is more accurate to justify these in terms of equal treatment of different groups and the importance of these group-based *identities* to most people. Protection of people's national identity does not necessarily mean the protection of unviable cultures, but the recognition of the people's identification with a particular community and the importance of membership in this community and political aspirations based on it. Unlike other forms of identity politics—such as gender, gay, racial, or ethnic identities, where it is possible to aspire to be treated fairly by the state—national identities are importantly bound up with political recognition and political power. It is precisely because the modern bureaucratic state is complicit in privileging a particular national identity that it can only be fair to other national groups through a policy of recognition and accommodation.

Conclusion

This chapter has examined the cultural argument for liberal nationalism. It argued that version (a) should be rejected because it confers rights only on those groups or cultures that respect autonomy. It then argued for a certain understanding, or modified version (b) of the cultural argument. Specifically, the empirical claim at the centre of the well-being (b) version of the cultural argument, and implicit in version (a), suggests a normative argument for recognizing and accommodating national identities. This is an argument from fairness: specifically, the fact that national identities *matter* to people—they care about them, and they are important to individual self-identity and well-being—combined with the argument that the contemporary state is not, and cannot be, neutral with respect to national identities, provides the basis for a normative argument that the state should recognize and accommodate national identities. This normative argument works even better if we try to move beyond considerations of culture to examine the issues of national or political identity.

This chapter also argued that proponents of the cultural argument misunderstand the relationship between nationality and culture. They tend to view the nation as an expression, and 'nationalism' a defence, of culture. This chapter pointed out that we may have sanguinary national conflict—as in Northern Ireland or the former Yugoslavia—where cultural difference is small; and we may have minimal conflict—as in Switzerland and Belgium—where cultural difference is greater.

This chapter proposes a shift, away from seeing nations as grounded in culture, to seeing them as grounded in 'identity'—often forged by historical forces having nothing to do with culture *per se*. This chapter therefore rejects the cultural argument for liberal nationalism, associated with the work of Raz, Tamir and Kymlicka, among others, precisely because it confounds national identity with common culture. Since nations are diverse despite a common culture, 'common culture' cannot explain them. Identity is more fundamental. It persists where culture changes.

This understanding of nationalism preserves the main normative point that I argued underlies version (b) of the cultural argument, associated with the work of Margalit and Raz and MacCormick. It also helps to bridge the false view that state action or institutional recognition of national groups involves preserving, in a static way, a particular culture or tradition. The main issue that nationalists are concerned with is that of jurisdiction: nations are primarily political communities, and this in no way implies that the political community will act conservatively to preserve their traditional culture.

CHAPTER 4

Instrumental Arguments (or, Why States Need Nations)

This book has examined several different kinds of arguments for the view that national identity should be given institutional recognition by the state and the international state-system. The most common kind of argument for the merits of national identity are instrumental in form—they link the national identity, or shared identification with the political community, with other goods. This chapter explores the strengths and limits of this kind of argument.

What is interesting about this kind of argument is that the direction of argument tends to be different: instead of focusing on the individual bearer of the identity, the argument focuses on the state and the kinds of goods or benefits that attach to the state when its members share a national identity. This raises the problem that the motivational basis for nationalism must be different than its justificatory basis: the nationalist has to believe for independent reasons—independent of this argument—in the merits of his or her nation. Moreover, for this argument to work as a normative argument, it is not sufficient simply to say that sharing this kind of identity is beneficial to the state, unless we link state action with the attainment of other goods.

This chapter proceeds by looking at the normative implications of the most prominent instrumental arguments for nationalism. The first section examines the arguments, frequently employed by historians and sociologists of nationalism, which are designed to explain the emergence of this phenomenon. This kind of argument shows why the state needs nations, but does not take the additional step of showing what it is about the state that is valuable. This chapter attempts to draw out the normative implications of this argument.

The two other instrumental arguments canvassed in this chapter do not explicitly draw on the modernist or functional explanations for nationalism, although their claims bear some affinities to the arguments examined in the first part of this chapter. However, they are more clearly normative arguments, because they directly link a shared national identity with the attainment of the moral goods of justice—second part of this chapter—and the smooth functioning of democracy—third part of this chapter. They also suggest the possibility of reconciling nationalism with more acceptable political doctrines, such as liberalism, democracy, and egalitarian justice.

The recent resurgence of these arguments in liberal political philosophy does not mean that they are new or original. The intellectual precursor of instrumental nationalist arguments is Rousseau, particularly in his *Discourses on Political Economy* and *The Government of Poland*. In these essays, Rousseau was concerned with the problem of achieving unity and maintaining stability. Rousseau argued that if the people were to be sovereign, they needed to have a corporate identity—to solve the problem of disunity.[1] He emphasized the need for common bonds of membership to unite the people and forge bonds of solidarity.[2] Rousseau's solution to the political problem of how to achieve and maintain unity and stability—which was thought to be especially difficult for a democratic regime—was to embark on a nation-building project to ensure that members share a common identity. Rousseau seemed to think that nation-building, to create a common (national) identity, would facilitate the mutual trust necessary to undergird consent and secure sacrifice.

Contemporary versions of instrumental liberal nationalism tend to fall into two basic categories. One argument, which is considered in the second part of this chapter, focuses on whether a free society can operate only if its citizens accept certain solidarities and certain liberal virtues. On this argument, the bonds of affection and solidarities nurtured by a shared national identity is useful to undergird these dispositions and support liberal justice.

---

[1] Jean-Jacques Rousseau, *The Social Contract and Discourses*, ed. G. D. H. Cole, J. H. Brumfitt, John C. Hall (London: Everyman, 1973), bk. 1, ch. 6, 191.

[2] Ibid., 149. The relevant passage from the 'Discourse on Political Economy' reads: 'If children are brought up in common . . . imbued with the laws of the state and the precepts of the general will; if they are taught to respect these above all things; if they are surrounded by examples and objects which constantly remind them of the tender mother who nourishes them, of the love she bears them, of the inestimable benefits they receive from her, and of the return they owe her, we cannot doubt that they will learn to cherish one another mutually as brothers, to will nothing contrary to the will of society . . . and to become in time defenders and fathers of the country of which they will have been so long the children.'

Another kind of instrumental liberal-nationalist argument suggests that a shared national identity is important to a well-functioning democracy. On this argument, democratic institutions require social solidarity and relations of mutual trust, and nationality is one means of providing this. The third part of this chapter is concerned specifically with this argument that nationality is (sometimes) instrumental to a well-functioning democracy. I argue in favour of this version of instrumental nationalism: specifically, I argue that a shared national identity is (sometimes) important to two constitutive elements in a well-functioning democracy: representation and participation.

The Normative Implications of a Gellnerian Theory of Nationalism

The most prominent instrumental arguments for nationalism are not normative arguments but explanatory arguments concerned with the conditions under which nationalism emerged as an important social and political force in the modern era. Many of the theorists—Gellner, Hobsbawm, Anderson, and others—who have emphasized the modern emergence of nationalism, and linked it with broad historical forces, explain nationalism in broadly instrumental terms, as a form of group-identity which serves an important purpose in the modern period.

One common normative reading of these arguments focuses on the socially constructed nature of national identities to suggest that these identities should be deconstructed. I argued in Chapter 1 that this does not follow; in this section, I argue that it is based on an incorrect reading of many works in history and sociology that link national identity with modernity.[3] Gellner's theory, which is the best-known and most complete modernist theory of nationalism, is often cited by those hostile to national identity for claiming that '[i]t is nationalism which engenders nations, and not the other way round'.[4] A careful reading of Gellner's argument, however, suggests the opposite: that national identity is ineluctably bound up with modernity; and that it is precisely the features of modernity—mass literacy, standardized modes of

---

[3] This view is expressed in Bhikhu Parekh, 'Discourses on National Identity', *Political Studies*, 42 (1994), 492–504, at 504. Parekh writes: 'Since national identity is a product of history, it can also be remade in history.' I agree with this view, but Parekh's terminology suggests that it is infinitely malleable.

[4] Ernest Gellner, *Nations and Nationalism* (Ithaca, NY: Cornell University Press, 1983), 55.

interaction, mass education, a bureaucratic state, and so on—that give importance to cultural and national forms of identity.[5]

Gellner's theory of nationalism drew on a philosophy of history, according to which agrarian society was both culturally plural and hierarchical. People in agrarian societies operated within carefully defined social and economic niches, and there was a great discontinuity between the life of the peasant and that of the aristocrat. This class division was often reinforced by a cultural discontinuity, with, in many cases, nobles speaking German, for example, and peasants speaking Hungarian or Czech or something else. In industrial societies—either societies that are beginning to industrialize or aspiring to industrialize—the relationship between the economic system and the culture is quite different. In this kind of society, it is necessary to have fairly standardized, accessible culture available to all workers. The worker/citizen is given a generic culture through a universal schooling system, which enables the worker to communicate in standard idiom, to be literate and numerate. These skills can be transferred from one part of the labour force to another, within the cultural or linguistic unit.

There are two implications of Gellner's argument that have an important bearing on a normative assessment of national identity. The first is that there are aspects of the transition from agrarian to industrial (modern) societies that explain why cultural and national forms of identity have assumed importance. These might not be important for all human beings, and certainly not in all contexts, but the requirement that they are universally true, embedded in the very nature of human beings, is a very strong requirement for treating them seriously. In the conditions of modernity, where these features are not likely to go away, national and cultural identities are extremely difficult to deconstruct and indeed, as Gellner's argument indicates, there are very good reasons why people do have this sense of attachment. The material basis that Gellner provides for a theory of nationalism does not make nationalism reducible to economic interests, but it does explain why national and cultural forms of identity become politicized in this type of society. This theory provides a material explanation, in terms of life-chances, of people's commitment to their own cultural/national group. For many people, their participation in the cultural life of the community, their employability, their status, and their skills are all acquired in an all-embracing education system operating in the context of a standardized cultural milieu supported by the state. This

---

[5] Gellner, *Nations and Nationalism*, 24–38.

instrumental argument about the salience of cultural and national forms of identity, and also the political significance of these identities, holds even if the historical story that Gellner tells is not absolutely accurate, as long as the connections that he makes between the economic, political, and cultural dimensions of life are roughly right.[6]

The second normative implication of Gellner's theory, which is brought out by Brendan O'Leary in an article on boundaries, focuses on the benefits from the state's point of view in ensuring that the national and cultural boundaries of the state in part coincide with that of the political unit. Specifically, O'Leary argues that the relationship that Gellner draws between national identity and modernity suggests a different view of the role of the state and the dimensions of the state.[7] Unlike agrarian society, which counted wealth in land and raw materials, and almost always regarded state expansion as beneficial, industrial states have to effectively harness the skills of the people. O'Leary argues that there are management imperatives involved in organizing an effective and legitimate industrial culture. This does not necessarily mean that all members of the state must be co-nationals or members of the same homogeneous culture, but it means that it is sometimes rational from the state's perspective to shed parts of the political territory where the people are mobilized in accordance with a rival national project. Unlike in an agrarian empire, where land and people are automatically equated with wealth and resources, there may be situations in which it is rational for the state to dispense with groups of people and bits of the territory that have proved indigestible. O'Leary does not argue that cultural and national divisions have to coincide— indeed, he argues that many states will contain small minorities that for historical or instrumental reasons attach themselves to the titular nationality, as well as many cultural groups who have migrated to the territory and accepted the state contours and dominant culture in exchange for the prospect of economic benefits and equal citizenship.[8] However, given the plural nature of many states, and the importance of cultural and national dimensions of life in this kind of society, we can expect that the most divisive issues are probably not those based on class within the same national or cultural group, but issues related to cultural or national identities between different cultural or national

[6] For an excellent critique of some of the problems with Gellner's theory, see Brendan O'Leary, 'On the Nature of Nationalism: An Appraisal of Ernest Gellner's Writings on Nationalism', *British Journal of Political Science*, 27 (1997), 191–222.

[7] Brendan O'Leary, 'The Elements of a General Theory of Right-Sizing the State', paper presented to the Social Sciences Research Council's *Right-Sizing the State: The Politics of Moving Borders* Conference, New York, USA, May 1998, 4.

[8] Ibid., 5.

groups. Managing ethnic and national conflict, not class conflict, will be the greatest challenge to state managers, and state policy with respect to cultural and national groups will be an important site of political contestation. Political units are better positioned if they have sufficient consensus and acquiescence from the population on these issues. The most optimally efficient and competent industrial states are liberal-democratic—where merit and transparency are important principles—and where there are no serious divisions on state boundaries, and no mobilized disaffected minorities within the state.

This view is also supported by Lustick's empirical study of the conditions in which states may be down-sized, which roughly follows the mounting political evidence of the fact that Ireland progressively became viewed—in nineteenth-century and early twentieth-century Britain—as not really part of the United Kingdom, due to the overwhelming empirical evidence of different Irish attitudes and identity; that Algeria became viewed, in the mid-twentieth century, as not really part of France, also as a result of mobilized violence there; and that one of the main effects of the intifada was to ensure that the West Bank was not viewed as part of Israel, despite deliberate state policy to foster a more expansive view of Israel.[9] Lustick's theory emphasizes that to some extent the problem confronting states is not simply Gellner's problem of how to create a common culture for an effective industrial society, but, rather, that unproductive tensions and violence arise in states where it is clear that people do not want to be part of the state. This is of course especially true for liberal-democratic states, but even authoritarian states feel the effects or consequences of rebellion by people who believe that they have been incorporated into a state against their will.

These two elements—the first, pointing to the commitments and identities of the population, and the second, pointing to the benefits for the state in ensuring the above—are different aspects of the same argument. However, the second element, which focuses on state benefits is not a clearly normative argument, unless the state can be linked in some way to the attainment of certain ethical goods or values. Recently, liberal-nationalists have developed their own instrumental arguments about the desirability of sharing a national identity, although, unlike Gellner, O'Leary, and Lustick, they have emphasized the goods that the state can facilitate.

[9] Ian S. Lustick, *Unsettled States, Disputed Lands: Britain and Ireland, France and Algeria, Israel and the West Bank-Gaza* (Ithaca, NY: Cornell University Press, 1993).

Liberal Justice and Instrumental Nationalism

In his book *Liberal Purposes*, William Galston argues that liberal citizenship cannot focus only on the justice or fairness of the political principles that are embodied in the state, but must also develop an emotional pride and identification with fellow citizens and with the particular institutions of the society. Because liberalism is operationalized everywhere within particular states, what is also required is a positive attitude of affection for the co-members of the state, and the political institutions and practices of one's particular community. He argues:

> On the practical level, few individuals will come to embrace the core commitments of liberal societies through a process of rational inquiry. If children are to be brought to accept these commitments as valid and binding, it can only be through a process that is far more rhetorical than rational.   (William Galston, *Liberal purposes: Goods, virtues and diversity in the liberal state* (Cambridge: Cambridge University Press, 1991), 243.)

In Galston's view, the sacrifices necessary for the realization of the common good require an emotional identification with the state and with its members. Although Galston typically terms this 'patriotism', it is extensionally equivalent to civic nationalism, both in terms of its requirements that there are bonds of affection for co-members or co-nationals, and sentiments of affection for the political project (the nation) that unites them.

This kind of argument—that citizenship requires bonds of attachment to the state and to fellow citizens or co-nationals—is an instrumental argument for a form of nationalism. It conceives of national identification as instrumental to achieving the good of liberal citizenship, which, in turn, is supportive of liberal political principles of justice and respect for diversity. Like many other theorists of nationality, Galston accepts that this kind of nation-building requires a reinterpretation of history that will function to secure the emotional ties of pride to fellow citizens and to the political project. In this respect, Galston is echoing the analysis of Ernst Renan who argues, in his famous 1887 essay, 'What is a Nation?', that nation-building requires 'getting one's history wrong'. According to Renan, the society has to be capable of forgetting those parts of its history that will interfere with the development of a sense of pride in it.[10]

---

[10] E. Renan, 'What Is A Nation?', in Alfred Zimmern (ed.) *Modern Political Doctrines* (London: Oxford University Press, 1939, 186–205, at 190 [originally published in 1882].

Other liberals have also expressed the view that national bonds can be instrumental to liberal justice. In his article 'Self-Government Revisited', Brian Barry argued that national sentiment could be instrumental to liberal justice, although he has since changed his mind.[11] In the earlier article, he claimed, echoing Mill's argument in *Considerations on Representative Government,* that 'the presence of fellow-feeling obviously facilitates co-operation on common projects and makes redistribution within the polity more acceptable.'[12]

This argument is supported by an interpretive reading of Lord Acton's opposite argument in favour of heterogeneous and multi-national states in his essay 'On Nationality'. Acton advocated a heterogeneous state on the grounds that this was conducive to liberty: more precisely, on Barry's reading, because Acton believed that the 'best way of confining a state to the pursuit of negative liberty is to ensure that its citizens cannot put together a majority for anything more positive'.[13] The greater the diversity of area and citizenry and political authority, the more difficult it is to institute positive state action, especially state action directed at redistribution.

A similar instrumental argument is made by Miller, in *On Nationality*, although in a more elaborate form, and focused almost exclusively on redistribution. In Miller's view, a shared national identity engenders trust among members and this helps to support a redistributive practice.[14] Miller's argument is a variation of the communitarian insight that, unless people feel bonds of membership to the recipients, redistribution by the liberal state will be experienced by the individual who is taxed as coerced and therefore as incompatible with individual freedom.[15] He also seems to be making the empirical claim that the political will supporting redistribution will not be there if the groups don't share a similar national identity, a similar sense that they are engaged in a common political project.

What can be said about the instrumental argument for liberal justice? The most striking aspect of this argument is that the link between

[11] Brian Barry now takes the view that reasonable individuals can be suitably motivated by impartial reason. See his *Justice as Impartiality* (Oxford: Clarendon Press, 1995), 164–8.

[12] Brian Barry, 'Self-Government Revisited', in *Democracy and Power, Essays in Political Theory I* (Oxford: Clarendon, 1991), 174–5.

[13] Barry, *Justice as Impartiality*, 165.

[14] David Miller, *On Nationality*, (Oxford: Oxford University Press, 1995), 92–4.

[15] For a parallel argument, explicitly set in the context of the liberal-communitarian debate, see Yael Tamir, *Liberal Nationalism* (Princeton, NJ: Princeton University Press, 1993), 118. She writes: 'The willingness to assume the burdens entailed by distributive justice . . . rests on . . . a feeling of relatedness to those with whom we share our assets'. For the communitarian argument, see Michael Sandel, *Liberalism and the Limits of Justice* (Cambridge: Cambridge University Press, 1982).

a shared national identity and redistributive practices is intuitively plausible, but the empirical evidence supporting it is unclear, at best. Indeed, if we think broadly and comparatively about societies that have strongly-felt national identities and try to correlate this with levels of redistribution, it is not at all clear that there is any evidence for this proposition.[16] The United States, for example, has a widely shared national identity and a strong tradition of patriotism, but a weak record on social justice. Indeed, redistribution from rich to poor is *more* effective in several nationally divided societies such as Canada and Belgium than in the United States. Much depends on the kind of national identity that it is. In the American case, there is a strong individualistic 'self-help' tradition and the discourse of social justice and state redistribution does not resonate as well as in countries where the state has historically played a much more active role in the economy and in social justice policy-making.

Indeed, the relationship between redistribution and shared national identity is even more complex than this. It is not merely the *content* of that identity that affects the levels of redistribution, but there is a large bureaucratic state structure that is an important intermediary in the relationship between national identity and the actual delivery of goods associated with social justice.   The case of Northern Ireland within the United Kingdom is interesting, from this perspective. At first glance, Northern Ireland belies this positive relationship between a shared national identity and social justice. Not only do 40 per cent of the population of Northern Ireland identify with Ireland, not the United Kingdom, and vote for Irish nationalist parties to reflect this, but the overwhelming majority of Britons do not regard the Northern Irish—whether Protestants or Catholics—as co-nationals. Yet, the British subvention to Northern Ireland, paid for by the British taxpayer, is one of the largest amounts of regional redistribution in the United Kingdom; and this occurs even though there is a sentiment, on the part of the mainland British, that Northern Ireland is not an integral part of the United Kingdom, and that Northern Irishmen are not British. This seems to fly in the face of the intuitively plausible instrumental nationalist argument that shared national identity facilitates redistribution.

In fact, however, this example does not demonstrate the falsity of the argument, only the enormous complexity of the relationship between social justice and national identity. At the time that the British

---

[16] Miller is aware of this potential objection in *On Nationality*, 94–5, but I do not find his response to it convincing.

welfare state was set up, British sentiments of national identity did include the Northern Irish as part of their nation and the territory as part of the United Kingdom. The territorial nature of the policies and rules for the kingdom as a whole reflected this sentiment. However, since that time, particularly since 'the Troubles' in the late 1960s, Britons have come to regard the province as 'a place apart' and the people who live there as unlike them. This suggests, at the minimum, that the instrumental nationalist account of the positive relationship between shared national identity and redistribution should be sufficiently nuanced to recognize that there is a large bureaucratic and legal structure that intervenes between political sentiments and public policy. This means that sentiments are not immediately reflected in public policy: at the very least, there is a substantial time-lag between the two, which can be accounted for in terms of the mediating bureaucratic, legal, and political structures.

However, with poll after poll showing that the British taxpayer would like to get out of Northern Ireland, there is also a desire on the part of the British for a solution there, with at least one of the two major political parties advocating withdrawal from the province, conditional on obtaining majority consent—Labour under Tony Blair— and a constitutionally recognized right to secession (to join Ireland) should the majority wish it. This desire to dissociate themselves, in legal, juridical, territorial, and public policy terms, from the province seems to reflect, at least in part, the asymmetry in national identity between Britons and (Protestant) Northern Irishmen. By asymmetry, I mean that Ulster Protestants think of themselves as 'British' and the mainland British largely regard them as not-British, and are implicitly prepared to reject them from their political community. Thus, the examples could be interpreted to suggest that the instrumental nationalist argument regarding a positive relationship between shared national identity and social justice is not without merit, but the situation is far more complex than the proponents of the argument suggest.

Another objection to the instrumental nationalist argument has been put forward by Daniel Weinstock.[17] He argues that national sentiments are unsuitable and unreliable instruments for ensuring that our redistributive obligations are met. They are unreliable, Weinstock argues, because our affective sentiments may include resentment toward the recipients of our redistribution, just as easily as attachment to them. And they are unreliable, too, because the scope of our

---

[17] Daniel M. Weinstock, 'Is there a Moral Case for Nationalism?', *Journal of Applied Philosophy*, 13/1 (1996), 87–100, at 93.

sympathy does not mesh easily with the bonds of the national community. Weinstock cites here the case of the person who is sponta-
neously sympathetic to the plight of the starving overseas. This leads
him to conclude that our moral sentiments do not necessarily, or even
usually, support liberal justice; rather, liberal legalism is a useful corrective to our sentiments, which are often unreliable as an indicator of
our obligations.

One partial answer to this objection is to point out that the reasons
that motivate us might not be the same as those that apply at the most
basic level of moral justification. The issue is only whether national
sentiments facilitate us in discharging our obligations, which, of
course, are independent of these sentiments, and independent, too, of
the kind of legalism that Weinstock talks about: tax laws, bills of
rights, regional and welfare redistribution policies, and so on.[18]

Even though the contrast Weinstock draws between liberal legalism
and sentimental attachment is too sharp, the underlying point implicit
in this analysis is that the state, with all its rules and laws and bills and
policies, is the main mechanism to deliver our redistributive obligations. And this suggests the same point that I alluded to above in the
United Kingdom-Northern Ireland example, namely, that the instrumental redistributive argument is too simple: that in fact, there is an
enormous bureaucratic structure that maintains our redistributive
obligations, despite our sentiments. However, the Northern Ireland
example also suggests that the instrumental nationalist argument cannot be dismissed, that, where there is a persistent feeling of non-shared
identity and substantial one-way redistribution—that is, the relationship cannot be argued for in reciprocal terms, as mutually beneficial—
the long-term continuation of this redistributive policy may be in
jeopardy. As David Miller argued, in the absence of reciprocity and
shared identity, the political will may not be there to discharge these
obligation over the long term.

It is important to recognize that, if we accept a nuanced form of the
instrumental nationalist argument, which takes into account the complexity in the relationship between shared identity and social justice,
the argument still doesn't support all forms of national ties but only
those that are demonstrably supportive of just regimes. If the instrumental nationalist argument is correct—including all the empirical
claims—then this would seem to mean that the nationalism or patriotism of just states should be supported. There are, of course, many

[18] Eamonn Callan, *Creating Citizens; Political Education and Liberal Democracy*
(Oxford: Clarendon Press, 1997), 97; Weinstock, 'Is there a Moral Case for Nationalism?',
92–3.

different conceptions of justice, but, at the minimum, this would seem to mean that states that respect liberal rights, the rule of law, and perhaps the redistribution of wealth according to principles of justice, are correct to nurture a national identification with co-members and with the political project, in addition to civic education on the political principles embodied in the state institutions and practices. Many forms of nationalism will be illegitimate on these criteria, because they are intended to support illiberal practices or unjust regimes.

Instrumental Nationalism and Democratic Governance

This part of the chapter is concerned primarily with instrumental arguments as they apply to democratic governance. This section considers the argument that a shared national identity helps to undergird democratic institutions. I argue in favour of this argument, suggesting that a shared national identity is not absolutely necessary, but that, in certain cases, it will facilitate democratic governance.

Many will disagree with the basic thrust of this argument on the grounds that, while, historically, the introduction of representative institutions has either preceded or proceeded alongside the development of nationalism,[19] it is also true, as Cobban noted, that 'nationalism has more often than not been the enemy of democratic institutions'.[20] However, if there is a positive, mutually supporting relationship between national identity and democracy, as I think there is, then, it is not the crude one that More Nationalism = Better Democracy; but, rather, one that suggests that a common national identity tends to facilitate the proper functioning of democratic institutions. This, of course, leaves open the role played by the content of the national identity or whether nationalism needs to be mediated by a flourishing civil society, and concepts of universal citizenship.[21] However, this section of the chapter shows that, in certain cases, a shared national identity is instrumental to achieving two constituent goods of democracy: representation and participation.

In the nineteenth and early twentieth century, many writers assumed a close relationship between national independence and

[19] Alfred Cobban, *National Self-Determination* (Oxford: Oxford University Press, 1945), 65; also John A. Hall, *Coercion and Consent; Studies on the Modern State* (Cambridge: Polity Press, 1994), 136–7.
[20] Cobban, *National Self-Determination*, 65.
[21] This argument is made persuasively by George Schopflin, 'Civil Society, Ethnicity and the State', Paper delivered at the *Conference for Civil Society in Austria*, Vienna, Austria, June, 1997.

democracy. The basis of this assumption seemed to be an association between the ideas of national and democratic sovereignty, internal and external self-determination. This is evident in Ernst Renan's definition of the nation as 'un plebiscite de tous les jours'[22], which suggests the consensual and democratic basis of national communities. In seeming support of this view, many nineteenth century and early twentieth century nationalists were committed to democratic governance. The potential for divergence between nationalism and democracy was not evident, as nationalists/democrats—often one and the same person— organized to fight the anti-democratic states of Russia, Austria, and Turkey.

In J. S. Mill's discussion 'On Nationality' in *Considerations on Representative Government*, he argues that democracy can only flourish where 'the boundaries of government . . . coincide in the main with those of nationalities'.[23] His argument in support of this contention is based on an analysis of the necessary conditions for a flourishing democracy: 'Among a people without fellow-feeling, especially if they read and speak different languages, the united public opinion necessary to the workings of government, cannot exist.'[24]

Mill's recognition of the need for a common national identity, combined with a nineteenth century view of historical progress and an ethnocentric view of the merits of different nations, led him to believe that the 'great nations' would enjoy independence and smaller nationalities would be assimilated into their 'orbit'. It is, however, no longer plausible to assume that the demise of smaller nationalities is historically inevitable, and it is difficult to justify policies of coercive assimilation in liberal terms.

This chapter argues in favour of the mutually supporting relationship that Mill points to between national identity and democracy. The strong version of this argument, as put forward by Michael Lind, holds that 'far from being a threat to democracy, nationalism—the correspondence of cultural nation and state—is a necessary, though not sufficient, condition for democracy in most places today.'[25] Lind supports his claim by listing the various linguistically and culturally divided societies in which democracy has not worked well: Cyprus,

---

[22] E. Renan, 'Discours et Conferences', (1887). Quoted in Cobban, *National Self-Determination*, 64.

[23] John Stuart Mill, 'Considerations on Representative Government', in *Utilitarianism, On Liberty and Considerations on Representative Government* (London: Everyman Library, 1993), 394.

[24] Ibid, 392.

[25] Michael Lind, 'In Defense of Liberal Nationalism', *Foreign Affairs*, 23 (1994), 87–99, at 94.

Lebanon, Sri Lanka, the Soviet Union, Yugoslavia, and Czechoslovakia are all examples of failed multinational states; and he explores the precarious nature of the three 'successes': Canada, Belgium, and Switzerland.

He does not, however, analyse the different reasons for the breakdown of the listed multinational states; nor does he show that it was cultural or national pluralism that threatened democratic institutions. Indeed, in some cases, the states he cites as empirical evidence had weak democratic institutions and/or few democratic traditions. This suggests that his empirical evidence merely supports the view that nationalism is dangerous for the unity of culturally plural states—not necessarily democracies. Indeed, one could interpret the evidence that he provides in a quite different way—namely, that democracies such as Canada, Belgium, and Switzerland, tend to cope better with multinational diversity than regimes without strong democratic traditions, for many of these have actually or already collapsed.

The weaker version of this argument, which is advanced here, claims that democracy may be possible in multinational states, usually by ensuring inclusive power-sharing or consociational arrangements, or by forging an overarching political identity. However, I argue that a shared national identity is sometimes important to a well-functioning democracy, because the relations of trust engendered by a shared national identity facilitate vertical dialogue between representative and constituent, and participation in political institutions.

Shared Nationality and Representation

This section of the chapter examines the relationship between a shared national identity and representation. I argue that a shared national identity provides a basis for unity that is important to the very idea that a person can represent others in a common institution or community. I also argue that there is a problem of trust in divided societies, but the problem is more acute in nationally divided societies, and so may necessitate institutional recognition of the various national identities and political communities in the society.

In a representative democracy, it is essential that the representatives can enter into commitments on behalf of members of the community/institution. Unless we are dealing with a very small participatory democracy, where citizens can directly vote on issues, it is essential that the people have sufficient unity and organizational structure to generate representatives. These must be seen as legitimate representatives of the people, as able to take binding decisions on behalf of the people, such as entering into war, making social welfare policy, and negotiating peace. The acts of the representatives are not, therefore, seen as belonging to individual agents, acting on their own; but must be seen as the genuine voice of a kind of collective will.

Of course, there is no logical necessity that the unity of the society depends on national identity, on a conception that all members belong to the same nation. However, in a world in which there are constant changes in the individual composition of the members—due to immigration, emigration, births and deaths—it is vital that all see themselves as members of a shared enterprise, as having an identity that can unify the whole and so render the political representatives legitimate.[26] In our (contemporary) world, national identities provide the basis for this sense of shared membership and unity.

The argument that there must be some basis of unity to generate legitimate representatives who can be viewed as acting on behalf of others is based on a Burkean conception of representation, where the representative's job is to advance the interests of the whole political community. On this conception, there is a clear connection between a shared identity and the legitimacy of the representative's act.

There is, however, an alternative conception of representation, according to which the representative is someone who speaks for a particular section of the community, and legitimacy derives from the fact that the system is procedurally fair, in that each group has a representative speaking for it and the final decision is arrived at in a forum which is inclusive of a number of groups, interests, and identities. It might be argued that all that is required in this context is the adequate representation of diverse identities, but that all members need not be committed to a common good, or share an identity as members of a common project.

This second conception of representation has some significant advantages over the Burkean one, especially in the context of divided societies. One of the most pressing problems in societies with severe divisions—and this may be true of ethnic, linguistic, religious, national, or ideological divisions—is the problems that they pose for normal electoral (democratic) politics. The majority vote rule that confers legitimacy in democratic regimes may function as a mechanism of exclusion. Moreover, I will argue, attempts to construct different democratic arrangements—beyond simple majority vote—to take into account the divisions in the state are extremely fragile or problematic.

[26] I owe this point to Margaret Canovan, *Nationhood and Political Theory* (Cheltenham: Edward Elgar, 1996), 22–3.

Let us take, as an example, a state with two main groups: A, which is the largest or majority group; and B, which is the minority group. In a case where these different national communities consistently vote for nationally-aligned parties—As vote for the party of As and Bs for the party of Bs—then elections proceed like a census, and the minority group is consistently excluded from power and the majority group consistently holds the reins of power.[27] The problem with this situation has nothing to do with preference-satisfaction, or with the minority Bs being upset because 'they don't get what they want'. The problem is the permanent exclusion of one segment of the population from a role in making rules that govern the state in which they live.

In this situation, the basic conditions for responsible democracy are not met. In *Democracy in America*, Tocqueville argued that, in a well-functioning democracy, the outvoted minority will respect the majority decision in the expectation that, at some later time, they will be part of a winning coalition and will require minority compliance.[28] The reverse would also seem to hold true—though Tocqueville did not spell this out—that a majority will tend to refrain from upsetting the minority because they anticipate that they will be in need of majority self-restraint when they are converted to minority status.[29] This dynamic does not occur in a state in which different national communities consistently vote for nationally aligned parties—there is no outlet for minority disaffection, there is no moderating influence on minority demands, and no mechanisms, at least internal to the democratic system, to prevent the majority from oppressing the minority.

This cycle of majority domination and minority exclusion is, of course, a disaster from a representational standpoint. On the majority-rule system of democracy, the legitimate representatives of community B are permanently excluded from a share of governing. Moreover, in this kind of divided society, there is so little trust between As and Bs that the members of the minority community are extremely reluctant to address their problems and concerns to representatives of the

[27] Moreover, because the governing party only needs to retain the support of the majority As, and any attempt to attract Bs to the party is likely to result in a loss of As' support—because these are two mutually antagonistic communities—there is little prospect of changing that alignment. There may be *some* movement at elections, of course, but not of the desired kind, that is, not across national lines. Frequently, a change in electoral support results if group A has two parties competing for the votes of As and group B, while a minority, only fields one candidate—in a first-past-the-post system—then a representative of group B may get a seat, even though Bs are a minority in that riding.

[28] Alexis de Tocqueville, *Democratie en Amerique* (Paris: Gallimard, 1961), 212.

[29] This implication is drawn out by Stephen Holmes, 'Tocqueville and Democracy', in David Copp, Jean Hampton, and John E. Roemer (eds.), *The Idea of Democracy* (Cambridge: Cambridge University Press, 1993), 23–63, at 30, 44–5.

government of the day, for these are themselves As, and are almost exclusively elected by As—and know that re-election depends on the support of As. Vertical dialogue between the minority community and the governing majority is therefore almost non-existent; and the particular concerns of the minority are also left unaddressed in the discussion *between* representatives at the government level, that is, in the corridors of power, when policy-making occurs. The special salience or interpretation that certain policies may have for the minority community go unspoken, and their concerns are left unaddressed.

This result poses difficulties for the most persuasive intrinsic and instrumental justificatory arguments for democratic institutions. Instrumental defences tend to argue in terms of the good consequences of democratic governance. The most persuasive of these argue that democracy is the form of government most likely to respect human rights, rules of justice, and allow people some measure of control or autonomy over their own lives. In this context, however, minorities have no influence on the government; they are alienated from the political process and there is no restraint on majority oppression. It is disturbing also for one of the most persuasive intrinsic justifications of autonomy, namely, the argument that democracy is intrinsically fair, and that at its heart is a neutral procedure that allows all individuals to have an equal effect in determining outcomes. Viewed in one way, of course, this defence still holds true: each person has a vote and the procedure—narrowly considered—treats each voter in the same way. But, in these circumstances, the majority rule for deciding 'winner' and 'loser' is not a neutral rule for arriving at collective decisions in the face of competing claims, for everyone knows who is in the majority and who is in the minority.

Many theorists, concerned about the exclusion of minority interests from democratic politics, and the idealized homogenizing influence of claims of 'common good', have argued for the need for representatives from marginalized groups, able to speak confidently on behalf of those groups, and have also suggested that this would facilitate participation of underrepresented groups in political life.

One plausible connection between representatives of different groups and participation is the need for vertical dialogue—that is, some discussion between the representative and the represented. The representative has to be sufficiently aware of, and receptive to, the concerns of her/his constituents. This is partly a matter of certain character traits, such as sympathy, and not a matter of national identity at all. However, there is strong evidence that sharing an identity helps to facilitate the kind of dialogue that is a component of good representative democracy. In the United States, for example, there is evidence that black constituents feel more comfortable with, and are more likely to voice their grievances or concerns to their representatives, if their representatives are black.[30] This, in turn, will ensure that government policy can be made with an awareness of the concerns and perspectives of this particular group. This is a good argument for devising electoral ridings or districts to ensure that such groups are more likely to have black representatives.

In societies such as the US, where there is a common national identity alongside groups who are excluded and marginalized along racial and gender lines, redistricting is an effective way to ensure that there are symbolic representatives of marginalized groups, and, particularly, to facilitate vertical dialogue between representatives and constituents in districts where the group dominates—although this only works for territorially concentrated groups.

In nationally divided societies, this solution is unavailable. Arguments for redistricting only work in societies where the excluded group wants to be included, wants a greater say in the governing of the society. Melissa Williams's deliberative democracy model, for example, attempts to include all marginalized groups and is successful in dealing with women and racial or ethnic minorities. However, it is unsuccessful in dealing with one of the most marginalized groups of all in North America—native people. In the first place, giving them 'voice' would help very little, for even if they were disproportionately represented, they would still be a small minority. Even more seriously, natives in North America are nationally mobilized—they call themselves First Nations and do not want simply to be included in central decision-making bodies. What they seek is not greater inclusion, but greater autonomy from central control.

The problem described above—the marginalization of one group from political power in divided societies—has also been used to justify a proportional representation system, which is designed to encourage smaller parties. The advantage of this system, in divided societies, is that it might lead to numerous interest-based parties, with cross-cutting cleavages, and to coalition-building that includes previously excluded groups. The evidence suggests that this may be effective in including groups of varying religious, ethnic and/or ideological

---

[30] Jane Mansbridge, 'What Does a Representative Do? Descriptive Representation in Communicative Settings of Distrust, Uncrystallized Interests, and Historically Denigrated Status', 21–4; Melissa S. Williams, 'Impartiality, Deliberative Democracy, and the Challenge of Difference', 9–12. Both papers prepared for the *Conference on Citizenship in Diverse Societies: Theory and Practice*, Toronto, Canada, October, 1997.

hues.[31] However, coalition-building is much more problematic in the case of strongly mobilized and competing national groups, which seek to be collectively self-governing. This is because proportional representation promises to allow the representation of diverse interests, reflective of different groups and identities and political opinion. This is suitable for ethnic or religious minorities, who aspire to have their identities expressed and included in the state. But in nationally divided societies, what is precisely in question is the existence of the state, and the legitimacy of the state. Nationally mobilized groups do not primarily seek greater representation of their interests or identity at the centre: rather, inclusion in the state is fraught with difficulty and is likely to be seen as an assimilationist measure.[32] These groups are mobilized around greater autonomy and political self-determination, not to improve their political or economic status. They seek not equality, but national rights, which typically involves not stronger central representation but institutional devolution.

There are other possibilities for democratic politics in nationally divided states, but these, too, are fraught with difficulty. In his books, *Ethnic Groups in Conflict* and *A Democratic South Africa? Constitutional Engineering for a Divided Society*, Donald L. Horowitz has suggested a system of 'vote-pooling' that would require that electoral systems have a 'distribution requirement' in addition to straightforward majoritarian rule. On this system, the party (or president) can only be declared a 'winner' if it or s/he gains support from a certain percentage of every state as well as a plurality of the overall vote. The idea behind this is to reduce political élites' incentives to make ethnically exclusive appeals. He cites the Nigerian electoral system as an example of such a procedure.[33] The problem with this requirement, in the context of an ethnically divided community (Nigeria), became apparent in 1979 when no one was able to fulfil the requirements.[34] This depressing event has certainly underscored the importance of

[31] See the discussion in Chapter 5 on the success of a proportional representation system in Israel, at least in so far as it has led to the proliferation of different parties based on different kinds of Jewish/Israeli identities.

[32] The evidence from Ireland and Israel on the problems with inclusion is discussed in Chapter 5.

[33] According to the Nigerian constitution, the president must win a plurality of votes nationwide plus at least 25% of the votes in two-thirds of the states (13 of 19).

[34] The leading candidate Shehu Shagari won a plurality of the votes overall and over 25% in 12 states and 20% in the 13th state. The electoral commission ruled that he could be president, anyway—they stated that this was 'equivalent' to meeting the constitutional requirements—despite the fact that he had obviously failed to do so. This type of exercise can only serve to undermine the view that governance should be in accordance with the constitution.

ensuring that institutional rules should be able to be met,[35] and the difficulty of finding representatives who are acceptable to all the people,
especially in an ethnically divided society. Moreover, while this *might*
work in ethnically divided societies, it is unclear whether it would
work in nationally divided societies, where the groups view themselves as constituting different political communities. Appeal to a
common interest, which is implicit in Horowitz's 'vote-pooling' procedures, presupposes that all see themselves as sharing a future
together and this is precisely what is in dispute.

This does not mean, of course, that there are no mechanisms available to try to treat national identities fairly. Complex power-sharing
arrangements may be helpful in such situations, especially if these are
accompanied by substantial self-government. Power-sharing is a possible solution to the problem of minority exclusion especially in non-
nationally divided societies. However, it is very difficult to achieve:
notable failures include Lebanon and Cyprus, although, in the case of
Lebanon, the power-sharing regime did last for 32 years, and so could
be considered a success.

Donald Horowitz, among others, has complained that the problem
with Lijphart's famous system of consociational (power-sharing)
democracy is that it only works in moderately divided societies, like
the Netherlands, Belgium, to some extent Canada.[36] In nationally
divided societies, there may be particular problems attached to the
level at which power-sharing takes place, and also to the boundaries of
the power-sharing unit. By this, I mean that power-sharing may be
adequate in ethnically or religiously divided societies, where disputes
are mainly connected to the kinds of symbols with which the state is
identified, and the policies that it enacts. In a nationally divided society, however, where the national groups are strongly mobilized in
favour of collective self-government, mere inclusion in the centre is
insufficient, and must be accompanied by some form of devolved
power in a federation or other kind of autonomy arrangement.

What I am suggesting, then, is that in societies with a common
nationality—even if there are other kinds of divisions, such as racial
divisions, gender divisions, class divisions—there are mechanisms
available to ensure that all groups have symbolic power; and—what is
important here in a discussion of representation theory—that there is
vertical dialogue between representative and constituent. In cases

---

[35] Horowitz is aware of this possibility, and says that other mechanisms should be in
place to provide for a government/presidency as a 'fall-back' position.
[36] Donald L. Horowitz, *Ethnic Groups in Conflict* (Berkeley, CA: University of
California Press, 1985), 568–76.

where a state has two groups with competing and mutually antagonistic national identities, the situation is quite different. The problem in nationally divided societies is that the different groups have different *political* identities, and, in cases where the identities are mutually exclusive (not nested), these groups see themselves as forming distinct political communities. In this situation, the options available to represent these distinct identities are very limited, because any solution at the state-level is inclined to be biased in favour of one kind of identity over another. That is to say, if the minority group seeks to be self-governing, then, increased representation at the centre will not be satisfactory. The problem in this case is that the group doesn't identify with the centre, or want to be part of that political community. Of course, from the point of view of marginalized national groups, increased representation may be better than the status quo even if only because it provides a forum in which minority representatives can press the case for what they really want, which is often some form of collective self-government.

Participation and National Communities

In his article, 'In Defence of Self-Determination', one of Daniel Philpott's arguments in favour of a majority-rule plebiscite to decide whether secession is justified is that it can sometimes have long-term good consequences. Specifically, he argues that creating smaller, more homogeneous units can make the government more participatory: '[B]y having their government closer to them, they may participate and be represented more directly, more effectually.'[37]

This is criticized by Allen Buchanan, who points out that, in many cases, a large federated political unit can offer more opportunities for participation, and more meaningful participation, than a small, relatively homogeneous unit.[38]

I argue here that both are right in their way: Philpott is right to correlate national homogeneity with increased participation, but his argument for it is weak or inadequately explained;[39] and Buchanan is right to point this out. Unless we are dealing with a small direct democracy

[37] Daniel Philpott, 'In Defence of Self-Determination', *Ethics*, 105/2 (1995), 352–85, at 359, n.16.

[38] Allen Buchanan, 'Democracy and Secession', in Margaret Moore (ed.), *National Self-Determination and Secession* (Oxford: Oxford University Press, 1998), 14–33, at 18–19.

[39] This, I will argue later (Chapter 7) is because his defence in terms of the exercise of autonomy or choice abstracts from the issue of national identity. Yet, it is precisely this element that would have helped to explain the insight that (nationally) homogeneous units tend to be more participatory.

in which individuals directly vote on issues, opportunities for meaningful participation are not a function of size. This section of the chapter suggests that there is an important connection between participation, which is a constitutive value in democracy, and a shared national identity.

There is an empirical tendency for language groups to become increasingly territorialized, in the sense that a particular language becomes more dominant in a region, but that, outside that region, the language is extremely vulnerable—Francophones in Canada, Germans in the former Soviet Union, Kurds in western Turkey.[40] This process tends to be accompanied by increased self-governing powers and/or demands for increased self-government in the territory where the language is dominant. This, of course, helps to consolidate the language group in becoming even more dominant over that territory.

Will Kymlicka notes this tendency and argues that democratic politics is 'politics in the vernacular'.[41] Genuinely popular processes tend to occur, when they do, only in units that share a common language. When institutions cut across linguistic lines, they tend either to be issue-specific and/or élite-dominated. Linguistic communities, then, are becoming increasingly important as the primary arenas in which political debate takes place. Kymlicka accounts for this in terms of 'the average citizen [who] only feels comfortable debating political issues in . . . [his/her] own tongue'.[42] Despite efforts to promote general bilingualism—in Canada and Belgium, for example—many people feel most comfortable debating issues in the vernacular: 'as a general rule it is only elites who have fluency in more than one language and who have the continual opportunity to maintain and develop their language skills.'[43] This means in practice that participatory processes tend to occur only within language groups, and that democracy in multinational states tends to function better when it is confined to political élites.[44]

---

[40] Jean Laponce, *Languages and their Territories* (Toronto: University of Toronto Press, 1987).

[41] Will Kymlicka, 'From Enlightenment Cosmopolitanism to Liberal Nationalism', Paper given to the *Conference on Minority Nationalism in a Changing State Order,* London, Ontario, November, 1997, 9.

[42] Ibid.   [43] Ibid.

[44] Kymlicka's argument certainly explains why language is an important axis on which political communities are constructed. However, it is important to emphasize that the sense of shared membership is crucial. Participation in a common project presupposes a desire to be included—or a belief that one already is a member of this shared community, shared political project. Individuals are likely to participate only when they see themselves as members of a community, as sharing a common project, and for this, a shared national identity is required.

One implication of the close link between participation and a shared national identity is that democracies in nationally divided societies might be able to accommodate multiple interests and be generally inclusive, but that this is inclined to be at the élite rather than grass-roots level.

The experience of some multinational states bears this analysis out. In Canada, a stable multinational system was possible when élite-accommodation was the norm, that is, when the various premiers of the different provinces and the federal government met behind closed doors to agree on a deal. But this method of reaching constitutional agreement came to an end in 1990, when, in an effort to increase Quebec's bargaining leverage *vis-à-vis* the federal government, the Quebec government stated that it would hold a referendum on any constitutional package agreed to. Naturally, this fuelled demands in all the other provinces that they also get a referendum on constitutional change.

It is generally accepted that the élite accommodation model of Canadian politics has given way to a more participatory model, in which any constitutional change would have to get the consent of all the people.[45] As this analysis suggests, this has made constitutional change extremely difficult: the same question, with the same wording, resonates differently in the two political communities, and is likely to elicit a different response.[46]

Moreover, this kind of participatory referendum is problematic because, while the majority of people in Canada do want to keep the country together, it is not clear that a referendum is the appropriate tool to achieve this. In the first place, a vote aggregates all kinds of interests and motives, and the reason for rejecting a constitutional package may be due to some other element in the package than the question of Quebec's relationship to Canada. Furthermore, and I think even more seriously, voting typically involves strategic decision-making. In the context of a multinational state, with two distinct polit-

[45] Alan Cairns, *Disruptions; Constitutional Struggles from the Charter to Meech Lake* (Toronto: McClelland & Stewart, 1991), 130–8; David V. J. Bell, *The Roots of Disunity* (Toronto: Oxford University Press, 1992), 189–91.

[46] Interestingly, one observer of Canadian constitutional debates prior to the current round of constitutional problems (correctly) *predicted* that genuinely participatory forums would be extremely problematic for the unity of the country. Back in 1971, S. J. R. Noel wrote, 'The lack of a pan-Canadian identity combined with strong regional sub-cultures is not necessarily a dysfunctional feature . . . as long as within each sub-culture, demands are effectively articulated through its political elite [and as long as there does not emerge] within any one of the provinces an elite who . . . are unwilling to [engage in] overarching cooperation at the elite level.' S. J. R. Noel, 'Consociational Democracy and Canadian Federalism', *Canadian Journal of Political Science*, 4/1 (March 1971), 16–18.

ical communities, the first choice of each of the two communities is different, and voting in a referendum is unlikely to reflect the common desire for unity. For example, the first choice of the Rest of Canada (ROC) is 'Canada status quo'; and so citizens may vote No to constitutional change on the assumption that Quebec will not leave, and compromise is unnecessary. However, many of them would be prepared to compromise if they thought it was absolutely necessary. The first choice of Quebec might be a federal state of two equal nations—that is, Canada in a renewed federal system—but many would be prepared to vote Yes to sovereignty/secession on the assumption that it would be necessary, to achieve concessions from the Rest of Canada. In other words, they may vote strategically, and on the basis of incorrect and unknowable assumptions—about the extent to which others are prepared to vote strategically, for example—and, in this way, end up in a sub-optimal arrangement. The problem here is the lack of dynamism in the voting structures, such that voters cannot accurately predict the consequences of their actions/votes. This, combined with their different political interests, tends to doom the process from the start, even though in this case, there is considerable shared ground.

This analysis of the relationship between participation and multinationality is supported by an analysis of both mechanisms—consociational democracy, 'vote-pooling' electoral systems—which are designed to produce a stable democracy in multi-ethnic and multinational states. Lijphart argued that one of the conditions of his consociational democracy is élite autonomy, in the sense that political élites are able to act in the interests of the group they represent, and this is in part a function of deference on the part of the general population—exactly the reverse of the attitude required in a strong participatory democracy.[47] Donald Horowitz's 'vote-pooling' model is also élitist in the sense that it depends on filtering out certain kind of appeals to produce political élites that are accommodating. It can do this because the electoral system is designed so that voters do not have an outlet to express their less accommodating preferences.

If this analysis is correct, there are trade-offs here: the value of participation has to be balanced against the importance of keeping together a large, multinational state which can incorporate different forms of (nested) identity and accommodate various interests and groups. Conversely, the desirability of maintaining a multinational state has to be balanced against other (positive) values, such as a

---

[47] Arend Lijphart, *Democracy in Plural Societies: A Comparative Exploration* (New Haven, CT: Yale University Press, 1977), 48–50.

democracy which can permit its citizens various avenues of participation. My conclusion, then, concurs with Philpott's contention that sharing a national identity may be positively related to participatory forms of democracy.

Conclusion

This chapter argues that there is some validity to contemporary normative defences of nationalism. First, the chapter considered the normative implications of instrumental arguments designed to explain the emergence and persistence of national forms of identity. It argued that there are important normative implications for our treatment of these identities, and in particular, we should respect these forms of identity, and try to accommodate them in non-violent ways in current political structures. The argument therefore dovetails in important ways with the argument from fairness considered in the previous chapter.

The Gellnerian argument not only suggests why national forms of identity would emerge and persist, but why cultural matters in general are politicized in the contemporary world. It suggests not only why nationalism is ineluctably linked to the form and practice of modern, bureaucratic industrialized societies, but also why multicultural identity politics would emerge in these types of societies. It explains the role of the state in reproducing and sustaining cultural practices and shows the importance of cultural uniformity for individual well-being.

The other two liberal-nationalist arguments link national homogeneity, not only with the functions of the modern state, but with the achievement of justice and the smooth functioning of democracy. The chapter first considered the argument that liberal values, and especially the value of social justice, will best be promoted in states whose members share a common national identity. In its strong form, this argument is vulnerable to counter-instances. A weaker version, which claims that in states divided in terms of national identities, social justice may be precarious over the long term, is more plausible.

The third part of the chapter argued that there is a close relationship between democracy and shared national identity. This is commonly accepted, and indeed is almost always supported by reference to J. S. Mill's rather quick argument in *Considerations on Representative Government*. This section tries to spell out precisely how a common national identity is needed both for representative institutions to function properly and for widespread participation on the part of ordinary citizens.

There is a strong statist bias in these arguments, because they point to the instrumental advantage of shared national identity for the state in its role as dispenser of justice and democracy. They tend to be employed by members of the majority national community, to indicate the problems that attach to nationally heterogeneous communities, and to explain the merits of embarking on a nation-building policy to assimilate national minorities, or at least to justify the non-recognition of minority national identities. From the perspective of this argument, national minorities do not have ethical value: indeed, they are potentially disruptive of the unity of the state and its capacity to fulfil its obligations to citizens and be governed democratically.

Arguments similar to these are often employed—by nationalist activists, not generally academics—to mitigate the potential tension between the national self-determination and nation-building components of nationalist agendas.[48] The two projects are potentially in tension. If the state attempts to facilitate the various national self-determination projects of different people within its borders, it runs the risk of not having a shared overarching national identity. If the state engages in nation-building to assimilate or incorporate national minorities into a common political project, then it denies their right to be self-governing or self-determining. Many nationalists have dealt with this possible tension by justifying national self-determination for their favoured groups, on the grounds that they could be or already are viable, just, and democratic states, and nation-building to 'mop up' the remaining minorities.[49]

This is, of course, extremely problematic, first, for the reasons given in Chapters 2 and 3, concerning the ethical value that attaches to these identities, the importance of these identities to the people who have them, and the requirement to treat these fairly. Second, the evidence

---

[48] An alternative strategy involves distinguishing between minority nations and national minorities, and claiming that only minority nations are entitled to rights to self-determination but that national minorities—defined as 'minority extensions of neighbouring nations'—are not. This strategy is developed by Michel Seymour, 'Une conception sociopolitique de la nation', *Dialogue*, 37/3 (1998) and Michel Seymour in collaboration with Jocelyne Couture and Kai Nielsen, 'Introduction: Questioning the Ethnic/Civic Dichotomy', in Jocelyne Couture, Kai Nielsen, and Michel Seymour (eds.), *Rethinking Nationalism, Supplementary volume of the Canadian Journal of Philosophy* (1996), 1–64; and is adopted by Kai Nielsen, 'Liberal Nationalism and Secession', in Margaret Moore (ed.), *National Self-Determination and Secession* (Oxford: Oxford University Press, 1998), 103–33. This argument is extremely problematic. I discuss the problems in 'Nationalist Arguments, Ambivalent Conclusions', *The Monist*, 82/3 (July 1999), 469–90, at 485–6.

[49] This point was made by Alan Patten to suggest that there is no necessary tension. The phrase 'mop up' is his.

suggests that state-sponsored assimilationist policies tend to be counter-productive, especially for national minorities in their own homeland, who have the demographic concentration to reproduce their own identity. Finally, it is a majoritarian fallacy that only large nations, or nations that already have their 'own' states, can be the bearers of the values of modernity, such as liberal justice and democratic citizenship. Many small minority national communities are also capable of supporting redistributive practices, of respecting basic human rights, and being governed democratically.

Another aspect of the instrumental nationalist argument, which is connected to its statist bias, is that it can explain what it is about national groups that is valuable, that is not true of other kinds of cultural or identity groups. Proponents of this argument tend to downplay the significance of other kinds of identity, and indeed, have tended to be acutely aware of the problems that attach to the celebration of religious, ethnic, sexual, or other kinds of identities. Miller, in particular, is at pains to note that the two are in practical tension, and is concerned that multicultural recognition should not take place at the expense of national identities.[50] This, of course, follows from the structure of the instrumental nationalist argument that he adopts: this argument considers only the value *to the state* in sharing a national identity, and this tends to reward not only functional—to the state—identities and virtues and beliefs, but also places a lot of weight on the importance of conformity and unity. In fact, of course, as the arguments of the two previous chapters suggested, these identities are not valueless: they may themselves be intrinsically valuable, as they express shared bonds of membership, and group affinity, and there are also important questions of fair treatment that attach to the state's role in dealing with issues that affect minorities.

Nevertheless, while the instrumental nationalist argument, by itself, is problematic, it does provide a valuable corrective to those theorists who argue for the celebration of all forms of identity, without regard for the consequences to the state or for the ethical practices that the liberal democratic state may perform. It is important to point out, as this argument does, that states are important to the realization of certain goals, and that national groups are also instrumental to these goals. A normative assessment of nationalism should not only focus on issues of identity and fairness, but also on the consequences that attach to claims to institutional recognition and fair treatment. In this context, it is an important fact that national groups are differently

---

[50] Miller, *On Nationality*, 133–9.

positioned than other identity groups, which lack the territorial basis or demographic power to argue for political autonomy, or political institutional recognition, as a remedy to the unfairness they experience. National groups typically *can* achieve some form of political or institutional autonomy without threatening the state system—although they may threaten the territorial integrity of a particular state—or the achievement of the goods that states can achieve.

The most persuasive element of the instrumental nationalist argument is the insight that we have to attend to the ways in which we can have a common life, or common framework in which people are able to meet and discuss their commonalities and to recognize each other as fellow citizens. This does not mean that we should negate or deny all other kinds of identities, but that the strategies of accommodation that we adopt should be consistent with a shared sense of ourselves as co-nationals, sharing a common political project.

CHAPTER 5

The Ethics of Nation-Building

This chapter argues that we need normative guidance on the kinds of nation-building policies that the state is justified in pursuing. Nation-building in the nineteenth century frequently involved the use of repressive state power to deny institutional recognition to minority national groups, and to marginalize minority cultural, ethnic, and religious identities.[1] Very few academics or political practitioners now advocate a nationalist policy of assimilation and denial of all kinds of identity. For most of the twentieth century, nation-building was mainly identified with state action to facilitate modernization—expanding communication and travel networks, encouraging industrialization and urbanization, raising educational standards and literacy levels—and increasingly complex and stratified economic activities. The basic premise has been that these forms of modernization will lead to an attachment to the nation, defined in statist terms, and erode more particularist cultural, ethnic, and religious forms of identity. However, the assumed empirical link between modernization and state-building is very questionable. In addition to the burgeoning number of minority nationalist movements, the main subject of this book, there are a number of minority cultural and other disadvantaged groups within the state who have mobilized around the theme that the policies of the liberal-democratic state disadvantage them.[2] In many countries, gays

---

[1] Mill's discussion of the progressive merits of assimilating smaller nations into the Great Nations in *Considerations on Representative Government* has been widely cited in the literature on nationalism. It is sheer anachronism to criticize him for these views, however, since they were widely held at the time.

[2] Revisionist liberals, multiculturalists, and minority nationalists have all pointed out that the liberal state is far from neutral on issues of cultural and national identity. Indeed, they argue that the institutions and policies of the liberal-democratic state tend to privilege particular cultural groups in the state. See Stephen Macedo, *Liberal Virtues: Citizenship, Virtue, and Community in Liberal Constitutionalism* (Oxford: Oxford University Press, 1990) and William Galston, *Liberal Purposes: Goods, virtues and diversity in the liberal*

have argued that the definition of the family in law and in state policies has served to exclude them and to deny them the benefits accorded to heterosexual married couples. Minority religious groups have been sensitive to the privileged status of the Christian religion in most Western democracies, in defining public holidays and rules regarding appropriate behaviour. Muslim girls in France and Quebec have challenged rules denying them the right to wear headscarves. Sikhs in Canada have argued that motorcycle helmet laws and the code of appropriate dress in the Royal Canadian Mounted Police—where the uniform includes a hat that is not compatible with the turban—discriminate against them. Orthodox Jews in the United States military have sought the right to wear the yarmulke. In each of these cases, the construction of the public sphere, which claims to be treating everyone as an equal, in fact is based on the majority culture. Its rules are compatible with the majority culture and religion, but disadvantages minority groups in the state, because its rules are incompatible with that culture and forces a difficult choice for minority groups. This movement, which I refer to in this chapter as multiculturalism, implicitly questions the homogeneity of the traditional state, and the vaunted equality of its citizens, and makes demands on the state for the recognition of difference from the norm.

Because of the questionable relationship between 'nation-building' and state action to facilitate the processes of modernization, this chapter does not address the traditional 'nation-building' policies of Western, liberal-democratic states. This chapter assumes that cultural pluralism is a permanent feature of most polities and that a variety of institutional and public policy mechanisms are necessary to accommodate these ties and identities to changing social circumstances. The term 'nation-building' primarily refers to the kind of relationship between national identity, culture, and the state that is appropriate and justifiable, and the legitimate role of the state in expressing a particular national community.

This chapter approaches this issue by examining two different kinds of identity politics: first, the claims of various—ethnic, gender, religious, sexual orientation, racial—identity groups, which I address under the rubric of 'multiculturalism'; and, second, the claims of minority nationalist groups. It accepts the basic distinction between two different types of diversity, developed by Will Kymlicka in his

state (New York, NY: Cambridge University Press, 1991) for a defence of some forms of state bias. See Iris Marion Young, *Justice and the Politics of Difference* (Princeton, NJ: Princeton University Press, 1990) for a criticism of it.

book *Multicultural Citizenship*.[3] Some states, Kymlicka argues, are comprised of different *national* communities, that is, historical communities on what they perceive to be their 'ancestral territory', and these groups are entitled to rights to self-determination. In other states—and here Kymlicka has in mind the immigrant societies of the United States, Canada, and Australia—diversity is largely, although not completely, a result of the immigration of people from a variety of cultural and ethnic backgrounds. This type of cultural pluralism is dealt with in this book under the rubric of 'multiculturalism'. In his book, Kymlicka argues that the two different types of diversity imply different kinds of rights.

Most of the work by liberals on multicultural policies has been concerned with whether these policies—of granting differentiated rights for disadvantaged groups—are compatible with liberal rights and rules of justice. Kymlicka, for example, suggests at the beginning of *Multicultural Citizenship* that the principal challenge to his project is that of demonstrating how minority rights might coexist with human rights. He endeavours, therefore, to outline the limits of minority rights, limits which are defined by the 'principles of individual liberty, democracy and social justice'.[4] His distinction between internal and external protections is designed to ensure that the individual rights of members of cultural groups are protected—groups have no rights against their members—although they do have rights against (more powerful) external groups.[5] The central concern of this chapter is not primarily with this debate,[6] but with a related debate in citizenship theory. This is the question of the relationship between multiculturalism and national identity politics, and, more specifically, with the kind of rights that are appropriate to these different types of groups. This chapter begins by questioning the basis of Kymlicka's differential treatment of these two groups. This chapter argues that, while Kymlicka is right to distinguish between the two types of cultural pluralism, the basis of his distinction, in terms of the aims of the different types of groups, is under-argued. The second and third sections

---

[3] Will Kymlicka, *Multicultural Citizenship* (Oxford: Clarendon Press, 1995), 11–26.

[4] Ibid., 6.

[5] Ibid., 35. For a criticism of the internal/external distinction, see Ayelet Shachar, 'Group Identity and Women's Rights in Family Law: The Perils of Multicultural Accommodation', *Journal of Political Philosophy*, 6/3 (1998), 285–305.

[6] Other theorists in this debate, most notably Chandran Kukathas, have argued that the pre-eminent liberal value is not personal autonomy, but toleration. From this perspective, he argues that liberals should tolerate all groups, even non-liberal ones, as long as members have a genuine right of exit. Chandran Kukathas, 'Are there Any Cultural Rights?' in Will Kymlicka (ed.), *The Rights of Minority Cultures* (Oxford: University Press, 1995), 228–56.

of the chapter examine the arguments put forward by marginalized ethnic, religious, or cultural groups and minority nationalist groups respectively. Both kinds of identity groups have argued that the liberal state is far from neutral on issues of cultural or national membership, and have tried to engage in a debate with liberals about the need to be sensitive to 'difference'. This chapter argues that liberal-democratic states fail the 'neutrality test' with respect to marginalized multicultural and minority nationalist groups. However, the chapter also argues that it doesn't follow from the success of their structurally similar critique of liberal polities that we should treat these two types of groups in the same way. The chapter justifies the differential treatment of multicultural and minority nationalist groups on the grounds (1) that these are different types of identities; (2) the different groups operate in different contexts and this poses limits to the kinds of remedies for unfairness that are appropriate; and (3) the context and type of identity are relevant to an assessment of the effect of institutional recognition on the state's capacity to realize the goods discussed in the previous chapter. Two underlying themes are also explored in the chapter: first, there is the issue of the appropriate relation of culture to the state; second, the issues of inclusivity and respect for diversity, raised by marginalized cultural, ethnic, gay and lesbian, and other groups, suggest the limits of justifiable nation-building that can be pursued by minority nationalists—and indeed all liberal nationalists. The chapter concludes by examining the more serious challenge that minority nationalist groups pose to the state.

Kymlicka's Distinction between Types of Cultural Pluralism

The view that multicultural groups are unlike nations because they seek the accommodation of their differences within the boundaries of a state forms the basis of Kymlicka's distinction between national groups and other kinds of identity-based groups. 'National minorities', he writes, 'typically wish to maintain themselves as distinct societies alongside the majority culture, and demand various forms of autonomy or self-government to ensure their survival as distinct societies'.[7] This is in contrast to immigrants, who 'typically wish to integrate into the larger society, and to be accepted as full members of it'.[8] While this is a broadly accurate characterization of national groups, this chapter takes issue with the automatic assumption of the relatively benign aims and effects of multicultural policies.

[7] Kymlicka, *Multicultural Citizenship*, 10. [8] Ibid., 10–11.

The distinction between multicultural and minority national identity groups based on the assumption about the integrative aims of multicultural groups is too simplistic, first, because it abstracts from the process of preference-formation on which the distinction is based, and, second, because it fails to give adequate importance both to the range of aims and policies espoused by the diverse versions of multiculturalism. Let me deal with each point in turn. First, the basis of this distinction between the two groups—national groups and other identity-based groups, which are mainly immigrants, in Kymlicka's work—is in the aims underlying their demands. But this raises an even deeper question about the context in which people formulate preferences and make demands. A reasonably dynamic view of the relationship between demands and contexts, between the aims of a group and what is achievable for a group, will recognize that what people demand, what people aim for, is partly structured by what they think they can get. The fact that one group demands more rights, or a different kind of right, might well be a function of their relative oppression, namely, the fact that they think that this is all they can reasonably aspire to achieve. The only argument that Kymlicka offers for treating multicultural groups differently than national groups is based on an empirical claim about groups having different types of aims, which begs the question about preference-formation.

Moreover, multicultural groups aspire to a wide range of rights, and some of these are not as integrationist in their aims and effects as Kymlicka assumes. Some of these policies do, indeed, aim at 'renegotiating the terms of integration', in Kymlicka's apt phrase,[9] and the empirical evidence of multicultural policies in Canada and Australia suggests that this integration is their main achievement.[10] But multicultural identity groups have a wide diversity of aims: some of the rights claimed are intended by the group claimants to reinforce their cultural distinctiveness, and these rights or policies may well have a disintegrative effect on the unity of society. It is unclear how Kymlicka

[9] Will Kymlicka, *Finding Our Way* (Toronto: Oxford University Press, 1998), chapter 3.

[10] Ibid., 18–24. In this book, Kymlicka offers empirical evidence to support the view that the official policy of multiculturalism in Canada has had integrative effects. 'Multiculturalism' in his book, however, primarily refers to the official policy of the Canadian government since 1971, whereas, this chapter is referring to the academic debate around multiculturalism, which is more radical—it includes group representation, group vetoes, support for Afrocentric education, and so on—and is mainly defended in terms of identity politics. It is confusion between the academic discourse and the official Canadian policy of multiculturalism that accounts for the confusion and ignorance that Kymlicka notes, with some puzzlement, in *Finding Our Way*, 22.

would respond, or could respond, to the cultural or religious identity group that did aim at institutional separation.

For these two reasons, I think Kymlicka needs another normative argument for treating their claims differently. The previous chapter of this book provided just such an argument: there I argued that the state is justified in pursuing a national agenda that socializes members into a common public framework in order to have economic opportunities, to participate in democratic processes, and to shape the public culture.

This book maintains Kymlicka's distinction between national groups and other identity-based groups. However, it argues that we need to further distinguish multicultural policies and group demands according to the kinds of aims they espouse and consequences that they are likely to have. It is possible, following from this, to identify three different kinds of multiculturalism.[11] (1) First, there are strong versions of multiculturalism. Proponents of this version of multiculturalism typically seek to maintain distinctive group identity and group solidarity by claiming rights which reinforce their separateness from other people in the society. They typically seek to exercise power which is normally exercised by the state to govern certain aspects of group life. This form of multiculturalism is problematic from the standpoint of the state's function in ensuring a common public life. (2) Weak versions of multiculturalism do not seek to challenge the jurisdiction of the state in a range of areas, but only to ensure that their cultural practices are included in the larger society. Their claims are primarily claims to be treated fairly, to be included in democratic debate and decision-making, to ensure that their history is part of the country's larger history. (3) Finally, there is a third type of group, who aspire to what Spinner-Halev has aptly termed 'partial citizenship' status. This refers to groups, like the Amish and the Hutterites, who are like strong multiculturalists, in the sense that they seek to maintain their distinctiveness by separating themselves from the larger society, but are unlike them in the sense that they do not make demands on the state, other than to be left alone.

There are, as well, important differences among national groups, which are mainly related to the kinds of demands that they typically make, and the context in which they operate. Just as I argued earlier, with respect to multicultural groups, that aspirations are sensitive to

---

[11] I draw these three types from Jeff Spinner-Halev, 'Cultural Pluralism and Partial Citizenship', in Christian Joppke and Steven Lukes (eds.), *Multicultural Questions* (Oxford: Oxford University Press, 2000). He refers to 'thick' and 'thin' multiculturalism. My (Irish) husband has pointed out, however, that 'thick' (t'ick?) is a pejorative word and I have changed the terms to strong and weak versions of multiculturalism.

context—sometimes, people ask for what they can get[12]—the demands and aspirations of national minority groups depends on their context and the current state form in which they operate. National minorities typically aspire, as Kymlicka has argued, to maintain themselves as distinct societies alongside the majority society. In some cases, however, the minority national group is either too small or dispersed to realistically aspire to self-government. In this case, they typically try to ensure that the state should not be identified with the majority national group on the territory, but should be conceived as a multinational or binational state, which confers rights on all nations in its territory. Italians in Slovenia, Swedes in Finland, Franco-Ontariens and Acadiens in English-speaking Canada all tend to seek language rights. Typically, they seek rights to use their language in official capacities or in their own region and rights to education in their own language. Sometimes they seek adequate representation in central institutions or power-sharing mechanisms, at least over certain areas of importance to them, to ensure that their interests are taken into account.

More typically, however, national minorities seek to maintain their own distinctive identity through some form of political self-government that potentially calls into question the legitimacy of the existing state order. If the minority nationalist group is sufficiently large and territorially concentrated to be able to effectively exercise authority within its own jurisdiction, it will typically demand some form of right to self-government or self-determination. This is the case with a wide range of minority nationalist groups, including the Québécois, Catalonians, and Basques.

Of course, these two kinds of rights often are demanded in tandem: Catalonian nationalists have focused on language rights, and have been very effective in advancing the position of the Catalan language, especially after the repression of the Franco regime; but they have, at the same time, also demanded various forms of political autonomy within Spain and as a region in Europe, consistent with their aspirations for collective self-government.

This more nuanced view of the diversity of aims and types of both multicultural and national groups raises questions about Kymlicka's assumption that multicultural groups have integrative aims. This extremely benign view of multiculturalism certainly helped him reach

---

[12] This isn't meant to imply that the state should minimize expectations and therefore demands. Sometimes, the state treats all group-based demands as ridiculous or unacceptable, and this leads to the radicalization of the demands, and the crystallization of antagonistic identities.

the conclusion that we should accord rights to various national and cultural groups, but the failure to take seriously some of the rights that were being demanded by multicultural groups has given rise to a new kind of criticism of multicultural policies. This is put forward most forcefully by Arthur M. Schlesinger Jr., in his book *The Disuniting of America*. He argues that multicultural policies are divisive, and that they reify difference. Schlesinger writes, 'The cult of ethnicity exaggerates differences, intensifies resentments and antagonisms, drives ever deeper the awful wedges between races and nationalities. The endgame is self-pity and self-ghettoization.'[13]

This chapter does not endorse Schlesinger's analysis. Indeed, I think that this blanket condemnation of multiculturalism makes the opposite error. It wrongly assumes that all kinds of multiculturalism, all references to group identity, are inherently divisive. It condemns multiculturalism on the grounds that it will lead, naturally, inexorably, to national separatism. Even more seriously, this claim about the deleterious effects of multicultural policies ignores the argument that many of these identity-based groups have made—namely, that their demands are required as a matter of justice. We do not want to automatically trade justice for unity and stability, but we should consider the merits of their case. Although I think that the errors implicit in this line of attack on multiculturalism are far more egregious than the one that Kymlicka and others make, we need to take seriously the kinds of concerns that give rise to this line of criticism.

In order to assess the claims of nationalist and multicultural groups to differentiated rights, it is necessary to consider the kinds of arguments that they have advanced in support of their claims. The next two sections of this chapter will consider the multicultural and minority nationalist arguments against the 'neutral' liberal state. It will not assume that all forms of multiculturalism, or indeed nationalism, are either inherently divisive or inherently benign, but will try to articulate the limits of both multicultural and national recognition.

Multiculturalism and the Non-Neutrality of the State

There are two normative considerations that provide some guidance on the rights that multicultural groups can legitimately claim. First, there is an argument from fairness, which leads to a presumption in

---

[13] Arthur M. Schlesinger, Jr., *The Disuniting of America. Reflections on a Multicultural Society* (New York, NY: W. W. Norton & Co., 1992), 102.

favour of removing any unnecessary disadvantage that a member of a group may suffer. The second concern is the creation of a unified political sphere. In many cases, this will involve making the political culture of the state permeable in the sense that a variety of cultural groups will feel included; that they will feel that it is possible to be both Muslim and French; Jewish and American; native and Québécois. This might involve removing any sort of special discrimination that the group suffers, which unfairly disadvantages the group. We have to recognize that demands on the part of multicultural identity groups to ensure that their history and cultural practices are included in the larger society are primarily claims to be treated fairly, to be included in democratic debate and decision-making, to ensure that their history is included in the larger history. These demands are ones of fairness and of justice, and will serve to strengthen citizenship by making the state more inclusive.

In her book *Justice and the Politics of Difference*, Iris Young defends radical multicultural policies on the grounds that this is necessary to redress various forms of oppression. She begins her analysis by rejecting the traditional liberal-democratic view of the state as justified in adjudicating between rival claims on the grounds that it is neutral and impartial: in fact, she argues, liberal theory and the liberal-democratic state are complicit in helping to perpetuate various forms of oppression. She distinguishes between five 'faces' of oppression from which groups may suffer: exploitation, marginalization, powerlessness, cultural imperialism, and violence. She then goes on to suggest a number of policies to redress this oppression: group representation, group vetoes over policies that affect the group directly, and public funds for interest groups to ensure that the 'voices' of oppressed groups are heard.

One problem with her account is that she fails to distinguish between different kinds of groups, and the aspirations that they have. As Will Kymlicka has objected, her account leaves more than 80 per cent of the population as oppressed.[14] Even more seriously, her account of 'oppression' lumps together economic factors and cultural issues. This is a problem, because it is more helpful, both in terms of analysing the problem, and arriving at a solution to it, to distinguish between these different forms. Economic discrimination or disadvan-

---

[14] Kymlicka, *Multicultural Citizenship*, 145. He cites Young on that passage that 'women, blacks, Native Americans, Chicanoes, Puerto Ricans and other Spanish-speaking Americans, Asian Americans, gay men, lesbians, working-class people, poor people, old people, and mentally and physically disabled people'. 'In short', Kymlicka writes, 'everyone but relatively well-off, relatively young, able-bodied, heterosexual white males'.

tages may be remedied by standard liberal anti-discrimination laws, rigorously applied, whereas other forms of oppression are based on cultural differences and seem to suggest that a group-based remedy is in order.[15]

Let us, for the moment, set aside the various problems with her particular formulation and examine what is most persuasive about this argument. This is the way she unmasks the particular identity lurking behind the universalist ideal. She contends that the abstract universal ideal fails to represent all people. Indeed, because it legitimates the existing biased structures, it serves to marginalize and oppress certain groups and perpetuate their disadvantages.

There is much that is true in this analysis. The languages of the public institutions and bureaucracy of the United States—to consider only one example of a Western liberal democracy—is English, not Spanish or Chinese or Farsi. Business customs and public holidays are consistent with the majority religion—Christianity. The design of many buildings and the requirements for many jobs presuppose that the basic norm or standard is that of the able-bodied person. The standard of beauty reflected in advertisements, television, and the political sphere reflect white physiognomy, as well as thinness. The dominant values and norms are those associated with white males. By questioning these norms, Young's analysis requires that we go beyond questions of distribution to examine the dynamics of decision-making and group power relations, and the biases inherent in the standards—of merit, beauty and much else—that legitimize inequalities in the society.

Young's argument draws attention to the fact that the neutral liberal-democratic state that abstracts from or ignores the cultural and group affinities of its members is a myth. In most cases, the state reflects the culture and traditions and practices of one group, and supports some ways of life over others. People with the right cultural background, the right career profile, the right kind of education—usually, with the imprimatur of a mainstream educational institution—will have advantages that others will not have. She is right to suggest that, in many cases, it is necessary to go beyond mere economic distribution of resources to examine the biases in the standards, policies and institutions that govern the structure of society. In order to

---

[15] See Nancy Fraser, 'Recognition or Redistribution? A Critical Reading of Iris Young's *Justice and the Politics of Difference*', *Journal of Political Philosophy*, 3/2 (1995), 168–70. This point is also made, with citation to the Fraser review, in Jeff Spinner-Halev, 'Land, Culture and Justice: A Framework for Group Rights and Recognition', *Journal of Political Philosophy*, 8/3 (2000), 319–42, at 321.

treat people fairly and equally, we must examine the ways in which people legitimately differ from one another. Some of Young's proposals to redress majority unfairness are very good ideas. She presents persuasive arguments in favour of comparable worth policies to combat sexism in wage structures, and bilingual-bicultural maintenance programmes for minorities.[16] Bilingual education, in particular, would go some way toward including speakers of a minority language in the public and economic life of the community. It would help to ensure that they develop the capacity to be full citizens in the political community and are able to take advantage of the economic opportunities that present themselves.

However, while these proposals seem to recognize the need for a common political language and identity, this does not flow from her analysis of oppression—in fact, it contradicts it—and her other, main proposal for redressing unfair structures, namely group-based representation, fails to take into account the possibility that this kind of electoral system will have the effect of undermining the common political framework in which people are able to meet and discuss their commonalities and to recognize each other as fellow citizens.

The first problem, then, is with Young's account of oppression, which tends to conceptualize all forms of minority status as a form of oppression. This seems completely unhelpful and unrealistic in contemporary circumstances. It is true that the liberal view of the state as not interfering in cultural matters is mythical. As Gellner has argued, since the rise of the modern bureaucratic state, with mass literacy, and increasingly standardized modes of interaction, the state is inextricably linked with the reproduction of values and cultures.[17] There are more than seventy different languages spoken, as mother tongues, by children in the Toronto District school board area.[18] It is not possible to have a modern state and give equal recognition to each of these languages. Signs, education, public debate has to be in one or two or three languages—I'm not sure what the upper limit is here—but there is a need for a common political language and identity, and some common framework in which different people are able to meet and discuss their commonalities and to recognize each other as fellow citizens.

A system of group autonomy is also unavailable in contemporary circumstances. The millet system, employed by the Ottomans, in which various groups were self-governing, was possible when the role of the

[16] Young, *Justice and the Politics of Difference*, 175–81.
[17] Ernest Gellner, *Nations and Nationalism* (Ithaca, NY: Cornell University Press, 1983), 17–40.
[18] Virginia Galt, 'Schools fear for immigrant students', *Globe & Mail*, March 3, 1998.

state was conceived of mainly as provider of protection and collector of tax. Quite apart from the theoretical question, raised by Kymlicka,[19] of whether liberals can justify the autonomy of groups that don't value autonomy, a contemporary version of the millet system is unavailable in the circumstances of modernity, or post-modernity, which presupposes standardized, literacy- and educational-based systems of communication, within which communication is rapid and readily understood, and labour mobile.

In contemporary circumstances, states are unavoidably bound up with the reproduction of cultures. Or, looking at the issue from the opposite end, culture is a collective property, in the sense that it is non-exclusive—it is not possible to affect one person's life without affecting others—and non-divisible—the benefit, or otherwise, of the property cannot be divided up into shares of resources.[20] It is entirely to be expected, then, as with other collective properties and collective goods—environmental regulation, zoning regulations—that disputes will arise and that not everyone will be satisfied by the resulting policy.

This raises two kinds of questions, which will be dealt with in turn. First, if some decision by the state is unavoidable, or better than not making a decision at all, does it make sense to think of being on the losing side of an issue—being in a minority—as itself constituting a form of *oppression*? Young seems to think that being in a minority is oppressive, but, in a culturally diverse society, we should expect to be in a minority on cultural issues, at least some of the time—perhaps even most of the time.

One of the reasons why disputes over cultural issues are so tricky is because culture is a collective property, not a collective good. It is not a collective *good* in the economists' sense, because a decision on some cultural matters—whether to put up a particular statue, say—may affect some people positively, and other people negatively. Even in the case of collective goods, there may be serious divisions over the level of provision of the good, and, in cases of limited resources, this might amount to a decision on which goods will be supported or provided by the state. But in the case of collective properties like culture, the

---

[19] Will Kymlicka, *Liberalism, Community and Culture* (Oxford: Oxford University Press, 1989), 170–3; Kymlicka, *Multicultural Citizenship*; Kukathas, 'Are There Any Cultural Rights?', 228–56; Joseph Raz, 'Multiculturalism', in Joseph Raz (ed.), *Ethics in the Public Domain* (Oxford: Clarendon Press, 1994); Spinner-Halev, 'Cultural Pluralism and Partial Citizenship'.

[20] See Thomas Christiano, 'Social Choice and Democracy', in David Copp, Jean Hampton, and John E. Roemer (eds.), *The Idea of Democracy* (Cambridge: Cambridge University Press, 1993), 173–95, at 186–8.

issue is even more contentious: what counts as a good for one might not count as a good for another. We should, that is, expect disputes over matters connected to culture, first, because of the cultural, linguistic, religious, and philosophical diversity of contemporary societies; second, because collective properties by their very nature—that is, the very conditions for counting as a collective property—involve a high degree of social interdependence; and, third, because conflicts revolve not merely over the levels of provision but over whether they should be provided at all.

At the same time, it does not follow that the state either can, or should, leave cultural matters alone, as if this neutral stance avoids the problem. First, it is doubtful that this approach is open to the state, because, as argued earlier, state policies on a whole range of areas are inextricably tied to the reproduction of language and culture. Second, even if state neutrality—in the sense of no state involvement on cultural matters—is possible, it is not at all clear that there should be a presumption in favour of state inactivity or state silence on these matters. In many cases of collective goods and collective properties, not making any decision would be tantamount to making a very bad decision in the sense that this might be everyone's last-place preference. It is precisely because people have an interest in living in an environment of a certain kind that it is important to arrive at a principled deliberative resolution of contested claims regarding collective properties, such as cultures. The alternative—leaving this kind of decision to the market—not only itself has certain biases, but the preferences that people have as consumers might be quite different from the collective judgements that they make as citizens and representatives in a deliberative sphere, where they try to shape the ground rules in which individual choices operate.

All this suggests that culture will inevitably be a contested area and that state policy with respect to culture will not satisfy all groups. People should expect to be in a minority at least some of the time, with regard to some matters. Simply being in a minority is not a form of oppression. In a culturally diverse society, it is unrealistic to expect that the public sphere is consonant with one's own particular culture and identity. There are many different kinds of identities and identity groups, and a full expression of one's particular culture and beliefs in the public sphere can only take place if other group's cultures and beliefs are excluded.

This suggests that a fair treatment of cultural issues would involve making the public sphere as inclusive as possible, and the public culture as permeable as possible, consistent with having a vibrant common life for the overarching political community. While one should not expect one's cultural beliefs to be fully instantiated in the public sphere, it is a claim of justice not to be unfairly excluded from full citizenship, and not to be discriminated against unfairly on the basis of cultural membership.

This leads directly to the second issue raised by Young's analysis. Once we realize that there is a need for a common public sphere in which we can make decisions, it becomes questionable whether Young's proposed solution of group-based policies and group-based representation is indeed appropriate. A vibrant public life and democratic processes presuppose some common sphere, some political space in which people can make collective decisions, can meet each other, not simply as blacks or women or Jews or Muslims or fundamentalist Protestants, but as *citizens* of a common political project, and deliberate over the best (fairest) ground rules to govern the basic structure of society.

Indeed, the need for a common political identity, a common sense of each other as citizens, is presupposed in Young's account, but she never addresses the conditions that are necessary to facilitate this recognition of commonality. At the beginning of *Justice and the Politics of Difference*, Young simply assumes that everyone accepts the fundamental equality of persons.[21] Later in her book, in her positive proposals for a more just society, she puts forward as the model of her solution Jesse Jackson's 'Rainbow Coalition', in which a number of oppressed groups—blacks, women, Hispanics, gays and lesbians, the disabled—join together under an umbrella organization to fight, politically, for an end to oppression.[22] The problem with this model is that it exaggerates the degree of common ground in the political projects of all these groups. It ignores the fact that there are also some serious differences between the various groups. The interests of women—conceived of as a group—in ensuring access to safe abortions may conflict with the interests of the disabled, who have an interest in ensuring that disabilities are not demonized, and want to prevent one manifestation of this, namely the routine aborting of disabled fetuses. The interest of fundamentalist Protestant and Muslim groups may conflict with the interests of lesbian and gay communities. (Interestingly, Young never cites these more conservative groups—Muslims, fundamentalist Protestants—as among her list of marginalized groups, although it is clear that they meet several of the

---

[21] Young, *Justice and the Politics of Difference*, 4–8.   [22] Ibid., 188–9.

criteria of an oppressed group.[23] Unfortunately, this may not be an oversight, for the inclusion of these types of marginalize groups in her list raises the question of the viability and unity of the Rainbow Coalition model.) Without some conception that these people are morally equal, first, as human beings, and also as fellow citizens engaged in a common political project, it is difficult to imagine how the various injustices can be addressed. A politics of difference, in other words, depends on the recognition of underlying unity; and yet, the proposals that Young puts forward, for recognition of difference, may in fact make it even more difficult for people to recognize their commonalities.

In many cases, as Kymlicka has pointed out in support of his distinction between national groups and other kinds of multicultural groups, the demands by minority cultural or religious groups can be met without jeopardizing the state's public and inclusive character. Often, the dispute arises in the first place only because of an excessively rigid, and of course false, view of state neutrality on cultural issues. Consider the debate in France concerning whether Muslim schoolgirls should be allowed to wear headscarves. Headscarves were prohibited on the grounds that religious symbols were disallowed, but at the same time these schools did not prosecute Christian schoolgirls who wore a crucifix. Even if that weren't the case, the requirement is not neutral between religious beliefs, because it is possible to be a Christian without any public displays of religious affiliation, whereas modest dress is required by Islam, and the requirement serves to prevent female Muslim believers from participating fully in the French public school system.

Demands by a particular racial or ethnic group to have their particular history taught in public schools are demands for a more permeable public culture, for a history that acknowledges the diversity of their contribution. Teaching this kind of history will show that the history of Canada, say, or the United States is not just a history of whites but that black communities made an important contribution to that history. As Spinner-Halev has argued, when this occurs, as it did with Martin Luther King Jr.'s legacy in the United States, the particular contribution that he made was not as a black; his legacy is not only for blacks; but as an American, and is a contribution that can be recognized and celebrated by all Americans.[24]

---

[23] This was pointed out by Tariq Modood, in response to questions at the conference on *Citizenship in Diverse Societies: Theory and Practice*, Toronto, Canada, October 1997.

[24] Spinner-Halev, 'Cultural Pluralism and Partial Citizenship'.

Demands to wear a yarmulke in the military or a turban in the RCMP, like the demand to wear headscarves in schools, are demands for cultural difference to be permitted and for exceptions to be granted when legislation adversely discriminates against them. These demands not to be discriminated against are not threatening to the *political* identity of the national community. On the contrary, ensuring that these various groups are included, that the common identity is constructed in a way which is consistent with the inclusion of various groups, may strengthen citizenship by ensuring that no one is left outside it, or marginalized by it, and so do not consider developing a separate identity which is threatening to the political project. It is, therefore, both normatively required, because fair, and good public policy, because it strengthens the national community.

Group-based representation is proposed by Young as a measure to redress current injustice—to ensure that marginalized groups are able to voice their concerns more effectively and thereby change the structures that perpetuate their oppression. It is conceived as a transitional measure, justified because we live in a non-ideal world, but which may no longer be required either when the state is more completely just, or when the group in question has become such a mainstream or accepted group in society that special rights are no longer necessary. The transition from marginalized to mainstream group has been well documented in relation to the Irish and Italians in the United States, and there are grounds for optimism concerning the similar progress of Asian-Americans and Hispanic-Americans in becoming part of the mainstream of American society. While other group-based measures—affirmative action for disadvantaged groups, or bilingual school programmes for linguistic minorities—can be framed in such a way that they apply generally, to any group that meets the criteria of disadvantage or has the desire and demographic concentration to justify bilingual education, this is hard to imagine in the case of special representation.

First, the empirical evidence surrounding institutional separateness suggests that it can lead to competing power bases in society, which depend on reifying or exaggerating the differences between the group and other members of the political community. This can be illustrated through the example of non-national federal systems, that is, those whose internal borders are not drawn to accommodate national minorities. In these kinds of federal arrangements, the argument for federalization is that the increased political autonomy gives voice to regional or local concerns and also may be more efficient. Now, of course, granting political autonomy to regional units of the state is inherently less problematic than giving autonomy to cultural groups, because these units are still part of the state, and governed by the constitution of the state. Nevertheless, even these types of federal arrangements have sometimes led political and bureaucratic élites to guard these privileges jealously, even when this is not necessary either from a democratic or efficiency standpoint. There is a large literature in Canada on provincial élites engaging in élite-driven province-building, which is out of step with the desires and aspirations of most (English-speaking) Canadians, who identify with the central government.[25] Indeed, this is a microcosm of precisely the problem that I am concerned with, for, in Canada, provincial leaders—in Alberta, British Columbia, Ontario, and elsewhere—have (falsely) equated their situation with that of Quebec, and have demanded to be treated in the 'same way' as Quebec, demanding more provincial powers and increased decentralization. As a result, even though opinion polls indicate that English-speaking Canadians desire a stronger role for the central Canadian government, and identify politically strongly as Canadians, they live in the most decentralized federal arrangement in the world with stronger interprovincial barriers than inter-country barriers.[26] They do so, because the institutional separateness and autonomy enjoyed by provincial leaders have been jealously guarded by provincial leaders, who have, in fact, tried to seek greater powers and more areas of jurisdiction. This experience suggests that non-*modus vivendi* arguments for institutional separateness for cultural groups, which are not part of the state, may threaten the unity of the society and reduce the capacity of the state to dispense liberal justice and function as a vibrant forum for public dialogue and debate on a range of issues. It suggests that granting political autonomy to groups when this is not required from a peace and stability perspective may create an institutional basis for exaggerating differences in order to expand power and jurisdiction.

[25] See David V. J. Bell, *The Roots of Disunity: a Study of Canadian Political Culture* (Toronto: Oxford University Press, 1992), 139–52; Garth Stevenson, 'Federalism and Inter-Governmental Relations', in Michael S. Whittington and Glen Williams (eds.), *Canadian Politics in the 1990s* (Toronto: Nelson, 1995), 402–23; Alan C. Cairns, *Disruptions; Constitutional Struggles from the Charter to Meech Lake* (Toronto: McClelland and Stewart, 1991); Philip Resnick, 'Toward a multination federalism', in Leslie Seidle (ed.), *Seeking a New Canadian Partnership: Asymmetrical and Confederal Options* (Montreal: Institute for Research on Public Policy, 1994).
[26] For English-Canadian identification with the central (federal) government and Canada as a whole, see Alan Cairns, 'Constitutional change and the three equalities', in Ronald Watts and Douglas Brown (eds.), *Options for a New Canada* (Toronto: University of Toronto Press, 1991).

The difficulty in getting élites to voluntarily relinquish the institutional basis of their power, when this is no longer required from the standpoint of transitional justice, is particularly relevant to the issue of group-based representation. Unlike in cases where the society as a whole frames a policy targeted at a particular disadvantaged group, or where the state delegates power to a group or local organization to run its own affairs, the issue here is: who has jurisdictional authority over the group and who is entitled to represent its interests. It is not clear that the rest of society would be able to exercise the authority to terminate the special group-based representation arrangement, even when the group was a rich and well-organized group, clearly no longer 'oppressed'—at least in the ordinary meaning of the term 'oppressed'.

The justificatory argument for representation rights in particular rests on the view that people outside the group do not or cannot represent the interests and perspectives of the group, and so cannot legitimately exercise jurisdictional authority over the group. If this is right, it seems that group-based representation will persist, even beyond the time that it is needed, unless the group's élites relinquish their power voluntarily. In short, the problem with Young's group representation proposal is not simply that this arrangement is justified as a temporary measure, but does not envision a state of affairs in which this measure would no longer be necessary. More seriously, group representation in particular, because it carries with it assumptions about who has authority to change the structures, seems to have a self-perpetuating character, which may well outlast the particular argument from current injustice that is intended to justify it. Moreover, its self-perpetuating character rests on the potentially divisive claim that those outside the group cannot be trusted or are unable to adequately consider or look after the interests of group members.

Minority Nationalism and the Non-Neutrality of the State

The arguments put forward by minority nationalists for recognition of their national distinctiveness, or for some form of national self-determination, are, like the arguments of multicultural groups, addressed initially to the false conception of the neutral liberal state. Like multiculturalists, who argue that the state tends to privilege certain identity groups in the state—white middle-class, relatively young males, in Young's theory—minority nationalists have argued that the liberal state is not in fact neutral amongst various national identities, and that policies of non-recognition tend to obscure the extent to which the state helps in reproducing the majority national community on the territory.

Many minority nationalists, however, have argued that political borders—or, more precisely, where political borders are drawn—can privilege some groups and not others. They do not mean here simply economic or material 'privilege' but are also referring to the fair treatment of certain kinds of identities. This section will discuss some ways in which minority status may involve a certain kind of unfairness, and the kinds of claims that might be considered appropriate for a broader conception of justice among national groups.

We are all too familiar with cases where being a minority carries with it a range of risks and insecurities, where being in a minority group involves a much higher risk of being a victim of serious violations of human rights. This is as true for religious and ethnic minorities as for national minorities: the treatment of Jews in Nazi Germany should dispel any notion that only national minorities suffer at the hands of majority groups. However, there is some renewed attention to the kind of problem that attaches specifically to national minority groups. In his book *Nationalism Reframed*, Rogers Brubaker focuses on national minorities 'trapped' on the 'wrong' side of borders, in nationalizing states.[27] His account of this relationship, with respect to Germans in interwar Poland, Serbs in Croatia after 1990, and Russians in the 'Near Abroad' since 1990, points to the vulnerability of national minorities. Especially in cases where there is a history of violence between groups, there is a possibility of a downward spiralling dynamic of mutual apprehension and mutual suspicion. In certain contexts, such as state break-up, people may become centrally defined by their national identity: even those who, previously, or in other contexts, had shared interests, can come to feel that they can only rely on, and hence have to be defined by, their own national group.

It is not difficult to understand how this dynamic takes hold. When you are a minority in a state peopled by other people who, historically, have distrusted 'your people', one's group identity is the only source of security one has and so comes to define which is an in-group and which is an out-group. In this context, people feel insecure when they are surrounded by people of another group, not because they might dislike individual members of the other group, but because they feel that members of the other group may distrust them, and the context of mutual suspicion and anticipation reinforces group solidarity. The fact

---

[27] Rogers Brubaker, *Nationalism Reframed. Nationhood and the national question in the New Europe* (Cambridge: Cambridge University Press, 1994).

that no one wants to be a minority should make us think about the problems that are associated with minority status.

This, of course, represents the ugly face of nationalist conflict, and some may object that this should not be used as a component of an argument for the recognition of national lines of identification. However, it is important to see that, in this situation, not only are national lines of identity almost and unfortunately unavoidable, but they are so partly because all parties recognize that minority status represents a serious disadvantage.

No one would deny that minority status is a problem when the regime is discriminatory and even murderous, or when it is a strongly nationalizing state, intent on privileging—economically, culturally— one national group on the territory. But what of the case of members of minority nations who operate in a situation where their basic (indi- vidual) human rights are not violated? There are many contexts where minorities live amongst the majority and are not oppressed, at least in the general meaning of the term oppressed. In this section, I want to suggest that disadvantages accompany minority status, even in this kind of situation.

Let us imagine, for a moment, a person who speaks X language, identifies with other Xs, and is culturally at home with other Xs. Borders are drawn and she finds herself in the state comprised of a majority of Xs. This person feels that the public culture is continuous with the culture and values that she believes in. The language that she speaks at home is not a mere private language: it is a public language, and speaking this language, being familiar with the patterns and nuances of the majority culture, translates into positions in the state economy, bureaucracy, and government.

Contrast this with an X who lives a village away. Borders are drawn and this person finds herself in a state peopled by a majority of Ys. There has been some historic enmity between Xs and Ys, but relations now are peaceful. Still, this person is aware, not only that she is a minority, but that this minority status carries with it a range of insecurities and disadvantages. The language that she speaks at home and in her community is not the language of the state: she must acquire facility in a second language, and ensure that her children acquire a second language, to have access to good jobs in the political and eco- nomic spheres. She may, indeed, be disadvantaged in numerous other ways, often unintentional, by the laws, procedures and public life of the state, which reflect the culture, history, and traditions of the major- ity community. Moreover, this person is acutely aware of her minor- ity status. Unlike members of the majority community, who can all be individuals in the sense that they are regarded by others as individuals, she is always regarded as an Other, as an X.

In addition to the economic implications of minority status, and the potential for discrimination and prejudice, there is significant psychological loss, in so far as the minority identity is denied or rejected. This has been well documented with respect to various groups in Central Europe in the period following the First World War. With the collapse of the German and Austro-Hungarian Empire, Hungarians found themselves converted from majority to minority status in Romania, Serbia, and Czechoslovakia. Germans in Czechoslovakia, Poland, and Denmark found themselves similarly converted from majority to minority status. The psychological loss associated with this transition is not just the notion of being transferred from dominant status to being dominated, but the psychological loss that accompanies the denial of their aspiration to be a political community. Nor is this loss simply connected to cultural or linguistic issues. In Chapter 3 I argued that national identity is not simply a knock-on effect of cultural differences, and the issue here cannot simply be conceived as a dispute over culture. The most significant problem is that the border, or more precisely where the border is drawn, denies their aspirations to be self-governing. Moreover, there is a sense of unfairness associated with this, for the border changes permit some groups to be collectively self-governing, to have institutional expression of their identity as members of a political community, but denies it to others (to national minorities).

The demands that national minorities make are justified as methods to redress various kinds of unfairness that attach to minority status, to ensure that the state they live in is not exclusively associated with the majority national group on the territory, and to give expression to their legitimate aspirations to be collectively self-governing.

In some cases, accommodation of minority identity will enable the group to accept its new political identity, and to identify with the state of which it is a part. The placement of many small minority nationalities on the 'wrong side' of the border may have at one time involved psychological loss, but many of these communities have made peace with this and are able to accept the political jurisdiction of the state because various kinds of accommodations—education rights, language rights, cultural rights—have been made, and their national identity is not necessarily incompatible with their political identity.

In many other cases—and these are actually the central because more problematic cases—national groups are not satisfied with mere cultural rights. The forms of unfairness that minorities experience can be addressed best through political self-government. This is so, first, because national identities typically involve an identification with a political community, and this identification involves its members feeling, in varying degrees, that they should enjoy some degree of collective self-government. Second, the aspiration to be collectively self-governing is related to the group's legitimate desire to maintain itself as a distinct group on their territory. In the current political order, where the state is inextricably linked with the reproduction of identities, this is ensured best through collective self-government.

This has important implications for a conception of fair treatment among national groups. In the case of the multicultural identity groups discussed in the previous section, state policies impact on these groups, advantaging or disadvantaging them in different ways, at different times, and these groups become politicized when they organize to change some government policy. The state cannot be neutral, and cannot be entirely fair—because there has to be some common public space and some standardized cultural practices—but the state can attempt to be as inclusive of these various identity groups as possible. The structural injustices that ethnic, religious, sexual orientation, and other kinds of minority groups face can be partially remedied by neutralizing the state. The state can, through policies of fairness, tolerance, and accommodation, try to ensure that these various ethnic or sexual orientation identities are compatible with the overarching political identity in the state. The main limit to this policy of accommodation is the need to maintain a common public life, which is itself also morally justified.

National groups, by contrast, are situated in a different context. First, they have the capacity to act as the carrier of the values of modernity, to be democratically self-governing, to dispense justice and create a common, public life in which people can participate. Second, and related to the first point, they are generally sufficiently territorially concentrated that the exercise of self-government is possible, and they typically aspire to this as a remedy to the minority disadvantage that they experience. Indeed, national communities are defined by the presence of aspirations to be politically self-governing. Of course, as discussed earlier, in some cases, where the group is too small or dispersed to enjoy territorial self-government, minority nationalists have attempted to secure other rights to express their identity and ensure that the state is not identified solely with the majority nation. In cases where political self-government is at least conceivable, and denial of this aspiration is not connected to natural causes—it is not demographic or territorial—questions of fair treatment arise. In such cases, whether the minority national identity is recognized or denied, their aspirations are fulfilled or unfulfilled, is inextricably bound up with the institutional structure of the state and majority willingness or unwillingness to countenance changes to the state structure. It is the state, controlled by the majority national community, which either functions to facilitate this political self-government through devolved power, or some other institutional expression of this aspiration, or serves to deny it.

In these cases, the only way to be fair to national identities—as distinct from gay identities or ethnic identities or other kinds of identities—is through creating the institutional or political space in which members of the nation can be collectively self-governing. In cases where the state is dominated by a majority national group, and political autonomy for the minority group is both possible and desired by the minority, fair treatment would seem to require that the minority national group also enjoy political recognition of its aspiration to collective self-government. Moreover, this kind of political autonomy and political recognition is entirely consistent with both justice and democratic governance—there is no imperative that democracy can function and justice be dispensed only at the highest levels of jurisdiction, rather than more local levels.

This suggests that accommodation of national minority groups through institutional separation—precisely what most national minorities demand—is a requirement of fairness. In cases where forms of self-government are neither demanded nor possible, cultural rights at least make their survival as a distinct group possible and also help to ensure that the character of the state is reflective of more than one majority national community on its territory.

Identity Politics and Other Kinds of Politics

There is, in addition to this normative argument about fairness, an important difference between national minorities—especially sizeable national minorities that aspire to self-government—and other kinds of minorities. This practical difference is relevant to the fact that national identities are primarily political identities, whereas other kinds of identities are not primarily political, and this political dimension means that national identities are potentially more divisive. This section argues that politics in nationally-divided societies is quite unlike the kind of politics that characterizes the multicultural societies of (English-speaking) Canada, the US, and Australia, and that it therefore makes sense to treat the claims of nationalists quite differently from the claims of other kinds of multicultural identity groups. The arguments of this section also provide some empirical basis for the view that the kind of group-based representation advocated by Young to deal with multicultural groups is problematic in a number of ways.

One of the most challenging aspects of establishing a genuine competitive democracy is the tendency, in seriously divided societies, of voting according to ascriptive identity. In many nationally and ethnically-divided societies, a segment of the society—a particular linguistic group, say, or a national group—will give a large proportion of its votes to political parties associated with this segment. Thus, the Xs vote for the party of Xs, and the Ys vote for the party of Ys. This tendency has been noted by a number of political scientists, and indeed has sometimes raised concerns that democracy itself is problematic, because communal identities offer a tempting basis on which to mobilize support.[28] When this occurs, as argued in the previous chapter, elections proceed like a census. Numerically small groups cannot form the government, and may indeed be consistently marginalized from political power. The group in power, knowing that its majority depends only on a particular strata of society, is intent on keeping support of its majority group. In this situation, political parties don't span the different cleavages in society, but antagonize them because there is no incentive for political leaders to compromise with the other groups in society. There is no incentive for compromise because the prospect of winning support from members of the other groups is very low.

This segmental division of electoral support is one of the features of nationally divided societies, although it also occurs with a different dynamic and different consequences amongst ethnic groups. In nationally-divided societies, democratic contests take place along national lines. Northern Ireland is a nationally-divided society, in the sense that it is divided between people who identify (politically) with Britain and people who identify (politically) with Ireland. In more than ninety years of democratic politics, in which elections were freely contested, no party that claimed to draw members from both communities has done better than 10 per cent of the vote.[29]

[28] Samuel P. Huntington, 'Democracy for the Short Haul', *Journal of Democracy*, 7/2 (1996), 1–13. The tendency for segmental voting has also been well documented in Donald L. Horowitz, *Ethnic Groups in Conflict* (Berkeley, CA: University of California, 1985) and Arend Lijphart, *Democracy in Plural Societies* (New Haven, CT: Yale University Press, 1977).

[29] John McGarry and Brendan O'Leary, *Explaining Northern Ireland* (Oxford: Blackwell, 1995), 154, 374–5. See also Paul Mitchell, 'Transcending an Ethnic Party System? The Impact of Consociational Governance on Electoral Dynamics and the Party

This is quite different from the kind of politics characteristic of the United States where the multicultural debate has raged most fully. The US is multicultural in the sense that the society is divided in terms of race, class, gender, and ethnicity. Nevertheless, it is possible in this type of society to have broadly-based parties, which span a number of different groups in society. Although blacks vote overwhelmingly for the Democratic Party, the Democratic Party is not a black party. The majority of Democrats are white. Because blacks, on the whole, are poorer than whites, their vote could be explained in terms of their class position and their interest in a strong redistributive state, rather than in racial terms. Moreover, there are also black Republicans. Other identity groups also find that their interests can be represented within the current political structure. Both political parties now compete for the Hispanic vote. Many Hispanics traditionally voted for the Democratic Party, but the Republican Party's message of strong family values and traditional small 'c' conservatism is appealing for many Hispanic voters. Republicans have also tried to lure Hispanics into the republican fold, particularly in Florida and Texas.[30] I don't want to suggest that this political system perfectly reflects the needs and aspirations of any of its voters—in fact, it is a feature of representative democracy that the voter necessarily has to aggregate preferences— but it is significant that blacks and Hispanics and Asian-Americans can be incorporated into the political system through competition between broadly-based political parties. While representation may not be perfect, and these groups may not be fully or adequately included, nevertheless, it is not true that only leaders of the black or Hispanic or Asian-American community can 'represent' the interests and identities of its members. A competitive electoral system, sensitive to its varying constituencies, can also address the needs and concerns of various groups and interests in society.

Of course, political strategies are devised against the background of what is possible and achievable. The fact that the United States has broadly-based political parties, which seem to incorporate a number of different groups in society, is partly a function of the structural and institutional biases of a single-member plurality system. This system makes it difficult for small identity-based parties to compete and win electoral representation. Single-member plurality systems are designed to encourage competitive political parties that span social

System', in Rick Wilford (ed.), *Aspects of the Belfast Agreement* (Oxford: Oxford University Press, forthcoming), 28–48.

[30] See 'The Happy 31', *The Economist*, November 28, 1998, and 'Out of the Dark, Republican Glimmers', *The Economist*, May 15, 1999.

cleavages, and help to mitigate conflict. If the electoral system was changed from single-member plurality to proportional representation, it is probable that this would encourage the proliferation of small group-based parties. It is not clear, however, that transforming the political sphere to reflect these social divisions and serve as a space for contestation is desirable, either socially or democratically. In social terms, it does have certain advantages: it helps to ensure a fuller representation of the range of diversity in society; it gives expression to the 'voices' of minorities and places their concerns on the political agenda. On the other hand, to the extent that this kind of politics may lead groups to engage in competition with each other for increased resources and power, it may exaggerate the divisions in society. There is no guarantee that these 'voices' will engage in a 'dialogue' about what is in the common good, rather than engage in interest-based politics to secure for their group the fruits of political power. In political terms, this kind of system may give increased power to very small groups in society to the detriment of the vast majority of citizens, who may feel that they are (politically) hostage to the demands of a small group who commands a swing vote in parliament. This has certainly been the experience of Israel: the Israeli electoral system rewards small political parties and this has sometimes meant that the religious right has wielded extraordinary power within governing coalitions.

It is certainly not clear that we should seek to replace the type of competitive electoral politics that spans cleavages with group-based politics. More expansive brokerage parties are motivated to deal with social divisions, because they must compete for support from the different segments of society.[31] Group-based politics, on the other hand, are often thought to be extremely problematic for democratic compromise and choice.[32] Admittedly, it is an important part of Young's argument that many of these groups are oppressed and their demands are justified on grounds of justice. But the evidence of

---

[31] One serious problem with single-member plurality systems is that they may ignore the interests of groups whose potential impact is small. This is true of very small groups or groups with very diffused populations. One of the best examples of this is aboriginal peoples in Canada. The major political parties have neglected their interests and done very little to improve their participation. In cases such as these, some additional mechanisms for effective consultation and participation may be necessary, as well as redistricting to ensure that the interests and concerns of the group are voiced. I am not suggesting that single-member plurality systems are perfect, only that specific rights to representation along the lines advocated by Iris Young raise concerns about group essentialism, lack of accountability, and common citizenship, and that proportional representation systems are not clearly superior.

[32] This has been argued by Seymour M. Lipset, *Political Man: The Social Bases of Politics* (Baltimore, MD: Johns Hopkins University Press, 1960), 12–13.

group-based politics in divided societies—and especially the lack of attention to the motive for compromise in her solution—suggests that her solution will exacerbate, rather than solve, social injustices and social divisions.

This conclusion does not apply to minority nationalist politics, which differ in important ways from the kind of group-based politics advocated by multiculturalists.[33] First, minority nationalists are sufficiently territorially concentrated that their interests and identities receive expression on both single-member plurality and proportional representation systems. Indeed, it is hard—given the territorial basis of the state and of democratic representation—to deny the expression of any territorially concentrated group. Nationalist politics can be expected in multination states, committed to freedom of expression, association, and democratic representation. Moreover, and just as important, national identities are primarily political identities and are bound up with the structure, boundaries, and membership in the state—indeed, in many cases, which state one wants to be a member of. Strategies of inclusion in expansive brokerage parties are therefore not available. Minority nationalists typically don't want to be included in current state structures: they do not seek access to the benefits of political power for their group, except in so far as this may advance the cause for self-government within structures that give them significant political autonomy or independence.

This tendency is apparent even in states which are diverse in a number of respects, and which encourage the flourishing of group-based parties. Israel is an extremely diverse society. Within the Jewish community, there are deep divisions—between religious and secular Jews, Sephardim and Ashkenazi, Russian-speaking, Ethiopian Jews, and many others—and the Israeli electoral system encourages representation of the different segments of Israeli society. Even in this situation—and with this degree of plurality and diversity—the differences between these various multicultural groups and national groups are apparent. The *political* divisions between Jews and Arabs are sharper in the sense that Arabs are not members of the political establishment. They are a segment of society which is not viewed as a legitimate party to government. This is because Israeli Arab parties have a double agenda: not only to improve the political and economic status of

[33] The conclusion does not apply to aboriginal people, either. The analysis offered here does not cope with aboriginal groups, who are unlike both multicultural identity groups and minority national groups. They are unlike multicultural groups because they seek self-government and autonomous political decision-making—like national groups—but they are unlike minority national groups because they typically lack the capacity to form anything remotely resembling a national political community.

Israel's Arab citizens, but also to affirm the national rights of the Palestinian people, even if they are content to remain citizens of Israel—although this, too, may be a matter of 'asking for what one can get'.[34] And unlike the other groups in Israeli society, from the left to the religious right, the Arabs are politically marginalized: no Arab party has been a member in a coalition government, and there has never been an Arab cabinet minister.[35] This suggests that, when the very existence of the state, and loyalty to the state, is at the heart of the division, inclusion is fraught with difficulty. It is difficult for the national minority, who typically seeks not merely improved political and economic status—that is, they do not simply seek equality—and difficult for the majority national community who find extending full political power to the minority problematic when there are questions surrounding the loyalty of the group, and the uses to which political power might be put.

A similar conclusion is evident in Northern Ireland, whose electoral system was changed from single-member plurality to proportional representation with single transferable vote, precisely in order to encourage numerous divisions in societies. The idea behind the change was that, under proportional representation, cross-cutting cleavages, such as class, would receive political expression and this would encourage coalition-building, and perhaps cut across the sharp national division between British (Protestants) and Irish (Catholics). As in Israel, there are divisions within the two national communities (Irish and British), but none cutting across them. There are, for example, a number of unionist parties, reflective of different groups and political opinion within the British (Protestant) community, but they are all *British unionist* parties, which Irish Nationalists do not, and would not, vote for. No attempt is made by these various parties to appeal to voters *across* the national divide. The same is true of the two dominant Irish nationalist parties—SDLP and Sinn Féin.[36]

In short, national identity is unlike other kinds of identities because it is fundamentally political, and nationalist politics is unlike other kinds of identity politics because the only way to accommodate them is through the kind of institutional separation that nationalists typically seek. We can ensure the inclusion of diverse multicultural groups

---

[34] The *Jerusalem Post*, Internet Edition, http://jpost.co.il/Info/elections99.

[35] This is related to concerns about the allegiance of Israeli Arabs to the state. See Nina Gilbert, '15th Knesset opens', The *Jerusalem Post*, 8 June, 1998.

[36] Voter transfers from first to second choice invariably occur within national blocs. There has been some limited evidence of pro-Agreement voter transfers following the 1998 peace agreement, in which Unionists supporting the Agreement supported pro-Agreement Nationalists, and pro-Agreement Nationalists supported pro-Agreement Unionists. This

in society—we can devise mechanisms to ensure that such minorities are included, that parties compete for their support—but this solution is not open to the state in its dealings with minority nationalist groups. Accommodation of their interests and their identity is therefore far more challenging, politically, than the accommodation of multicultural groups such as ethnic minorities, gays and lesbians, disabled people, and women.

Conclusion

The recognition of the non-neutrality of most states on national questions raises a number of normative issues, which did not arise when the state was (wrongly) presumed to be neutral on such issues. First of all, it raises the question of *fairness*. Issues of fairness arise in terms of national self-determination projects, for these frequently involve rival and incompatible—at least in their maximal form—claims to political autonomy by groups intermixed on the same territory. This is the subject of the next two chapters. Issues of fairness arise also in terms of nation-building projects, particularly when these operate in the context of states characterized by a diversity of identities. The issue of fair or justifiable nation-building is closely bound up with the related question of the appropriate relation of culture and identity to the particular policies of states. This chapter approached this issue by examining the claims of various 'identity' based groups in a multicultural context and minority nations incorporated on the territory of a larger state.

This chapter argued that the multicultural and minority nationalist critiques of liberal-democratic neutrality are broadly right. The liberal-democratic state was not, is not, and cannot be, neutral on issues of culture and membership and boundaries. Proponents of multiculturalism are right to point to ways in which minority groups are disadvantaged by the majority construction of the public sphere and to alter it so that they are not unfairly disadvantaged. However, it also argues that neutrality is unachievable. It is not possible for the state to be neutral in the sense that it makes no decision on these issues. Nor is it possible to be neutral in the sense of incorporating all traditions, all cultural, ethnic and national claims. The public sphere can only be expressive of a certain number of identities. This means that there are

can be attributed to the fact that the Agreement introduced an important division within the Unionist community. In any case, the extent of the cross-communal transfers, in comparison to a normal society, was 'negligible'. See Mitchell, 'Transcending an Ethnic Party System?' at 40.

genuine limits on the extent to which accommodation is possible. This can be conceptualized in terms of a dispute over culture, conceived as a collective property. This suggests that, while minority nationalists have to recognize the reality of people's multiple identities, and that no one group identity is automatically entitled to subsume all others, so multiculturalists have to recognize the need for an overarching political identity and some common political institutions in which we can work out our aims as citizens.

National identity politics is somewhat different from other kinds of identity based politics because it is primarily concerned with the issue of jurisdiction—with increased political autonomy and self-government, rather than inclusion. Ethnic or cultural identities may matter as much to individuals as national ones, and they may also find that they do not operate in a neutral context. An important difference between multicultural identities and national ones is that the latter involve a commitment to collective self-government, and are potentially consistent with a democratic forum and vibrant public life. Further, because these identities are primarily political, fairness requires that minority national groups are 'compensated' differently for the unfairness that they experience than other kinds of minorities.

This chapter emphasized that civic integration—by which is meant a policy of full inclusion, and equal treatment—is advantageous to the majority national group on the territory, for they are operating in the context of a state in which they are the majority, in which their language is the public language, in which their culture, norms and history are central to the history and norms of the state. But the minority nation is at a disadvantage in these regimes of equal treatment. With no recognition of their language rights, they often have to learn a second language in order to function in the political and economic spheres. They have no forum in which their particular interests, which flow from their shared culture and history and identity, can be expressed. In fact, most minority nations correctly regard civic integration as an assimilationist move, which fails to give them the political power to protect their minority culture, and thereby denies the uniqueness of their cultural identity. Treating them equally as individuals, and abstracting from the cultural and national context within which this individual equality operates, means, in practice, that they will be denied the political power, the political mechanisms, to democratically decide as a community, what kinds of protections for their culture might be warranted, or how their identity can be safeguarded. This is not a concern for the majority nation in the state, since majoritarian democratic decision-making—as well as legal devices such as 'community standards' and the legal fiction of the 'reasonable person' pre-supposes the majority view of the world, and gives effect to the major-ity's decision-making powers.

While minority nationalists have important claims of fairness with respect to jurisdiction and collective self-government, there are important limits on the kinds of policies that minority nationalists can pursue. Specifically, minority nationalist claims are based on fairness, and are therefore justifiable only as long as they involve the fair treat-ment of other kinds of groups in minority nationalist areas. These lim-its are suggested by the legitimate claims of multicultural identity groups to be fairly included. Nation-building should proceed in ways that are sensitive to the disadvantages some groups suffer as a result of the construction of the public sphere. It suggests that the political cul-ture of the state will have to be made, as far as is possible, permeable in the sense that a variety of cultural groups will feel included; that they will feel that it is possible to be both Muslim and French, both native and Québécois.

This differential treatment of the two types of identity groups was justified on three grounds. The first affirmed Kymlicka's point that there are different types of identities, which typically seek different types of rights. However, I offered additional arguments, which do not depend on an empirical claim about the aims of the group. The sec-ond argument was practical: both groups experience minority disad-vantage, but minority nations, because they are ensconced in their own homeland, can remedy these through political self-government, whereas other identity groups cannot. Context matters.

This chapter also advanced the third related argument that demands for institutional separateness on the part of multicultural identity groups are not conducive to democratic governance and the pursuit of justice by the state. Minority nationalist demands are often compatible with territorial government, and challenge the jurisdiction of the state, but not the institutions of democratic governance and redistributive justice which the state also provides. Indeed, it is a majoritarian preju-dice, or fallacy, that only large states, or nations within already exist-ing states, have a monopoly on universal values. Minority nations should be assessed by the same standards of tolerance and inclusive-ness as majority national communities.

Finally, this chapter argued that many of the claims of multicultural identity groups, at least in places like the United States and Canada, can be accommodated within the current state structure. There is much that we can do to accommodate these groups and ensure that they are included fairly in the state. Accommodation within the state of minority nationalist forms of identity is far more difficult. Indeed, it is hard to see how a multination state, committed to freedom of expression, association, and democratic governance, can avoid addressing the kinds of demands for political self-government that typically characterizes national communities.

Part Two

TERRITORY

CHAPTER 6

Just-Cause, Administrative Boundaries, and the Politics of Denial

So far in this book, I have outlined and assessed a number of arguments that suggest that national communities have both intrinsic and instrumental moral value. I have argued that we have good reason to recognize (institutionally) and accommodate national identities. However, there is a serious problem with the recognition of national identities, which I have not yet confronted, and which is related to its territorial dimension. The arguments outlined thus far all suggest that there is moral significance in recognizing *identities*, or that moral value attaches to the *ties* or *bonds* of affection among people, or that recognizing national identities will contribute to *individual* well-being. None of these arguments deals with the fact that an important component of national identities is the belief that the collective group has a homeland, an attachment to a particular part of the globe, a particular soil, and does not simply consist of attachments to co-nationals. In some cases, the beliefs about homeland do not correspond to the land that the group occupies.

Moreover, I have suggested earlier in this book that nationalism typically involves appeal to two distinct types of projects: nation-building projects, the justifiable limits of which I explored in Chapter 5, and national self-determination projects. Any adequate analysis of the limits of national self-determination projects involves an examination of the issue of boundaries, and also the various arguments generally put forward in the context of secession concerned with the conditions under which a group can justifiably remove itself from the authority of the state. This chapter analyses both issues, for they are closely related. Most of the normative theories of secession on offer wrongly abstract from the fact that secession is inspired by nationalist arguments and nationalist mobilization, and they appeal to a conception of boundaries that ignores nationalist lines of division.

Finally, so far in this book, I have argued for the need for recognition and accommodation without addressing the fact that many of the dominant forms of recognition—independence, federalism, even forms of consociationalism—are territorial in the sense that the jurisdictional authority is divided into geographical areas or regions, and that everyone within the geographical area is subject to the authority of the rules of that legal/political regime, and the rules do not apply outside the geographical area. This is a problem because most geographical regions are not homogeneous but are characterized by identity-pluralism—they have, in other words, a dominant national group, and a minority group, or number of groups, which do not share the dominant national identity—and it is very difficult, if not impossible, to draw a line on a map to correspond exactly with the national identities of all the people. To some extent, of course, this problem of identity-pluralism has been discussed already, in Chapter 5, on the ethics of nation-building, which addressed the need to reconcile various forms of diversity with the need for political unity, and suggested that a pluralistic and flexible political culture represented the best way to strike the balance between unity and practical flexibility in the long run. This argument was insufficient, however, since it does not address the prior issue of the state in which these kinds of accommodations should take place.

The next two chapters are concerned with the question: how should boundaries be drawn? If most forms of institutional recognition require some kind of boundary, what normative principle should we follow in establishing these boundaries? This chapter, and the next, will examine various normative arguments designed to secure a group's legitimate control over territory, or rights to territory. In many cases, these normative arguments about territory presuppose other normative values—the value of autonomy, of collective self-government, or the sentiments of attachments that people feel. This book does not put forward a unitary theory of the kinds of arguments that will 'trump' all other arguments: rather, it suggests that different kinds of considerations are appropriate in different kinds of contexts, and that various arguments should be considered and sometimes addressed, even when they cannot provide a basis for the general or principled resolution of conflicting claims, because they are important in the context of specific attempts at conflict-resolution.

Inter-state and Intra-state Boundaries

My plea to consider the issue of boundaries, and the treatment of this issue in the context of the ethics of secession, is not intended to imply that this discussion is relevant only to boundaries between states. Of course, secession constitutes the most dramatic and potentially destructive form of boundary-alteration. However, it is implicit in this discussion—and international law and political practice on the issue— that a full normative theory of boundaries would encompass boundaries *within* states, as well as between them.

This is so, first, because jurisdictional authority, and boundaries between jurisdictional authorities, are not always, or even typically, an all-or-nothing matter.[1] In federal states, subunits have jurisdictional authority over some areas of life—for example, in Canada, education and health are within the domain of the provinces—and other areas— defence, monetary policy, foreign policy—fall within the authority of the central government.[2] Boundaries between states are clearly not the only morally relevant boundaries: subunits of states may operate over important areas of human life; they may be important to the protection of the local and regional flavour of an area; and they may allow for limited forms of political autonomy and recognition within the state.

Moreover, in this era of mutual defence alliances, regional economic associations, and international human rights covenants, sovereignty is increasingly blurred even for unitary states. This is because some policy-areas, previously within the jurisdiction of the state, have become transferred upwards, to supra-state institutions. In this context, we should not talk about the borders between states as characterizing clear divisions of jurisdictional authority. Rather, there are a number of overlapping areas of jurisdiction, both larger and smaller than the state, with no clear hierarchy among them.

Secondly, it doesn't make sense to limit our discussion to boundaries between states when, in current international law and political practice, intra-state boundaries are extremely important in defining the jurisdictional units along which secession can legitimately take

---

[1] This point is ably made in Allen Buchanan, 'The Making and Unmaking of Boundaries: A Liberal Perspective', in Allen Buchanan and Margaret Moore (eds.), *The Making and Unmaking of Boundaries: Diverse Ethical Perspectives* (Princeton, NJ: Princeton University Press, forthcoming). However, he views it merely as a 'further complication' to any discussion of secession and territory. A serious consideration of the issue would affect his own analysis in important ways: specifically, it would not make sense to regard the 'taking of territory' alone as creating a presumption against secession.

[2] This rough, and incomplete, list of the division of jurisdictional authority characterizes the Canadian state.

place. While international law is contradictory and unclear on a number of areas, as I will discuss in Chapter 7, there is, on this matter at least, a clear move to try to limit the right to self-determination to the internal administrative units of the disintegrating state.

The question of whether the right to self-determination could be used to change republican boundaries—the republic being the internal administrative unit in this case—was posed by Serbia to the Badinter Arbitration Committee on the former Yugoslavia, a committee set up by the EU. The Serb minorities wanted to change the borders that had been drawn for administrative reasons at the end of the Second World War to ensure that most Serbs could be kept in one country.[3]

Much of the international community—the UN and the EU in particular—sought to recognize the self-determination of peoples as members of specific republics, but not as national groups. This view was also expressed by the Badinter Committee, which argued that federations could disintegrate along the lines of their constituent units, but that there could be no reconsideration of borders, 'no secession from secessions'.[4] The justificatory argument for this decision, emphasized in the Committee's ruling, and by many other critics of the idea of self-determination, was that the 'stability of frontiers' must be maintained. The Committee also justified its decision in terms of the principle of 'territorial integrity', which it described as 'this great principle of peace, indispensable to international stability'.[5]

In view of decisions and policies such as these, a moral theory of boundaries would have to take into account the *internal* boundaries of the state in question. The relationship between the two is a close one, because, as argued earlier, self-determination claims are typically made along administrative lines, and, when they are not, they encounter enormous international resistance, as Serb minorities in the former Yugoslavia discovered. Secondly, the relationship between the two is not one-way, but dynamic and mutually supporting. One of the chief reasons why a state may resist devolving power to its minority is that it fears that the minority will use its political platform and its jurisdictional authority to mount a campaign for increased autonomy, or even secession.

[3] For an excellent discussion of this, see Mihailo Crnobrnja, *The Yugoslav Drama* (Montreal and Kingston: McGill-Queen's University Press, 1994).

[4] Donald L. Horowitz, 'Self-Determination: Politics, Philosophy, and Law', in Margaret Moore (ed.), *National Self-Determination and Secession* (Oxford: Oxford University Press, 1998), 181–214, at 191–3.

[5] A. Pellet, 'The Opinions of the Badinter Arbitration Committee: A Second Breath for the Self-Determination of Peoples', *European Journal of International Law*, 3 (1992), 184.

For these reasons, it doesn't make sense to think about boundaries or territory as solely the jurisdiction of sovereign states, or view the only morally relevant boundaries as those between states. A full moral theory of boundaries would encompass a range of self-government and jurisdictional claims, from the demands of aboriginal peoples to be self-governing, though usually within the state context, to the aspirations of small minority nationalists to some form of devolved power or autonomy within the state. This book doesn't offer a full normative theory of boundaries, but its arguments and conclusions apply to intra-state as well as inter-state forms of institutional recognition.

Conceptions of Territory and Self-Determination

The issue of defining jurisdictional units is a distinctively modern problem, connected to the interrelationship between self-determination and democracy, and self-determination and nationalism. In the past, the sovereign was related to the jurisdictional unit that s/he reigned over in a way roughly analogous to the relationship between a property-owner and his/her land: it was something s/he (largely) controlled and was transferred by inheritance, just as individual property-holdings were. The jurisdictional territory of the sovereign was carried with the sovereign into marriage, just as property might be. Many dynastic marriages were designed to gain or secure territory for the realm, just as aristocratic marriages were often decided on the basis of the lands that the marriage partners brought with them. Many of the current boundaries of European states have been defined in this way: modern-day Spain was largely a product of the marriage of Ferdinand of Aragon with Isabella of Castile. The Union of England and Scotland was facilitated by the ascension of James VI, King of Scotland, to the English throne.

Of course, in many cases, the sovereign king was not an absolute monarch, but one whose power was limited in various ways, most notably by the historic privileges of certain nobles and regions of the country. This meant, in the Scottish case, that Scotland remained institutionally distinct from England in a dual-monarchy arrangement until the Act of Union in 1707, when the Scottish nobles voted in favour of union with England. This is still partly analogous to the relationship of a property-owner to his/her property, for, in many cases, alliances between property-owners did not result in the full incorporation of the various properties. For example, in a case where the daughter inherited an estate in Kent, and then married, this became part of her husband's properties, along with 'his' estates in Essex and

Norfolk. In this type of situation, the Kent estate would probably be run separately from the other property-holdings, with its own bailiff, and with certain tenants enjoying historic rights and privileges.

Under this conception of territorial jurisdiction, the wishes and well-being of the people who lived on the territory did not matter at all. There were, of course, conceptions of 'good governance' and numerous guides to how a prince should behave, but these are analogous to conceptions of how a lord should treat his vassals, and rule over his own property. Not only were territorial jurisdictions subject to dynastic alliances and marriages, they were also considered part of the 'spoils' of war. For example, the European powers sometimes exchanged North American lands as part of peace settlements for wars fought in Europe, without regard for the wishes of the people living on the land.

It follows from this rough conception of territorial jurisdictions as analogous to property, held by the sovereign authority, that they could be purchased. This was unusual, since territorial expansion was almost always regarded as a benefit to the state, and a measure of its power and importance. Nevertheless, it did occur. Most notably the US bought Alaska from Russia in 1867. Even as late as 1916, the US purchased Denmark's territories in the West Indies from Denmark.

This is quite different from the modern conception of territorial jurisdiction, in which the territory is conceived as in some sense belonging to all the people, and for the benefit of all the people. On the modern conception, it is unclear whether the state can dispense with bits of territory (outposts) that the state no longer wants—such as the Falkland Islands in the case of the United Kingdom—especially when the majority of the people on that outpost seek to be part of the political jurisdiction.

This problem arises because, in both liberal and democratic theory, the state, including its territory, is not conceived of as the 'property' of the monarch or sovereign authority, but as 'belonging' in some sense to all the people.[6] Territory refers, not to property, or even land, but to a geographical area or domain of legal and political rules. It is implicit in the notion of popular sovereignty that the whole territory of the state stands in a special relationship to the people as a whole, and that the people exercise sovereignty within that jurisdiction.

There is, however, a crucial ambiguity in the modern conception of self-determination, and the modern idea of boundaries. This is the issue of whether it is justifiable to distinguish between groups of

---

[6] See here Buchanan, 'The Making and Unmaking of Boundaries: a Liberal Perspective'.

people in the state, and establish their right to jurisdictional control over territory. Scholars in international law have identified two distinct conceptions of the principle of self-determination, which are linked to distinct historical periods, and which have different implications for the drawing of boundaries and state control over territory.

Throughout the nineteenth century until the end of the First World War, or even, arguably, until the Second World War, self-determination of peoples was conceived in ethnic terms. As US President Woodrow Wilson made clear in his famous Fourteen Points speech, he sought to secure 'a fair and just peace' by employing the 'principle of national self-determination'.[7] The 'peoples' entitled to exercise the right to self-determination, according to the Paris Peace Accord of 1919, were ethnic groups, which had become nationally mobilized, and numerous states were carved out of the ruins of the Russian, Ottoman, Austro-Hungarian, and German empires on broadly ethnic lines.

Since the Second World War, however, the self-determination of peoples has been conceived in a non-ethnic or non-national way. International law has been careful to elaborate that the right-holders— if indeed, self-determination is a right—should not be conceived of as ethnic groups or national groups. Rather, they are multi-ethnic people under colonial rule. Whereas self-determination in the Wilsonian period was conceived of as the political independence of ethnic or national communities, in the post-Second World War period, self-determination has been conceived of as 'the right of the majority within an accepted political unit to exercise power'.[8]

In many cases, of course, the confusion surrounding the appropriate grounds for claiming territory is used by groups to maximize the territory to which they are entitled. Consider, as an example, the German nationalist argument for including the Duchy of Schleswig in the German empire in 1848.[9] The Duchy of Schleswig had not been part of the Holy Roman Empire or the German Confederation of 1815. Therefore, the German case for its incorporation into Germany had to be based on the ethnic or demographic principle. But this

---

[7] This was articulated in US President Woodrow Wilson's 'Fourteen Points' speech of 8 January, 1918. This is quoted in Alfred de Zayas, *A Terrible Revenge: The Ethnic Cleansing of the East European Germans, 1944–50* (New York, NY: St. Martin's Press, 1986), 14.

[8] Rosemary Higgins, *The Development of International Law through the Political Organs of the United Nations* (Oxford: Oxford University Press, 1963), 103–5. Quoted in Rupert Emerson, 'Self-determination', *American Journal of International Law*, 65/3 (1971), 464.

[9] Otto Pflanze, 'Characteristics of Nationalism in Europe: 1848–1871', *Review of Politics*, 28 (1966), 129–43.

jeopardized the German case for the entire duchy, because Danes occupied the northern parts. But here, German nationalists appealed to the idea of the duchy as a unified administrative unit, arguing that the territorial integrity of the duchy as a whole must be preserved. The simultaneous appeal to two contradictory principles was of course partly self-serving, but it also indicates genuine confusion as to the criteria for determining the nation that is supposed to be determining itself. Is it the ethnic group? Is it shared history in a national homeland? This of course translated into confusion about what principles should be followed in delimiting territory. Does self-determination follow administrative boundaries or can new boundaries be established to encapsulate the group? In this case, German nationalists appealed to previous administrative boundaries; and were able to secure more territory on this principle than any other principle.

Contradictory principles to delimit boundaries, and therefore the units in which self-determination should occur, were also employed by various parties to the conflict in the former Yugoslavia in the 1991–9 period. The Croats in the republic of Croatia appealed to the principle of self-determination, arguing that they should be self-determining within the administrative borders of Croatia that they had inherited from Tito's Yugoslavia, which included a large and geographically concentrated Serb minority. Croats in Bosnia, however, appealed to the ethnic or demographic principle to argue for their inclusion in a Greater Croatia.

The Serb leaders, in Bosnia, but also many in Serbia itself, argued in favour of changing the borders that had been drawn for administrative reasons at the end of the Second World War to ensure that most Serbs could be contained in one country. Serbs in the Slavonia and Krajina areas of Croatia and the eastern and northern regions of Bosnia-Hercegovina appealed to the principle of self-determination, defined in ethnic or demographic terms, to argue that they should determine their future and join the republic of Serbia.[10] Meanwhile, Serbs in Serbia and Kosovo appealed to the historic and administrative boundaries principle to argue that Kosovo was historically Serb territory, and also an integral part of Serbia.

Academic analysis alone will not prevent nationalists from making these arguments, but these arguments will be deployed only if nationalists think that they have resonance. A rigorous analysis of the validity of these arguments may be helpful in legitimizing or delegitimizing certain kinds of arguments. The aim of this chapter and the next is to

---

[10] See Crnobrnja, *The Yugoslav Drama*, 234.

offer some clarity on the kinds of principles that are employed, the strength and validity of the various arguments, and the contexts in which they might be appropriate.

This chapter examines the dominant conception of self-determination in the decolonization period, according to which self-determination occurs within existing administrative units. I argue that this conception of self-determination—civic integration within administrative boundaries—is ethically attractive, and is appropriate for multi-ethnic societies in which there is no dominant majority. However, in other cases, where there is a national majority, it is not appropriate. It is inadequate normatively, in the sense that the internal boundaries are themselves normatively problematic, and from a conflict-resolution perspective. By the latter term, I mean that repeated emphasis on this conception of self-determination has failed to allay the grievances of minority groups in states, who aspire to recognition of their distinct status, in a situation where the dominant national majority group implicitly enjoys such recognition.

The administrative boundaries conception of self-determination has been linked with a particular ethical view of secession, according to which secession is viewed as justified only when there is just-cause. Although this theory is advanced in the context of secession only, not boundary-drawing in general, it is importantly related to the administrative boundaries conception of territorial jurisdiction, first, because it presupposes the view that self-determination should only occur along the lines of previous administrative boundaries, and, second, because they both share the view that cultural, ethnic, or national identities are inappropriate bases for public policy and boundary-drawing.

This chapter will proceed by first describing and assessing just-cause theories of secession and then move on to assess the appropriateness of the theory of drawing boundaries, on which it is based.

Just-Cause Theories and the Ethics of Secession

In his 1991 book, *Secession: The Morality of Political Divorce from Fort Sumter to Lithuania and Quebec*,[11] Allen Buchanan begins by pointing out that the issue of the morality of secession has received very little consideration from a normative standpoint. Now, however, there are, broadly, three distinct theories of the right to secede, each of which specifies the ground for the right and the conditions under

[11] Allen Buchanan, *Secession: The Morality of Political Divorce from Fort Sumter to Lithuania and Quebec* (Boulder, CO: Westview Press, 1991).

which there is a right (or justified claim) to secede. These theories are: choice theories, just-cause theories, and national self-determination theories. In this chapter, I consider just-cause theories; and, in the next, I consider the other two, as well as related arguments for assigning territory to groups within the state.

Just-cause theories, among which the best-known is Buchanan's, typically argue in favour of a remedial right to secede. The term 'remedial right to secede' means that there is a general right to secede for groups that have suffered certain kinds of injustices, and for which there are grounds for believing that these injustices could not be ended until the group is no longer in the state. Different just-cause theories focus on different kinds of injustices: some on prior occupation and seizure of territory; some on serious violations of human rights, including genocide; others view discriminatory injustice as sufficient to legitimate secession.[12] In Buchanan's argument, a group is required to demonstrate both that it has a valid claim to the territory it wants to withdraw from the state—such as showing that the group was illegally incorporated into the state—as well as that the group is a victim of systematic injustice or exploitation or that its culture is seriously imperiled.

Buchanan's right to secession is in important respects analogous to Locke's theory of the right to revolution: there is a legitimate right (to secede/to revolt) only if it is necessary to remedy an injustice. The political theory implicit in a just-cause theory of secession suggests, like Locke's right of revolution, a conception of the legitimacy of states. On this view, states exercise legitimate authority over territory only if they treat citizens justly.

One advantage of this type of theory is that it suggests a strong internal connection between the right to resist tyranny—exploitation, oppression, genocide, wrongful seizure of territory—and the right to self-determination, or secession. By suggesting a strong link between secession and human rights, this kind of argument grounds the ethics

---

[12] In Wayne Norman's elaboration (and defence) of just-cause theory, he cites five kinds of injuries to a group that are considered to give just-cause: '(i) that it has been the victim of systematic discrimination or exploitation, and that this situation will not end as long as the group remains in the state; (ii) that the group and its territory were illegally incorporated into the state within recent-enough memory; (iii) that the group has a valid claim to the territory it wants to withdraw from the state; (iv) that the group's culture is imperiled unless it gains access to all of the powers of a sovereign state; (v) that the group finds its constitutional rights grossly or systematically ignored by the central government or the supreme court.' Wayne Norman, 'Ethics of Secession as the Regulation of Secessionist Politics', in Margaret Moore (ed.), *National Self-Determination and Secession* (Oxford: Oxford University Press, 1998), 34–61, at 41.

of secession within the generally accepted framework of human rights, and a generally accepted theory of state legitimacy.

There are, however, three serious objections to just-cause theories of secession. The first objection applies to institutional forms of just-cause theory. It does not deny the central claims of just-cause theory—that justice is central to state legitimacy, or that unjust states are illegitimate and that secession is therefore justified—but it raises concerns about institutionalizing such a right. These objections apply to the main just-cause theories on offer,[13] both of which conceive theories of secession as forms of institutional morality. The second and third concerns are connected to the implicit weight in the argument on the conception of the state and its relation to territory. I argue that this favours the status quo, and is not argued for sufficiently.

(1) The first problem emerges mainly when we think about how a just-cause theory of secession might be institutionalized, either in the international system or in domestic constitutions. Because claims to justice are strongly contested, and there is no neutral international arbiter to decide on the merits of any such claims, just-cause theories frequently end up relying on procedural mechanisms in order to approximate the relative justice or injustice of the seceding group's claims. This is true of Wayne Norman's argument in favour of institutionalizing a right to secede. He argues in favour of erecting fairly large hurdles in the path to secession and so restricting secession to groups that have just cause.

However, it is not at all clear that these procedural mechanisms approximate the relative justice or injustice of the seceding group's claim. This is true for both practical and philosophical reasons. One serious practical problem with the proposal is that it is likely that a group that is unjustly treated—subject to exploitation, oppression, denied democratic governance—will also be denied the opportunity to exercise their right to secession. This means that groups that have just cause will probably be unable to give effect to the right, and groups that are able to exercise that right, using the procedural guidelines that Norman outlines, are quite unlikely to be able to demonstrate positive injustice. This doesn't impugn just-cause theory in itself, conceived in non-institutional terms, but it does suggest that proponents of this approach, who seem to pride themselves on their 'realistic' assessment of the power dynamic behind secession, ignore it in this case, and tend also to abstract from the extent to which international law and

---

[13] I examine Allen Buchanan's theory as elaborated in *Secession* and numerous other articles since then, and Wayne Norman's theory, especially as it is formulated in 'Ethics of Secession'.

international relations would need to change to give effect to a just-cause theory.

Moreover, it is unclear whether mobilization for secession is after all strongly related to current injustice. Norman's just-cause argument, for example, ultimately relies on the group's choices, on the assumption that a group that has been unjustly treated will be more likely to satisfy the procedural hurdles that he places along the way. He writes:

[I]t is [natural] . . . for liberals concerned with promoting justice to opt for democratic procedures and to attempt to 'rig' them in a way that encourages just outcomes . . . [T]hose supporting the just-cause theory must seek fair rules that will make it relatively easy for those with genuine just cause to secede, and relatively difficult for those without it to do so. Of course democrats must always accept that it is a feature of such 'imperfect procedural justice' that even the best rules will sometimes prevent a legitimate secession and permit a 'vanity' secession (i.e. one without just cause). (Wayne Norman, 'The Ethics of Succession', 14.)

In this passage, Norman assumes that there is a positive relationship between support for secession and the perpetration of injustice by the state. This is an empirical relationship, which is intuitively plausible, but unsupported. The important point here is that, as Norman recognizes—but not in a way that seems to put into question his basic assumption—nationalist mobilization can occur for other reasons than unjust treatment. A group may become nationally mobilized for historical reasons. It may even be because of past injustice or exclusion by the majority group in the state, but not due to any current injustice committed by that group or the state.[14] In other words, although the positive relation between injustice and secession that Norman posits is intuitively plausible, there needs to be greater analysis of the social forces that lead to nationalism, since nationalism is crucial in explaining support for mobilization. Here, Norman's confidence in the correlation between injustice and support for secession is in some tension with his own view of nationalist politics, which, at other places, he describes as manipulative, opportunistic, and élite-driven, rather than grounded in grass-roots, legitimate grievances.

One possible response to the recognition that there is a tenuous link between support for secession and justice is to reject Norman's procedural argument, and rely solely on justice-based criteria. This manœuvre would require considerable changes in current inter-

---

[14] Conversely, another group may be economically and socially marginalized, the victim of widespread abuses, and unjust treatment, and not be nationally mobilized. Such a group may not seek to remove itself from the state because it is in such a weak position that the prospect of 'going it alone' is not an attractive one.

national law: at the minimum, it presupposes an international tribunal or court to assess the legitimacy of these claims. The problem with this, as Norman's procedure hints, is that it will fail to provide a basis for the resolution of national conflicts. By this, I mean that, if a group is strongly mobilized behind a national self-determination project, then rulings based on *individual* justice will simply fail to address their concerns about self-determination, and will fail to provide a peaceful resolution of the conflict. This is a problem for democratic states, because the basis of democratic legitimacy lies in the assumption that a state's authority is accepted by those who are subject to it. It is unclear how democratic politics can continue when the legitimacy of the state is called into question, and a majority of people do not wish to belong to the state in which they live.

(2) Despite the problems with the procedural criterion, there is no doubt that just-cause theories satisfy many of our basic beliefs and intuitions about secession. It is difficult to deny that a group that has been the victim of widespread violations of basic human rights or the target of a genocidal campaign has a right to secede. This is relatively uncontested, since it is grounded in the widely accepted view that the state's authority and political legitimacy are forfeited when it commits such injustices. Another problem with just-cause theory is the requirement that a group must demonstrate that it has been wronged according to the criteria established by liberal conceptions of legitimate governance.

One interesting aspect of Buchanan's argument, which I think throws into relief some of the problems with it, is that it is unclear whether the would-be secessionist group must demonstrate that it has been wronged in order to have a right to secede. Buchanan argues that the desires and claims of the secessionists have to be weighed against the claims of the state, which, if it is a just state, is the 'trustee for the people, conceived of as an intergenerational community'.[15] The just state, therefore, has an obligation to protect all (existing and future) citizens' legitimate interests in this political and territorial community. Because the claim to secession by a group within the state cannot be reconciled with the territorial integrity of the state, which is trustee of the interests of all citizens, Buchanan ultimately endorses the view that secession is permissible only when the state fails to fulfil its justice-based obligations and hence forfeits its claims to being a legitimate trustee.

This theory doesn't seem to require that the group itself be the victim; rather, it requires only that the state that is being dismembered is

---

[15] Buchanan, *Secession*, 109.

the perpetrator of injustice. Kurds, in Iraq, who were the victims of a nerve-gas attack, have a strong claim to secession; but, this is primarily because the Iraqi government of Saddam Hussein, through its action, lost political legitimacy and failed to fulfil its trusteeship role. Its claim to a right to territorial integrity therefore does not need to be weighed against the desires of the secessionists', and this is so even if the would-be secessionists are some group in the state other than the Kurds.

One important question that Buchanan's theory raises is: on what grounds does the state acquire the status of legitimate trustee of all the people, conceived of as an intergenerational community? This is crucial to his argument, for it is this conception that ultimately defeats arguments based on national self-determination or democratic choice. The only answer that Buchanan gives is in terms of a traditional liberal conception of legitimate states, namely, a democratic state that upholds basic individual rights. Within this conception, there is little, if any, room for a model of political legitimacy based on shared group identity. Indeed, when Buchanan does consider the issue of national or cultural identity, he reveals a careful but negative view of the nature of such forms of identity. For example, as I've already outlined in Chapter 3, in *Secession*, Buchanan rejects the indigenous group's claim to state protection of their culture on the grounds that another (non-indigenous) culture is on offer to them. More recently, he has argued that granting nations political rights to self-determination is in violation of the liberal requirement that all people should be treated equally.[16] This argument, as I've suggested earlier, is flawed in many ways, not least because it completely ignores the non-neutral character of most existing states, and therefore that the demands in question are not for special rights, but for equal treatment.

Buchanan's negative assessment of national and cultural identity is shared by the other dominant just-cause theory of secession, advanced by Wayne Norman. Although his argument mainly focuses on the destabilizing and counter-productive consequences that would follow from institutionalizing a permissive right to secede, Norman's critique of such permissive theories reveals a similar underlying negative assessment of nationalist claims, as motivated by manipulative élites who seek to mobilize groups along national lines in order to gain

---

[16] Allen Buchanan, 'What's So Special about Nations?', in Jocelyne Couture, Kai Nielsen, and Michel Seymour (eds.), *Rethinking Nationalism*, *Canadian Journal of Philosophy*, Supplementary Volume (1996).

access to greater resources.[17] There is no cause to deny that élites are party to such mobilization and that some rules can lead to perverse incentives. Nevertheless, the general tenor of Norman's work on secession emphasizes the manipulative and opportunistic character of this kind of politics. This assumption ignores the evidence that, sometimes, nationalist sentiments are genuine expressions of democratic politics, and it begs the question of why this form of mobilization is likely to be successful rather than, say, class mobilization.

Since Buchanan implicitly rejects national or cultural claims in his conception of justice, it is hardly surprising that he concludes that national or cultural claims to self-determination cannot trump a state's claim to territory. But the critical source of the state's claim to territory and the crucial element in the concept of political legitimacy is the idea of individual justice, and this is precisely what is contested.

One problem with just-cause theories, then, is not what they propose, namely, that victims of injustice have a right to secede, but that their restrictive right to secession is based on a conception of justice that cannot incorporate national lines of identification or group-based identity into their theory, and these are precisely the basis for secessionist movements. Since secessionist leaders are very likely to believe and argue that they have just-cause—either because they believe they have a democratic right to be self-determining, or because they are nationalists and believe in the legitimacy of nationalist discourse and the illegitimacy or injustice of denying these kinds of claims—a theory based on (individual) justice will be essentially contested. It is hardly likely that applying this theory of justice to particular secessionist movements will wither or dampen secessionist demands.

(3) Finally, and related to the failure to move beyond considerations of individual justice, the just-cause argument presupposes that a legitimate (just) state automatically has jurisdictional authority over the whole territory, and that all the people in the state stand in an equal relation to all the territory in which rules are applied. This is suggested by Buchanan's conception of the state as a 'trustee' for '*all* the citizens' (my emphasis) and by his argument that, in the absence of just cause, a group or portion of the state can secede only by mutual consent. Buchanan's argument about the relationship of the state to territory— and especially the idea that the state has legitimate authority over all the territory—raises a problem implicit in the idea of self-determination. Chapter 1 discussed the problem of indeterminacy as it applied to who counts as a 'nation' or 'people'. There is a similar indeterminacy

---

[17] Norman, 'Ethics of Secession', 36.

problem in specifying the jurisdictional unit in which self-determination can occur, or in which a referendum can be held, and Buchanan's conception of the relationship of state to territory and people assumes only one answer to that problem.

The issue of indeterminacy applies regardless of whether one endorses a just-cause theory of justified secession, or some other theory of secession. Even if all groups agree on democratic procedures, and agree that there is a primary right to secede if a majority of people vote in favour of secession in a fair referendum, the jurisdictional unit in which a plebiscite is held may be essentially contested. As Brian Barry has argued, in a case where the majority of people in an area want the boundaries of that area to be the boundaries of the state and a minority do not, the 'issue is in effect decided by the choice of the area of the plebiscite'.[18]

The issue of jurisdictional unit first arose in terms of the secession of Ireland from the United Kingdom. Was the appropriate jurisdictional unit the whole of the United Kingdom? Or the island of Ireland? Or should majorities in the historic provinces or local government areas *within* Ireland be able to determine their own destinies? In the contemporary case of Quebec, a referendum on secession would probably yield different results if the jurisdictional unit is taken to be the whole of Canada, or the province of Quebec, or only part of the province of Quebec.

In other words, territory is frequently viewed as derivative of a conception of self-government; yet the idea of self-government does not tell us where boundaries should be drawn. At the very least, it is indeterminate between the view that all inhabitants of the state exercise the right to be self-governing, and this means that all members of the state are involved in the exercise of the right to draw boundaries; and that groups within the state, such as territorially concentrated national minorities, have a unilateral right to alter the boundaries of the state, either through seceding from it or through devolved areas of jurisdictional authority within the state.

The next section of this chapter analyses the problems associated with the first (statist) view that identifies the state with all the people on the territory. It argues that this conception of territory and of boundaries as purely administrative, or not designed to express or recognize the ethnic, cultural, or religious identity of the people living there, is appropriate in some cases, but that there is a wide range of

---

[18] Brian Barry, 'Self-Government Revisited', *Democracy and Power* (Oxford: Clarendon Press, 1991), 156–86, at 162.

cases in which it is problematic or otherwise inappropriate. This contextual analysis is relevant to just-cause theory, because, if it is broadly right, it brings into question the weight in Buchanan's argument on the notion of 'territorial integrity' and the idea that the whole state has legitimate authority over all the territory and all the people in the state, without any distinction among them.

Administrative Boundaries and Self-Determination

Buchanan's conception of the relationship of territory to the sovereign authority has been the dominant one in international law and practice, which has mainly defined the nation in statist terms. Thus, the 1992 UN Declaration of Human Rights endorses a right to self-determination but then goes on to claim that this right is not intended to authorize or encourage any action 'which would dismember or impair . . . the territorial integrity or political unity of sovereign and independent states', and then goes on to describe such (sovereign and independent) states as 'possessed of a Government representing the whole people belonging to the territory without distinction of any kind.'[19]

The view that self-determination should take place within administrative boundaries, without regard for the cultural, ethnic, and national identity of the people living there, draws its normative appeal from two powerful moral ideals. First, it is consonant with the idea of equality, and in particular, the idea that everyone should be equal under the law, and should enjoy equal citizenship and equal political rights. This is a fundamental norm in both liberal and democratic theory, and is so fundamental to the modern outlook that its moral status is rarely disputed, even by those critical of liberal democracy, though they may question what equal citizenship or equal rights actually entails.[20] Secondly, the administrative boundaries conception is also based on the idea that national/ cultural/ ethnic identities are inappropriate bases for public policy and for state action. It appeals to the idea, forcefully presented in Hollinger's book *Postethnic America*, of

---

[19] Vienna Declaration 1993, part 1, para. 2 . Cited in Rainer Bauböck, 'Self-determination and Self-government', March 1999 version of unpublished manuscript.

[20] A good example of this is Iris Marion Young, *Justice and the Politics of Difference* (Princeton, NJ: Princeton University Press, 1990) which is mostly devoted to criticizing the liberal (and representative democracy) conception of equal citizenship and equal rights as 'formalistic', but which presupposes the norm of equality and says as much in the introduction to her book, at 3.

moving beyond ethnic or (ethno-) national divisions, and particularist forms of identity, to forge a transcendent, post-ethnic identity, as *citizens* of a particular polity, and that this identity should not be based on ascriptive markers or group affiliations.[21]

This is an attractive vision, and an important aspirational ideal. The vision of a multicultural America, inclusive of people of all races, religions and cultural backgrounds, is undeniably attractive; and, where possible, it should be pursued.[22] A non-racist South Africa, in which all share a common identity as South Africans, regardless of their race or cultural/linguistic group, is an appealing one, and in sharp contrast to the hierarchical divisions and oppression of the apartheid era. In societies where there are few national divisions, or where the political community is relatively homogenous, there is a strong basis for encouraging a common—that is, inclusive—political identity with which all can equally identify. However, the discussion that follows argues that the context in which this conception is appropriate is rather limited, and that, in many cases, an administrative boundaries conception is both politically and normatively flawed.

Administrative Boundaries in Highly Diverse States

In some cases, an administrative boundaries conception, at least for external boundaries, makes sense, not because there is a strong basis for a shared political identity, but because the best hope for democratic governance and stability lies in the attempt to forge such a political identity. In these cases, the ethnic /linguistic groups are so numerous that none can hope to have its own state. Therefore, the administrative boundary conception of self-determination, at least as regards the external frontier, may be the most appropriate. There are at least 120 different ethnic groups in Tanzania.[23] In this context, it doesn't make sense to talk about minority rights in the same sense in which that term is used in Europe.[24] There is no 'minority' defined in relation to the majority: everyone is in a minority. Nor does it make sense to talk

[21] David A. Hollinger, *Postethnic America; Beyond Multiculturalism* (New York, NY: Basic Books, 1995).

[22] Of course, that vision, by itself, does not address the difficult public policy issues that still remain, and which are the subject of Chapter 5. It does not, that is, address the issue of how a culturally diverse society can be inclusive, and the kinds of group-specific policies that are necessary to redress various kinds of structural disadvantages that minorities suffer.

[23] Donald L. Horowitz, *Ethnic Groups in Conflict* (Berkeley, CA: University of California, 1985), 37.

[24] Ibid., 37.

about drawing boundaries *around* ethnic (potentially, national) groups, since the widespread application of secession by these groups would lead to sadly sub-optimal results. In this situation, perhaps the best one can hope for is to foster, amongst each of these various groups, a sense of a common Tanzanian political identity.

This view was widely held during the decolonization period. The administrative boundaries of the imperial power were the basis on which boundaries were drawn in most of Africa and Asia. Imperial powers were unconcerned with ethnic or linguistic relationships, and made little attempt to draw boundaries to take into account these potential bases for identification. In part, this could be attributed to the disfavour with which ethnic nationalism was regarded in the post-Second World War period, and the related dominance of a civic or post-ethnic conception of nationhood. In part, it was due to the general optimism amongst academics and policy-makers alike concerning the transformative effects of the forces of modernization and state-sponsored 'nation-building' projects on particularistic (tribal) attachments. In part, however, it was because it was difficult to predict the extent to which these new states would experience difficulties accommodating or managing ethnic diversity peacefully and in accordance with democratic principles.

This is related to an important, but often overlooked, difference between decolonization and secession. Secessionist movements tend to be driven by the region's largest group, and are sometimes opposed by local ethnic minorities.[25] This pattern of mobilization for secession provides some evidence of the potential for ethnic / national conflict in the post-secessionist state. In many cases of decolonization, by contrast, there was widely shared support for the new state. However, these pan-ethnic, pan-tribal coalitions were mobilized mainly by opposition to imperial rule, but broke down in the post-colonial period. They did not, in other words, translate into post-ethnic coalition politics. In many cases, politics degenerated into ethnic-based politics, where the dominant person or party, generally drawing support from a particular ethnic group, used political power for the benefit of his own particular group or party or person. In these cases, the state, which should be impersonal and differentiated, has become

[25] Secession has been contested by local ethnic majorities in Kashmir, Northern Cyprus, Croatia, Kurdistan, Sri Lanka, Quebec. Historically, secessions or imperial breakups led to differential support (by majorities and minorities) for the new state in Ireland, Poland, and Greece and Bulgaria—when the last two broke away from the Ottoman empire in the nineteenth and early twentieth century. Evidence is taken from John McGarry, 'Orphans of Secession', in Margaret Moore (ed.), *National Self-Determination and Secession* (Oxford: Oxford University Press, 1998), 215–32, at 218.

personalized (corrupted) by the dominant group in the territory, or even, as in the case of Mobutu Sese Seko's Congo, the territory has become completely subordinated to its ruler, and treated as his own personal fiefdom.

While not every bad thing in Africa can be attributed to the failure of nation-building and to ethnic divisions there, the evidence surrounding this legacy is pretty grim. The artificial boundaries left by the imperial powers—artificial because they did not correspond to any social, religious or historic entities—have started to unravel. It is doubtful whether either the Congo or Angola can function as single political entities; Eritrea has broken away from Ethiopia; and the future of Nigeria—sub-Saharan Africa's most populous state—is shaky, at best.[26]

It is true, following a Gellnerian or modernist account of the functional attributes of nations, that a shared civic identity and common culture is probably the most optimal from the point of view of developing a modern state. As Spinner-Halev has argued with respect to the application of cultural rights 'to diverse and industrializing places'— he cites Nigeria with between 200 and 400 different ethnic or national groups—some form of assimilation to reduce the number of distinct groups is desirable, to ensure equal citizenship and equal opportunity for all.[27] This might, in certain contexts, be a normative goal, but it is difficult to conceive of how the state can be neutral with respect to cultural/linguistic/issues; and therefore how these divisions can be kept out of the political arena, particularly as the society becomes more democratic.

Recent studies of the problems of African polities have (partially) agreed with Spinner-Halev's analysis. One of the problems distinctive to Africa is the weak sense (or no sense) of civic responsibility or shared citizenship. This is related to the 'strongman' tradition in African politics and the tribal divisions of allegiances and systems of patronage.[28] It is difficult, however, to know how to get from here to there, as it were, or how to foster a shared civic identity where none exists.

Even in places where the external boundaries cannot reflect the incredible ethnic or cultural diversity of these societies, and therefore

[26] See 'The New Geopolitics', *The Economist*, 31 July–6 August, 1999.

[27] Jeff Spinner-Halev, 'Land, Culture and Justice: A Framework for Group Rights and Recognition', *Journal of Political Philosophy*, 8/3 (2000), 319–42, at 321.

[28] Jean-Francois Bayart, Stephen Ellis, and Béatrice Hibou, *The Criminalisation of the State in Africa* (Bloomington, NY: Indiana University Press, 1999); Patrick Chabal and Jean-Pascal Daloz, *Africa Works: Disorder as Political Instrument* (Bloomington, NY: Indiana University Press, 1999).

where an external frontier may have to reflect the administrative boundaries of previous political orders or of the extent of imperial rule, it does not follow that a crude conception of equal citizenship, abstracted from ethnic/national/cultural forms of identity is the best. It may well be that the sheer ethnic/cultural/linguistic diversity of the society necessitates a state inclusive of a number of groups. The state must be larger than any particular ethnic group because this is functional from the point of view of capital mobility, military logistics, economies of scale, capitalist markets, and an effective political and administrative state. However, there is still a number of mechanisms— including internal boundaries, that permit strong forms of local government or federated units—that are aimed at giving institutional recognition to local—cultural, tribal, linguistic—forms of identity. These are apposite, first, because they may be desired by groups themselves, and, second, because they may help to consolidate stability within the political unit by ensuring that each group has a stake, but not an all-or-nothing stake, in the institutions of state.

In other words, where there are strong ethnic/linguistic/cultural lines of affiliation, some kind of recognition of these forms of identity may be necessary to secure rights, opportunities and freedom in the community as a whole and thereby foster the political and social conditions in which democratic governance and justice are possible. An administrative boundaries conception, at least as regards external boundaries, is appropriate for states that are so diverse that it doesn't make sense to draw external boundaries *around* each of the groups. However, even in this situation, it is probable that some internal forms of recognition and boundary-drawing would be helpful to secure the commitment of different groups in the state by recognizing their identity and their particularist ties.

Administrative Boundaries in Majority-Dominated States

In cases where states are characterized by identity-pluralism, and where the state is viewed as the political expression of only one nation on that territory, the principle that self-determination should occur only within the confines of previous administrative boundaries, or is an act of the whole people within the territory, is extremely problematic. In these situations, there is a majority national community that can be said to be able to control the state, using standard democratic (majoritarian) principles. Appealing to the borders of previous administrative units may be a way for the dominant nationality to increase its territory, and still be a majority in the state, and able to govern without the participation (in government) of the minority community. In this situation, an administrative boundaries conception of self-determination is inappropriate, even as an aspirational ideal, and unlikely to lead to stability and justice.

In cases where there is a dominant national majority that can control the state, the administrative boundaries principle does not have the moral force, the legitimating force, to persuade those people whose aspirations are denied by this conception. The lack of legitimacy is connected to two different, albeit related, problems: first, there is the problem of the arbitrariness of boundaries themselves, and second, there is the problem that seemingly inclusive citizenship may, in this context, be both unwanted by the minority and unfair to them.

First, let us consider the problem of the arbitrariness of the boundaries themselves. In the nineteenth century, nationalists did not assume that boundaries were artificial, or, at least, they thought that only imperial boundaries were artificial, but that it was possible to discern the 'natural' boundaries in which a people could be self-determining. Hence, there were many discussions of the natural shape of France. Mazzini thought that it was possible to discern the 'natural boundaries' of Italy—which, unsurprisingly, encompassed parts of Slovenia, southern France, and many places which we do not think of as Italian! This project failed, mainly because any attempt to specify the 'natural' boundaries of one particular national group came up against another group's assertions of 'its' natural boundaries, and the contested nature of these claims became apparent.

It is apparent that the general view that there are 'natural' boundaries is not sustainable, even if we accept the more moderate proposition that there are some limits to the extent to which rule can be effective and that some of these limits may indeed be 'natural'. For example, there is a reason why the United States and Canada are not politically joined to the UK, and this reason has to do with the Atlantic Ocean that separates them, which makes or did make government less effective over that distance, as well as contributing to the flourishing of separate identities.

In any case, today, it is hard to find anyone who defends a general 'natural boundary' conception. It is generally accepted, even by nationalists, that boundaries are created; they are wholly artificial creations, the products of war, or the vagaries of power politics, or the limits of former imperial rule. This has given rise to a new problem: once we admit that boundaries are wholly artificial human creations, it is clear that they can be unmade by human beings too; and that many of these creations merely embody the exigencies of power and politics, but have no strong moral basis.

In many cases, national minorities are correct to point out that administrative boundaries frequently have no moral basis themselves, or that they were often drawn in accordance with a moral or political conception that is irrelevant in the current political situation, or drawn by the central state in order to facilitate assimilation of the minority or its control by the dominant group. It is therefore hard to see why these boundaries should be cast in stone, as the only unit in which self-determination can take place.

Another way to see this point is to consider the fact that, while much attention by political scientists and normative philosophers has been devoted to the idea of internal boundaries as a mechanism to recognize and grant political space to minorities, political practice has been quite different. Just as often, perhaps more often, internal boundaries are drawn either haphazardly, and by ignorance or inattention, the aspirations of people are denied; or to deliberately frustrate the aspirations to collective self-government of people who share a sense of common national identity.

Internal boundaries in the former Soviet Union were often drawn in a way that ensured that many members of the titular nation were outside the boundaries of their (titular) republic. In Armenia, for example, Walker Connor argues that one of the reasons why the central state (Moscow) included the Nagorno-Karabakh Autonomous Region, with more than 80 per cent Armenian population, in the region of Azerbaijan, was that it was advantageous to them. It helped to ensure links between the Republic's titular ethnic groups and the federation as a whole, and the resulting friction between ethnic groups—Azeris and Armenians—enabled the centre to more easily control events in these republics.[29]

In Romania, gerrymandering was used to control the Magyar minority, which predominated along the Hungarian-Romanian border and in the centre of the state where they were surrounded by Romanian-dominated territory. Along the border, no devolution of power or recognition was given to the Magyar character of the population. In 1952, the Magyar Autonomous Region was established to give some autonomy to this minority living in the centre of the state, but, following the pro-Budapest uprising in 1956 on the part of the Magyars, two districts with strong Magyar majorities—83.3 per cent

---

[29] Walker Connor, *The National Question in Marxist-Leninist Theory and Strategy* (Princeton, NJ: Princeton University Press, 1984), 368.

and 90.2 per cent—were detached from the region and Romanian-dominated districts were added.[30]

In Communist China, too, ethnic Tibetan and Mongolian areas have been incorporated into districts dominated by Han Chinese. Even in areas still formally devolved, the Chinese authorities have encouraged massive in-migration to reduce or dilute the Tibetan or Mongolian share of the population. The boundary drawings have been particularly effective in facilitating Han Chinese control of the area, and in reducing the local (Tibetan or Mongolian) flavour of these areas.

Administrative boundaries are not simply morally *arbitrary*. In many cases, their role is more insidious than this. They are an important mechanism of control: they are a means by which the majority group can oppress minorities and render them powerless. This is the reality that Philpott has hinted at, in his claim that self-determination is not analogous with divorce. Divorce, he says, is negative; it is the failure to realize the goods of marriage.[31] However, self-government for ethnic or national groups is more positive; it is the realizing of a good, that is, of collective self-government. It is this good that is denied by majority gerrymandering.

The second, closely related problem with the administrative boundaries conception is not directly concerned with the moral status of the boundaries, but with the majoritarian bias of the territorial conception of citizenship. Most secessionists who appeal to the administrative boundaries to define the jurisdictional unit in which (their) self-determination should occur, state their aims in terms that ignore minority nations in their midst, and indeed downplay divisions of all kinds. They appeal to the people as a whole, as in 'the people of Croatia' or refer to the territory as if it is wholly united in its aspirations, as in 'Quebec's historic aspirations'.[32] In fact, of course, most secessionist movements are not united in this way, but are driven by the largest ethnic group in the region. These local majorities typically aim to break up the state so that they can constitute an overall majority in 'their' unit, and use their control over the political and administrative apparatus of the state to promote their own culture and language. Not surprisingly, these secessionist movements, supported by local ethnic majorities, are opposed by local minorities.[33] This majority–minority dynamic, in which secession is supported by local

[30] Connor, *The National Question*, 340.

[31] Daniel Philpott, 'Self-determination In Practice', in Margaret Moore (ed.), *National Self-Determination and Secession* (Oxford: Oxford University Press, 1998), 79–102, at 82.

[32] For an excellent discussion of this tendency, see McGarry, 'Orphans', 217–8.

[33] However, this is not always the case, see McGarry, 'Orphans', 219.

majorities and opposed by local ethnic minorities, was a feature of the secession of Greece and Bulgaria from the Ottoman Empire, and is also found in a large number of recent or current examples, from Northern Cyprus to Palestine, Kurdistan, Croatia, and Kashmir.[34]

In many cases, then, secessionist projects are contested, and the idea of equal citizenship within a certain defined territory—it all depends on how the territory is defined—is a method by which the dominant nationality can extend its control and encompass more territory. In some cases, including (some) people who disagree with the secession-ist cause—either co-ethnic dissenters or members of other national groups—is unavoidable, because of territorial intermixing. There is no way to separate the groups cleanly, and in a way that permits all the people to remain in the state of their own choice/that they identify with. This does not, of course, justify the non-recognition of minority nations. This is hypocritical, even if the context and circumstances necessitate less extreme forms of self-determination than secession or only collective (linguistic, cultural) rights or modest self-government within the state structure.

Indeed, in many cases, as in the duchy of Schleswig case discussed earlier, the administrative boundaries principle has been employed to justify the acquisition of more territory. In the former Yugoslavia, republics like Croatia appealed to administrative boundaries to assert control over the whole territory of Croatia, including the parts such as Western Slavonia or the Krajina that were ethnically Serbian, but appealed to the ethnic principle in support of their co-ethnics in Bosnia.

The problem with a territorial (administrative boundaries) concep-tion of citizenship is that it enables local majorities to assert their own claims—for territory, self-determination—while denying the collect-ive claims of other groups, with similar aspirations. Not only are the consequences of implementing this principle often unfair, but the principle itself is in tension (contradiction) with the national sentiment that underlies the original secession. Secessionist movements are fueled by nationalism, and are accompanied by rejection of the idea of equal citizenship in a state in which they are not a majority. It is there-fore hypocritical that their own self-determination combined with this idea of administrative boundaries involves imposing this status on their own minorities.

Sometimes the groups that are denied in this way are the ones who have the strongest case from the point of view of just-cause. In the

---

[34] See McGarry, 'Orphans', 218.

case of the natives in northern Quebec, who have no clearly demar-
cated administrative unit or territory within which they could be
(internally) self-governing in the state, the administrative boundaries
principle serves to deny their nationalist aspirations, while according
these rights to the much-better-off and much-better-treated
Québécois. The fact that the group has been denied any kind of
devolved power or institutional recognition of its identity is often a
sign of the relative oppression and powerlessness of the group, or of
the extent to which it has been controlled in the past by a dominant
group. This principle has the perverse consequence of perpetuating
this unfair treatment, and indeed justifying it, into the future.

This suggests that there are two serious problems with the administrative boundaries conception. One is the moral status (or lack
thereof) of the boundaries themselves; the second is the fact that
boundaries may themselves be instruments of group oppression. The
first point goes some way to suggesting why an appeal to administrative boundaries will not silence minority grievances or answer minority nationalist aspirations. The principle is not, therefore, satisfactory
from a conflict-resolution perspective. However, the most serious
problem with this conception, at least from the normative point of
view, is that it fails to address the most egregious cases of group injustices, where people have been denied any kind of recognition of their
distinct identity.

Conclusion

While liberal-democratic theory has a conception of state legitimacy
that can be applied to the issue of secession, to yield just-cause theory,
it does not have a rich theory of boundaries, or even much discussion
of the principles on which they are drawn. However, implicit in just-
cause theory is the standard view in international law and practice in
the post-Second World War period that the state is for all the citizens
on the territory, and that boundaries are merely administrative in
nature, necessary to delimit the domain of state jurisdiction.

The problem with this view is that it ignores the sentiments, attachments, and group-based identities of people within the state who may
not identify with the state or with all the people in the state. It grants
an effective veto to the majority group on the territory in designing the
political and institutional structures of the state, and treats as morally
insignificant the group-based aspirations of national communities
encapsulated on the territory of the larger state.

Implicit in this critique of just-cause theory and the related view of administrative boundaries is the need to consider various institutional mechanisms to recognize group-based identities and to consider the group-based claims to territorial jurisdiction. In some cases, an administrative boundaries conception, at least as regards the external frontier, is necessary, but even in this case, the statist conception of the nation implicit in just-cause theory is problematic. Against that view, I have advanced a vision of the state based on the acceptance of pluralism and equality of the different communities in the state. Political autonomy is an important element of group recognition, either defined territorially for groups that occupy local majorities, or in certain areas of jurisdiction that are important to the group like religion or education. The idea behind this is to ensure that all groups are included in some form of power-sharing arrangement, either in the form of a Grand Coalition that encompasses the main groups in society, as in Lijphart's consociational model, or a government that is not a simple majority or plurality but has mechanisms that guarantee inclusive government at the executive and legislative levels.

Ideally, these kinds of mechanisms secure the rights, identities, and opportunities of the different national communities—or at least those that are parties to the bargain—and create conditions in which each community must co-operate with, not control, the other. This may not be as stirring a moral ideal as equal citizenship, regardless of race, religion, ethnicity, or sex, but recognition of this kind is certainly better than the destabilizing ethnic politics that characterizes many heterogeneous African, and some Asian, states.

This chapter has also argued negatively against the view that the exercise of self-determination involves all the citizens in the territory. This is to pave the road to the next chapter, which advances a more positive and detailed argument in favour of the view that minority national groups in the state have rights to self-determination. Territorial integrity is an important value—which will be discussed in the next two chapters—but it should not automatically 'trump' the claims to recognition and self-determination that minority groups make on their own behalf. If it does, as on Buchanan's version of just-cause theory, it will fail to provide a basis for the fair adjudication of nationalist demands, and indeed can lead to the oppression of minorities by intolerant majorities anxious to repress and deny the existence of minority groups on their territory.

CHAPTER 7

Self-Determination, Rights to Territory, and the Politics of Respect

The previous chapter argued that we should view rights to territory as implicit in the idea of self-government. The view that the self-determining group is somehow 'taking' land that 'belongs' in some sense to the larger state is based on a dubious analogy between the relationship of state to territory and the relationship of an individual to his or her private property-holding. This is dubious because the state does not 'own' the territory. Territory simply refers to the domain of jurisdictional authority, to the geographical area in which self-government operates. This is partially recognized by Buchanan, when he argues that the central problem is connected to justifying the state in the exercise of its powers, but he nevertheless holds on to the notion that the liberal-democratic state must be sovereign over the whole territory.

It follows from the conception of the relationship of territory to self-government advanced in this book that territory is a moral good because a necessary or essential component of the good of self-government. Collective self-government is an important good: it gives expression to moral communities; it reflects people's identity; it is a forum in which citizen autonomy can be expressed; in which citizens are empowered to shape the context in which they live, and realize their political aspirations. When a group is deprived of its territory, it is also deprived of the main institutional conditions or means to exercise self-government. This is of course the goal of many tyrannical governments, who seek to silence potentially or allegedly disloyal minority groups, and indeed destroy them as a people by depriving them of a demographic basis to reproduce their culture and sense of identity. In the Soviet Union, many groups were forcibly expelled from their homeland: they had to leave their homes and neighbour-hoods, and became scattered in isolated communities, where they could not mobilize or exercise any form of collective self-government. This was the fate of the Crimean Tatars, Chechens, Kalmyks, Volga Germans, the Karachai and the Ingush, among others, who were exiled to Siberia during the Stalinist period.[1]

However, as argued earlier, viewing territory as derivative of a conception of self-government does not tell us where boundaries should be drawn. The previous chapter addressed the view that all inhabitants of the state should exercise the right to be self-governing and the associated argument that all members of the state should be involved in the exercise of the right to draw boundaries. In cases where the state has lost its right to carry out the agency/trusteeship function implicit in the notion of territorial sovereignty, the seceding group is able to show that it ought now to have territorial sovereignty.

This chapter focuses on a rival conception of the relationship between self-government and self-determination, according to which groups of people within the state have a right to determine the boundaries of the political community within which they govern themselves. Of course, any appeal to democratic choice or the will of a group of people within the state still requires some administrative boundary within which votes are counted, and there will of course be debates about whether the administrative boundary should be a large unit such as a historic province, or small units such as individual ridings. However, unlike the straightforward administrative boundary conception canvassed in the previous chapter, these boundaries would be drawn in an attempt to encapsulate the group, not deny the group's existence. This model—or a hybrid version of it—seems to have been implicit in Woodrow Wilson's (inconsistent) carving up of territory along national lines as part of the First World War peace settlement. Wilson recognized that areas of overlapping national communities, or disputed territory, pose problems for this general conception and suggested that local plebiscites would settle boundary disputes.

The idea that groups of people within the state should have territorial jurisdiction does not preclude the possibility that the area that they claim for the exercise of self-government is different from the area that they actually occupy. In many cases, groups are attached to a particular territory, for religious reasons, or because they view it as their historic homeland, or because they are indigenous to that area, even if

[1] Details of the groups expelled by Stalin in the former Soviet Union are found in Robert Conquest, *The Nation Killers: The Soviet Deportation of Nationalities* (London: MacMillan, 1970).

they no longer constitute a majority in that area. This chapter will also consider these special claims, first, because they are advanced by the groups themselves and have to be considered in any attempt to arrive at a fair resolution of competing claims, and, second, because the idea of a nation involves the idea of a homeland, and it would be inconsistent to ignore the sentiments, attachments, and feelings of the groups within the state as regards territory, but treat as relevant sentiments of membership.

There are, roughly, two variants of the view that groups or individuals within the state should be permitted to redraw state boundaries. Both variants reject the view, discussed in the previous chapter, of the state's relationship to the whole territory. In contrast, they suggest that the people themselves must in some way authorize the government, and that this authorization may be withheld or borders may be redrawn by individuals or groups within the state.

Choice Theories of Secession and the Individual Autonomy Argument

One version of this argument is identified in the secessionist literature as a choice theory of justified secession. Choice theories of the right to secede, such as those advanced by Christopher Wellman, Harry Beran, and Daniel Philpott, typically require that a territorially concentrated majority express a desire to secede in a referendum or plebiscite for the secession to be legitimate, and do not require that the seceding group demonstrate that they are victims of injustice at the hands of the state or the majority (remainder) group on the territory.[2] Typically, those who adopt this line of argument view the right to self-determination, including a right to secession, as based on an argument about the right of political association. The right of political association is then grounded in a deeper argument about the value of individual autonomy.

There are mildly different versions of the individual autonomy argument (or choice theory), put forward by Beran, Wellman, and Philpott, all of which emphasize the foundational value of individual autonomy. Beran develops the liberal idea that consent is the basis of political obligation and confers legitimacy on the state, and then

---

[2] Daniel Philpott, 'In Defence of Self-Determination', *Ethics*, 105/2 (1995), 352–85; Christopher H. Wellman, 'A Defence of Secession and Political Self-Determination', *Philosophy & Public Affairs*, 24/2 (1995), 142–71; Harry Beran, 'A Liberal Theory of Secession', *Political Studies*, 32 (1984), 21–31.

applies this to the issue of secession, and, specifically, the redrawing of political boundaries. He argues that the only coherent and consistent liberal theory of political obligation is based on individual consent—although he concedes that this is ineffectively operationalized in so-called liberal states.

This view of the basis of political obligation and state legitimacy is deployed in support of the view that individuals *within* the state should be able to define and redefine political boundaries. Specifically, Beran argues that the secessionists should be able to nominate the area for referendum, and that this nomination should be 'recursive' in the sense that minorities within this area also have the right to hold referenda on secession. This procedure not only makes the boundaries of the state voluntary, but it ensures that the aggrandizing aspirations of majority groups, who may tend to define jurisdictional areas expansively, are prevented from doing so.[3] Beran's procedure is vulnerable to the objection that this may have a dangerous domino effect. One response to this concern is the claim that, in fact, it will serve to inhibit local majorities from being secessionists, if they know that the same procedure may be used to carve up their chosen area of jurisdictional authority.[4]

Like Beran, Philpott and Wellman have each developed a theory that links individual autonomy with the right to secede. They both argue that liberalism and democracy can be justified by appealing to

---

[3] Rainer Bauböck denies that this is a problem. He writes: 'The first paradox of plebiscitary self-determination need not arise as a practical problem as long as all groups involved accept given borders as starting lines. National self-determination demands are rarely claims for the largest possible territory where a group can muster a majority, but refer more often to a particular and well-defined territory which the group regards as its historic homeland.' See Bauböck, 'Self-determination and self-government', unpublished manuscript, March, 1999 version, 16. He cites the partition of Ireland in 1920 as a counter-example, because the six provinces of Northern Ireland did not correspond to the historic region of Ulster and included areas with a Catholic majority. Indeed, its only rationale seems to have been that this permitted the Protestant Unionists the largest area in which they were still a stable majority. However, I think that this isn't a single counter-example, but indicates a general problem with over-holding states, of which the Protestant Unionists are an example—they identified with Britain. Indeed, if Bauböck's optimistic view were correct, we wouldn't expect states to so vehemently resist secession—and many of them do—nor would we expect states to try to keep groups within their territory, and under their jurisdiction, especially when the state encompasses land beyond its so-called 'historical' territory. Bauböck is too optimistic: aggrandizement is a problem, especially for the over-holding state, which is accustomed to a certain territory, accustomed to borders of a certain shape, and for the majority ethnic or national group in the state, which is accustomed to a pre-eminent position within that state.

[4] Brendan O'Leary, 'Determining Our Selves: On the Norm of National Self-Determination'. Paper presented to the *International Political Science Association*, Berlin, Germany, August, 1994, 13.

the value of autonomy; and then argue that this value is also the basis of the right to self-determination. The exercise of the right to self-determination involves the individual in exercising positive freedom in shaping the kind of society s/he lives in and the very conditions of his/her own existence.

Wellman's 'hybrid' model of political legitimacy is like Philpott's in so far as it also emphasizes the importance of individual autonomy to ground a fairly robust right to secession. His theory differs from Philpott's in so far as he has, in addition to consent, a 'teleological' component to his theory of political legitimacy. However, this merely amounts to the requirement that both the seceding group and the remainder state must be capable of performing the functions of a state. The same restriction is presented as a 'practical' limitation on the exercise of the right to secede in both Philpott's and Beran's theories. In both cases, the relatively permissive view of secession is justified through an appeal to the autonomous ideal of the person. The term 'autonomous' refers to the view that people are not merely negatively free but are self-forming beings, capable of acting reflectively in making choices over their own lives and the conditions of their existence.

All three choice theories appeal to the idea of a majority vote in favour of secession as an operational guide to the choices of individuals within a particular area. They extend the right to secede to any territorially concentrated group, provided, in Philpott's case, that it is likely to be as protective of human rights as the state from which they are leaving, and, in Wellman's case, that both the seceding group and the remainder state are capable of exercising the functions of government, and in Beran's case, that the areas are territorially contiguous and viable.

At this point in the argument, one may raise the objection that the principles of individual autonomy and freedom of association do not help us to define the jurisdictional unit or territory within which the group should be self-governing. Indeed, Philpott acknowledges that viewing secession as an exercise of democratic choice, or autonomy, may seem to require that *everyone* in a state vote on the separation of a group within its borders—since the contours of their state are affected, too. This is the position identified in the previous chapter with the civic equality model, international law since 1945, and with just-cause theory. Against this view, Philpott argues:

[O]ne does not have the autonomy to restrict another's autonomy simply because she wants to govern the other. The larger state's citizens cannot justly tell the separatists, 'My autonomy has been restricted because, as a member of our common state, I once had a say in how you were governed—in my view, how we were governed—which I no longer enjoy.' A right to decide whether another self can enjoy self-determination would make a mockery of the concept . . . I am not [entitled] . . . to decide who will and will not be included in my state, or how another group governs its own affairs.   (Daniel Philpott, 'In Defence of Self-Determination', 362–3.)

In this passage, Philpott's argument seems to be based on something like the liberal principle of freedom of association. Freedom of association involves the ability to associate with other freely consenting individuals, and to dissociate from some others. If dissociation is implicit in a freedom of association principle, freedom of association cannot imply a right to associate with others against their will. It cannot amount to decision-making powers over the associational freedom of others, or to a possible veto over the wishes of others. It is, Philpott suggests, a requirement of individual autonomy that the individual should have the capacity to associate and dissociate with whomever s/he chooses.

However, this understanding of secession as an extended form of individual freedom is problematic in a number of ways. Most of these problems are related to the general problem of deriving a collective right—collective here meaning a right that must be exercised in common with others—from the value of *individual* autonomy. This is a significant transition because the exercise of collective choice over institutional decision-making does not always result in increased individual autonomy. In fact, as Buchanan has persuasively argued,[5] neither democratic decision-making by majority or plurality vote, nor a majoritarian plebiscitary right to secede, should be conceived as an expression of individual autonomy, for in neither case is the individual self-governing. Rather, he or she is governed by the majority and may end up worse off, in the sense that the decision made by the majority rule runs counter to his/her most strongly felt preferences.

One problem arises in cases where the permissive implications of choice theory results in a sub-optimal situation that is actually counter to the choices of most individuals in the state. Because the right to secede is conceived as justified in terms of individual autonomy, or choice, there are very few limits, internal to the theory, on the possibility of unrestricted and destabilizing secessions-from-secessions. In one sense, this is because choice theory grants such a strong presumption in favour of individuals to freely choose not only the kind of life they wish to lead but also the kind of state they wish to live in and

---

[5] Allen Buchanan, 'Democracy and Secession', in Margaret Moore (ed.), *National Self-Determination and Secession* (Oxford: Oxford University Press, 1998).

which state to live and participate in. However, I think that the argument also runs into this difficulty because it pays insufficient attention to the question of *who* should justifiably exercise this right. All three authors seem to confine their examples to national groups; indeed, Philpott anticipates a response to the question of how to identify the group in question with the claim that we do in fact know national groups when we see them. However, none of the choice theorists discusses the special political claims that follow from nationhood or why their theory of secession should be limited to national groups.

In fact, however, the individual autonomy argument is not limited to national groups but is applicable to any territorially concentrated group seeking to secede from the state. Consider the case of a right-wing anti-state 'Militia' group, which had bought land and trailers in a park in Texas and then claimed a right to secede.[6] They were territorially concentrated—in a trailer park near Fort Davis, Texas—ideologically similar, and their claim to the right to secede from the United States was informed, in part, by a historical argument about their fidelity to 'true' American values. It is hard to see how choice theory could deny this kind of claim.[7] They are clearly exercising positive freedom in the sense that they are determining the conditions of their existence, and the kind of state that they want to be subject to, and the kind of values that they want such a state to endorse. But nevertheless, I think we are right to try to resist this kind of logic, both because such a right, if it was institutionalized, would have perverse consequences, and also, because, ultimately it fails to respect the first-place preferences or choices of the vast majority of people in the state.

Let me deal first with the problems of institutionalizing such a right. I take it as a relatively uncontested axiom of internal institutional design that we should try to avoid institutional structures that provide perverse incentives. The flaws in the institutional design of such a right to secession in the domestic constitution of a state may be readily apparent, but, at the risk of belabouring the point, let me elaborate on the kinds of problems that are attached to encouraging groups to exit

---

[6] There were other members of the 'Militia' scattered throughout west Texas. See *The Economist*, 8 June, 1996, and *The Economist*, May, 1997.

[7] This point is made in a different way, by Wayne Norman, 'Ethics of Secession as the Regulation of Secessionist Politics', in Margaret Moore (ed.), *National Self-Determination and Secession*, 34–61, at 37: 'Choice theories are, in effect, nationalist theories shorn of the moral complications of ethnicity. Groups do not have to prove they are nations in order to qualify for a right to secede, and this allows choice theories to avoid entirely the problem of explaining why some often very apolitical cultural traits should take on such enormous moral weight in arguments for secession.' I take this criticism of choice theory to be exactly right, although not the description of nations.

for ideological reasons. The first and most obvious problem is that this may undermine the democratic exchange of ideas and perspectives, as ideologically similar groups simply set up their own self-governing states, and thereby threaten the pluralist and multifaceted character of contemporary democracy.

Further, institutionalizing this kind of right may encourage people to gain increased rights through becoming territorially concentrated and asserting majority control over the area in which they settle. One concern is that the effect of this rule will result in states taking defensive measures to discourage perfectly natural and ordinary migration patterns within the state. Immigrant groups, for example, have long congregated together, so that people who speak the same language and share some of the same experiences can feel more at home in their new country—the United States, Canada, Australia. They can integrate into the general public life of the host society, without assimilating entirely into the majority culture. But if small pockets of groups who share some of the same views and values can secede from a state merely through a majority vote, then it is to be expected that the state will seek to discourage this kind of settlement pattern, and so interfere in people's freedom to move and settle freely in their new country.

More seriously, for choice theory, it is hard to justify this policy in terms of autonomy. At one level, of course, the option of secession increases the range of choices. For the immigrant discussed above, there are now three options. There is, of course, option # 1, of staying in one's home country, with the political or economic uncertainties that that choice may entail, and option # 2, of coming to a new country, which is perhaps more just and more prosperous, but also a difficult cultural adjustment. But institutionalizing this right gives rise to a third option of settling *as a group* in a more attractive society and then seceding from it to form one's own state in which one can be self-governing. This might seem ideal, for it leaves the individual with even more choices. But this is to ignore the feelings of Americans, Canadians, and Australians who find their country dismembered and their own chosen (political) project snatched away from them. Not only is the end-result a sadly sub-optimal one, as the former country is dotted with pockets or enclaves of sovereign units throughout its former territory, but many people's choices for their own state, and their own political project are not respected in that scenario. This makes it very difficult to defend this policy in terms of autonomy.

Problems attached to the transition between the value of individual autonomy and collective rights also arise in cases where some individuals vote in favour of secession, and some individuals vote against it, and the pro-secessionist and anti-secessionist people cannot be separated territorially.

All three choice theories consider the issue of territorially inter-mixed groups, with different political aspirations, at the end, or as a *practical* difficulty attached to the exercise of the right, rather than as a core problem in their philosophical discussion. Philpott develops his principal argument in favour of a right to secede by abstracting from the problem of national diversity and minorities who do not consent to secession. Indeed, the first half of the article, where he develops his main principles, is confined to determining the appropriate principles for an imaginary group that he calls the Utopians, who are nationally homogeneous, territorially concentrated, and united in their aspirations for secession.

Wellman, too, after an extended discussion of political legitimacy and its implications for secession, finally comes round to consider the problem posed by those who do not seek to secede *in a footnote*. The relegation of this important problem to a footnote in itself demonstrates an amazing lack of realism about the actual circumstances in which secessions occur, the prevalence of multinational states in the world, and the difficulty of separating most national groups by a line on the map (or border).

Indeed, Wellman is quite explicit that the problem of rival and contested nations is not a significant problem in the ethics of secession. His 'hybrid' model of political legitimacy, as we have seen, combines features of choice theory with teleological considerations. The consent component of his theory grounds a presumption in favour of political liberty or political self-determination. However, the teleological component of his theory of political legitimacy leads him to argue that 'the case for liberty is defeated only in those circumstances in which its exercise would lead to harmful conditions.'[8] He then specifies the likely harmful conditions or circumstances:

[B]ecause harmful conditions would occur in only those cases in which either the seceding region or the remainder state is unable to perform its political function of protecting rights, secession is permissible in any case in which this peril would be avoided. Therefore we can conclude that *any* group may secede as long as it and its remainder state are large, wealthy, cohesive and geographically contiguous enough to form a government that effectively performs the functions necessary to create a secure political environment. (Christopher Wellman, 'A Defence of Secession', 161–2.)

---

[8] Wellman, 'A Defence of Secession',161.

What is clear in this discussion is the complete ignorance of the dynamic of most secessionist movements. In almost every case of secession, and every serious secessionist movement, the people who seek to secede are culturally and/or linguistically distinct from the majority population, with a somewhat different history and different relationship to the majority group and the state, and who are situated on their ancestral territory—not recent immigrants. Secession is not simply an issue of political legitimacy or fulfilling the functions of a state but is closely tied up with sub-state nationalism, and the inter-play between the state and the community's culture, symbols, and identity.

Since this is so, one crucial factor in determining whether there are likely to be problems is the extent to which the secessionist project itself is contested, especially by local minorities. The question that Wellman thinks is crucial—indeed, he thinks it is the *only* question— is whether viable states result; but 'viability' in the ordinary sense is rarely important in determining whether peace, justice, and stability will result. Rather, since most secessionist projects are fuelled by minority nationalism, and are aimed at producing a state with which these local minorities will identify, and which will promote the culture and language of the group that will be, post-secession, an overall majority, the crucial question is the extent of and demographics of support for, and opposition to, secession in the seceding region.

In many cases—Quebec, Northern Ireland, Kashmir, Northern Cyprus, Croatia, Kurdistan, and Sri Lanka—support for secession breaks down along ethnic lines, and, in some cases, results in minority campaigns resisting the newly-created state *after* its successful seces-sion.[9] In some cases, these are aimed at improving the minority's posi-tion in the new state; but they also sometimes involve massive population movements as minorities migrate to be on the 'right' side of state borders; and sometimes they involve violent rebellions against the new states which then poses a serious challenge to the stability of the otherwise viable post-secessionist state.

In his footnote, ostensibly addressing the problem of those who do not consent to a particular secession, Wellman offers as a general rule the claim that 'the hybrid account allows for maximal political self-determination consistent with political stability'.[10] One problem with Wellman's formulation—in terms of 'political stability'—is that this has quite different implications than the term that Wellman seems to

[9] John McGarry, 'Orphans of Secession', in Margaret Moore (ed.), *National Self-Determination and Secession* (Oxford: Oxford University Press, 1998).
[10] Wellman, 'A Defence of Secession', 163, note 25.

use interchangeably with it—'viability'. 'Stability', as I have argued, is partly a function of the absence of nationalist discontent, whereas 'viability' suggests the kind of criteria that Wellman explicitly employs in his theory, such as wealth, size, access to resources, and military capacity.

This is very similar to Beran's argument, which also mixes a Kantian freedom of association model with more utilitarian or 'real world' considerations. Although he derives his right to secession from a freedom of association principle, which is grounded in terms of the value of individual autonomy, in the end he recognizes that not everyone will end up in their preferred association. His recursive secession model is designed to achieve the maximization of preferred political associations, but he acknowledges that in some cases people will end up in political units that they did not choose, and this is partly due to considerations connected to political stability, viability, and territorial contiguity.

This abstraction is problematic not only because the real world is not like this, but because the fact that there are minorities or dissenters is a serious problem for an individual autonomy argument. On Philpott's, Wellman's, and Beran's argument, self-determination is grounded in considerations of free association and individual autonomy. This means that the right to secession is problematic for every case other than the Utopians—where the desire for secession is unanimous—that Philpott initially focuses on, and which Wellman tends to assume throughout. In any case where there is disagreement among citizens, and this disagreement is not amenable to a partitionist or recursive secession solution, it would seem that the resulting state violates the individual autonomy of (dissenting) citizens, and their freedom of association, by forcing them (the dissenters) to be in association with people they do not wish to associate with.[11]

This problem with the individual autonomy version of this argument seems to me to be decisive. It is a serious problem for this argument that all existing states, and indeed almost all conceivable states, would be classified as unjust in the sense that they violate individual autonomy of their members and their rights to freedom of association. The appeal to practical considerations and utilitarian-type maximization is hardly compelling, since it applies to the central value of freedom of association on which the theory is erected.

---

[11] Alan Patten, 'Democracy and Secession', Paper presented to the *Conference on Secession and the Quebec Reference Case*, London, Canada, April, 1999, 16.

National Self-Determination and the Collective Autonomy Argument

A more plausible argument to justify boundaries drawn *around* the group focuses on the collective autonomy of the 'nation' or 'people' concentrated in the secessionist region. The collective autonomy argument is like the individual autonomy argument in so far as it supports a democratic vote in the self-determining area, although not a state-wide vote throughout the over-holding state. This is justified in terms of the collective autonomy of the nation or people. It is this which justifies them in being able to decide as a group who to associate with, and it is the collective autonomy of the nation that would be violated by a state-wide vote.

Of course, this account presupposes that respecting the collective autonomy of nations is of moral importance. In this book, I argue that there is moral value in giving institutional recognition to national identity. Nations are moral communities, and the bonds of membership and shared identity that co-nationals feel have ethical value. Institutional recognition is important to members' sense of identity and gives expression to their political aspirations.

One problem with appealing to a national self-determination argument is that there is a range of different principles for drawing boundaries that is consistent with this argument. First, there is the occupancy principle, which suggests that national groups that aspire to be self-governing should exercise that right in the jurisdictional area that they occupy. This is similar to Wilson's (inconsistently applied) appeal to the ethnic principle following the peace settlement of 1919, since, it was assumed that many of the large ethnic and linguistic groups had the potential to become nations.

I have also argued, especially in Chapters 2 and 3, that a normative theory of nationalism should consider the constitutive elements of people's identities, and this may include the role played by the group's conception of their homeland, and the bonds of attachment to territory that they feel. In other words, nationalism is not simply based on group membership, but also has an important territorial component, involving an attachment to a homeland or area of the globe. If people *care* about their homeland, and if these feelings have developed legitimately—because the area in question is in fact their home, their ancestors are buried there, their mothers and fathers have tilled the soil there, their national monuments are erected there—then it only seems proper that this should be taken into account to define the territory to which the group is entitled.

In many cases, however, arguments to justify entitlement to territory that the group does *not* occupy have been deployed precisely in order to undermine some other group's legitimate claim, and particularly the claims of groups already settled, and subject to their own government on the territory. The idea that the people who live on a land, especially if they have not recently—within living memory—acquired the land unjustly, should have more rights, or greater entitlement, to that land than anyone else is so intuitively plausible that it has rarely been defended. Indeed, in many cases, the other justificatory arguments—based on religion or superior culture or something else—were employed precisely to undermine entitlements that attach to people who live there. For example, after the European discovery of the New World, and the prospect of gold and other riches, the Holy Roman Emperor Charles V, in 1550, summoned the learned men of the age to Valladolid to debate the question: 'How can conquests, discoveries and settlements (in my name) be made to accord with justice and reason?'—and while they considered this question, there was a moratorium on further expeditions to the New World.[12] Additional justifications were found—mainly in terms of the uncivilized, unChristian nature of the indigenous people, or, in the case of the great civilizations of the Aztecs and Incas, much was made of the fact that they practised ritual cannibalism, and therefore were clearly uncivilized. This was deployed to justify both conquest and settlement of the New World by the more 'civilized' and Christian Spanish. My point is not to show that some version of an occupancy argument was generally respected, but that it was sufficiently plausible and intuitively attractive that there was at least a recognition of the need for special justifications to override it, or to present special cases where occupancy alone was insufficient to justify rights to territory.

The four kinds of arguments most commonly employed by nationalists to claim superior entitlement to land, are based on Divine right; superior culture; indigenousness; and historic claims. In assessing these rival and competing claims to territory, I adopt two different criteria or 'tests'. One criteria is dictated by the moral importance of conflict-resolution. In many cases, we can only achieve some resolution of

---

[12] David E. Stannard, *American Holocaust; Columbus and the Conquest of the New World* (New York, NY: Oxford University Press, 1992) 210–11. See also Anthony Pagden, *The Fall of Natural Man: the American Indian and the Origins of Comparative Ethnology* (Cambridge: Cambridge University Press, 1986), 38–9; and Anthony Pagden, 'The Christian Tradition', in Allen Buchanan and Margaret Moore (eds.), *The Making and Unmaking of Boundaries: Diverse Ethical Perspectives* (Princeton, NJ: Princeton University Press, forthcoming).

a territorial conflict by taking into account some of these special claims, especially when they rest on a strong feeling of attachment.

However, there are limits to the rights which can arise out of these 'special' claims, because these types of arguments are difficult to generalize and hence of limited applicability for conflict-resolution and for a fair treatment of rival national claims. The criterion of generalizability is an important one, especially in the context of two rival claims, by different national groups, for the same territory. These 'special' arguments are problematic, because in many cases the justificatory argument is non-generalizable in the sense that the argument is internal to a specific tradition or culture and cannot provide the basis for a neutral adjudication of national conflict.

For this reason, I argue that, while these special claims for rights over territory do sometimes generate rights, they often fall short of the kind of full jurisdictional authority over the territory that the groups typically seek. In what follows, I will examine four different kinds of 'special' claims to superior entitlement to land, the problems attached to them, and the extent to which they are valid.

Chosen People and Divine Rights to Land

One important kind of claim to territory arises from a conception that a certain group of people is entrusted with a divine mission: they are God's chosen people, and they were granted the land by God.

The idea of a covenant between God and his chosen people is central to Judaism, and the idea that the terms of the covenant involved a divine right to land has been used, politically, by certain elements in Israel. A similar argument, based on the same passages in the Bible, but, of course, with a different view of who constituted the chosen people, was employed by early American colonists in the New World, Dutch settlers in South Africa, and Protestants in Ireland.[13]

There are some key passages in the Bible[14] which suggest that land is a crucial element in the covenant between God and His chosen people. At Genesis 17:8, Abraham agrees to obey God's laws and worship him, and in exchange he receives a promise of land. Specifically, God promises: 'And I will give unto Thee, and to thy seed after thee,

---

[13] See generally Donald Harman Akenson, *God's Peoples; Covenant and Land in South Africa, Israel, and Ulster* (Montreal and Kingston: McGill-Queen's University Press, 1991).

[14] The first five books of the scriptures—the Torah, the books of Moses—are nearly identical in both the Jewish and Christian religions, although arranged in slightly different order and with different titles.

the land wherein thou art a stranger, all the land of Canaan, for an ever-lasting possession.' The promise of land in exchange for the covenant is repeated to Moses, but it is explicitly extended not just to Abraham and his descendants, but to all people who worship God according to the ways God has outlined. God reminds Moses: 'And I am come down to deliver them out of the land of the Egyptians, and to bring them up out of that land unto a good land and a large, unto a land flowing with milk and honey.' (Exodus 3:8). There are many references pinpointing the exact location of this land, references to Jerusalem as the centre of Judea, the centre of the earth, and as a sacred place.[15]

The importance of the territorial element in Judaism itself has been the subject of much dispute amongst Biblical scholars;[16] but there is little doubt of the *political* importance of the belief that the land was given to the Jews by divine right. These religious beliefs, and attachment based on religious belief, were important in the Zionist movement's rejection of the 1903 Uganda proposal, put forward by Theodore Herzl to the pre-state sixth congress of the Zionist movement.[17] Since then, as Lorberbaum has shown,[18] the secular left in Israel has alternated between a functionalist interpretation of the territory of Israel, which is concerned with the defensive integrity of Israel as a sovereign polity, and a more symbolic and religiously infused interpretation of that territory. The incorporation of the Jewish tradition's concept of a divine entitlement to the land into nationalist discourse has been very selective: the Jewish tradition explicitly links that entitlement with a requirement to live a holy life, and this has been overlooked or ignored in Israeli nationalist ideology.

Appeals to the idea of a divine entitlement to the land is even more striking in the discourse of the religious-right. The settler movement is a largely right-wing religious movement that justifies Jewish occupation and settlement of the land of Israel as described in the Bible, and rejects functionalist treatments of the land. As Rabbi Abraham Isaac Kooks has claimed: "It is impossible to appreciate the content of the sanctity of the Land of Israel and to actualize the depth of love for

[15] See Ezekial 38:12. For a discussion of this, see W. D. Dawes, *The Territorial Dimension of Judaism* (Minneapolis, MN: Fortress Press, 1991), 1–12.

[16] See Dawes, *The Territorial Dimension of Judaism*, 14.

[17] The Uganda proposal was a proposal that Jews settle in the present state of Uganda, which was then part of the British Empire. This proposal was put forward by Herzl and other Zionist secularists, but was rejected by the majority of the movement. See details in Dawes, *The Territorial Dimension of Judaism*, 74.

[18] Menachem Lorberbaum, 'Making and Unmaking the Boundaries of the Holy Land', in Allen Buchanan and Margaret Moore (eds.), *Making and Unmaking Boundaries* (Princeton, NJ: PUP, forthcoming).

her by some rational human understanding—only by the spirit of God that is in the soul of Israel."[19]

The legitimating discourse of the settlers' movement places theological justifications for the territory at the centre. However, they too have selectively interpreted the relevant Biblical passages. They do this, first, because simply establishing that the territory is morally important or significant does not really determine its weight in the hierarchy of values or tradition, and this may be strongly contested.[20] Second, there is a tension between the religious role of territory in Judaism, and its role in legitimating a *political* entity. There is, Lorberbaum argues, a serious question whether one wishes to live in the state of Israel (*medinat yisrael*) or in the land of Israel (*eretz yisrael*), for the Biblical narrative does not necessitate the former.

What is being claimed by extreme elements in the settler's movement to justify Israeli settlement in the West Bank, and Israeli control over these lands, cannot be straightforwardly deduced from the Biblical passages. It is intended by its proponents as a knock-down kind of argument in the sense that it ignores demographic facts and alternative claims to the territory. That the West Bank is 95 per cent Palestinian Arab, that these people overwhelmingly resist the settlements, that the rules surrounding the dispossession of Palestinians are biased and unjust, are not relevant facts if the land belongs to the Jews by divine right. On that conception, the Palestinians are trespassers anyway.

The colonization of the Americas, and the accompanying dispossession of native Indian tribes, was justified in a variety of ways, but one prominent form of justification involved the idea that it was God's will that Christian people tame the wilderness. Indeed, early colonists argued that God was making a place for his Christian children there by unleashing destructive plagues of Biblical proportions on the native peoples, and they noted that these pestilences seemed to afflict Indians selectively. Not all was left to divine action, however: the settlers occasionally helped God to secure his plan, by deliberately sending blankets infected by smallpox.[21]

The development of doctrine in the Presbyterian and Dutch Reformed Church by Ulster-Scots in Northern Ireland and the Afrikaners, respectively, also drew on the idea of a chosen people with a divine mission. In both cases, the integrity and purity of the chosen

---

[19] Rabbi Abraham Isaac Kook, *Orot*, 89. The quote is from Lorberbaum, 'Making and Unmaking'.

[20] Lorberbaum, 'Making and Unmaking'.

[21] Stannard, *American Holocaust*, 239.

people were maintained by endogamy, and the territory was justified in terms of divine sanction, with the Ulster-Scots and Afrikaner Volk carrying the torch of Christian civilization to backward Catholics and heathens, respectively.[22]

The basic problem with all these justifications, of course, is that they establish the 'right' of a particular (chosen) people to particular pieces of land only in the eyes of those who accept the authoritativeness of the text and the particular interpretation of the text being advanced. There are different authoritative texts and, even when all accept the same text as authoritative, there are, as I've tried to show with respect to the Israeli debate, contested interpretations of the same text. Appeal to divine sanction, therefore, cannot provide a basis for a rule or mechanism to adjudicate conflicts between people over land, since all parties to the conflict could base their rights to the same piece of land on divine sanction. What is needed, therefore, is some impartial standpoint—impartial not in the sense of being outside all morality, but in the sense that the standpoint or basis of the argument is not acceptable from one position alone, but is comprehensible and accessible to all points of view.

The Argument from Efficiency: Superior Culture Claims

Another argument that has been employed, and is still sometimes employed, to justify rights to territory is based on the moral importance of efficiency. This argument was used to justify the taking of land in the New World and in Israel.

In the sixteenth century, Sir Thomas More argued that land could justifiably be taken from 'any people [who] holdeth a piece of ground void and vacant to no good or profitable use'.[23] This conception was applied to the Colonization of the Americas by John Winthrop, the first governor of Massachusetts Bay Colony, just prior to the Great Migration to Massachusetts in the 1630s. He anticipated the possible objection that 'we have noe warrant to enter upon that Land which hath beene soe longe possessed by others' with an argument appealing to efficiency, and which anticipated Locke's more famous justification of private property in the *Second Treatise of Government*. Winthrop wrote:

That which lies common, and hath never beene replenished or subdued is free to any that possesse and improve it: For God hath given to the sonnes of men

---

[22] See Akenson, *God's Peoples*, 120–1, 208–10.
[23] Stannard, *American Holocaust*, 233.

a double right to the earth; theire is a naturall right, and a Civill Right. The first right was naturall when men held the earth in common every man sowing and feeding where he pleased: then as men and theire Cattell encreased they appropriated certaine parcells of Grownde by inclosing and peculiar manuerance, and this in time gatte them a Civill right . . . As for the Natives in New England, they inclose noe Land, neither have any settled habytation, nor any tame Cattell to improve the Land by, and soe have noe other but a Naturall Right to those Countries, soe if we leave them sufficient for their use, we may lawfully take the rest, there being more than enough for them and us.   (John Winthrop, 'Reasons to be considered, and Objections with Answers', quoted in Stannard, *American Holocaust*, 235–6.)

Locke, in *The Second Treatise of Government*, argued that the right to property was based on the person's right to his body; that the person can appropriate things in the external world through labour and that these became his goods as long as he leaves as much and as good for others. Like Winthrop, Locke justifies a certain form of (private) property-holding, for he goes on to argue that enclosure is more efficient than holding the land in common, and that, while it might seem to be taking land away from others—because others cannot use it—it is possible to produce more efficiently on private property and so, effectively, 'leave as much and as good for others'.

In these passages, the right to territory is premised on a particular conception of land use, in which land is improved and transformed through private ownership. The native conception of the appropriate relationship between land and people, which involved communal holdings, and emphasized a sustainable relationship between people and resources, was not even seen as 'use'.

In the first half of the twentieth century, when early Zionists began to settle in Israel, the 'efficiency argument' was used to justify rights to land. Although some early Zionists claimed that there were few people or no people in Palestine, this wasn't meant literally—for the demographic reality was unavoidable and indeed of great concern to early Zionist leaders. The idea, rather, was that there were no people using the land. Zangwell, a leading Zionist, made this point well: "If Lord Shaftesbury was literally inexact in describing Palestine as a country without people, he was essentially correct, for there is no Arab people living in intimate fusion with the country, utilising its resources and stamping it with characteristic impress: there is at best an Arab encampment."[24]

---

[24] Quoted in Nur Masalha, *Expulsion of the Palestinians: The Concept of 'Transfer' in Zionist Political Thought 1882–1948* (Washington, DC: Institute for Palestine Studies, 1992), 6.

The same basic idea is still expressed today, even in doveish circles, although less crudely. In 1986, the then-Prime Minister of Israel, Shimon Peres, described the early period of Zionist settlement in an article in the *New York Times*: "The land to which they came, while indeed the Holy Land, was desolate and uninviting; a land that had been laid waste, thirsty for water, filled with swamps and malaria, lacking in natural resources. And in the land itself there lived another people; a people who neglected the land, but who lived on it."[25]

Implicit in this description is that the people who lived on the land, the unnamed Palestinians, were not attached to it: they had 'laid waste' the land, neglected it, and, so it seems, had no rights to it.

The basic idea here—that land should be allocated to those who use it most efficiently—has two basic problems: lack of generalizability and the disastrous consequences of implementing the rule. The first difficulty is that what counts as efficient use depends on the values of the people and their vision of desirable land use. It is impossible to assess one culture's 'efficiency' against another if they value different things, if one culture values low density and open spaces, for example, while another values a more intensive, transformative pattern of land use.[26]

The second, equally serious problem is that if this was adopted as a general principle or rule, it would not provide a secure basis for rights, but would lead to an unstable and counter-productive situation where borders are constantly being redrawn.[27] If applied generally, this rule would seem to dictate that land rights should be conferred according to who is most effective in exploiting the resources. Because this would change over time, the rights to particular pieces of land would also shift. Changing technology, changing land-use patterns, and demographic shifts would lead to a situation in which one area of land, previously best exploited by one group, now might be used more efficiently by another group; thus, one group would lose their rights to the land and another would gain rights. Because efficiency, or expected efficiency, is the foundation for rights, it would follow that the actual amount allotted to different groups would constantly change. Not only might this be undesirable in itself, causing instability and insecurity—and perhaps even less efficient use of the land because of this—but there would be a greater likelihood of conflict over the terms of the

[25] Quoted in Edward W. Said and Christopher Hitchens (eds.), *Blaming the Victims* (London: Verso, 1988), 5.

[26] This point is made in Ian Lustick, 'What Gives a People Rights to a Land?', *Queen's Quarterly*, 102/4 (Spring 1995), 60.

[27] Ibid., 60.

transfer, especially given that there are difficulties measuring efficiency across cultures.

Indigenousness: Grounding Superior Entitlement to Land

One of the most widespread and generally recognized arguments for a right to territory is based on a claim to indigenousness. Many groups in all parts of the world claim to be indigenous: Australian Aborigines, New Zealand Maoris, and native Cree, Ojibway, Cherokee, Mayan and many others in North, South and Central America; Malays in Malaysia, Fijians in Fiji, Sinhalese in Sri Lanka, the Kannadigas of Karnataka state in India, the Bankonjo and Baamba of Western Uganda, the Kinshasa in Zaire, to name a few.[28] Rights which flow from indigenousness are also becoming generally recognized at the international level. The Draft Declaration on the Rights of Indigenous Peoples, for example, outlines numerous rights which attach, as it were, to indigenous people.

Some of the rights which are claimed by indigenous peoples, and which are recognized internationally, seem no different from minority rights. It does not seem that a special claim to *indigenousness* is necessary to ground the rights; rather, indigenous people are beneficiaries only because many indigenous people are also *minority* groups. For example, the UN Declaration grants rights to practice and transmit distinctive customs and to provide education in the indigenous language.[29] It is hard to see why this should apply solely to indigenous people and not other minorities, especially national minorities, in the state.

Other arguments made in support of rights of indigenous people are premised on considerations of justice. Many indigenous people, particularly in Australia and the Americas, are economically and socially marginalized, with lower literacy rates, lower socio-economic status, and higher mortality rates than the population as a whole. It is therefore an important issue of justice that these people are given rights which are designed to overcome their disadvantage. What is noteworthy is that these rights are based on an equality argument, and do not require any special claim to indigenousness, or first occupancy. They

---

[28] Donald L. Horowitz, *Ethnic Groups in Conflict* (Berkeley, CA: University of California, 1985), 202.

[29] Draft Declaration on the Rights of Indigenous Peoples, articles 12–16. Quoted in Donald L. Horowitz, 'Self-Determination: Politics, Philosophy and Law', in Margaret Moore (ed.), *National Self-Determination and Secession* (Oxford: Oxford University Press, 1998), 201, note 65.

attach to indigenous people only because indigenous people are, in many cases, a disadvantaged group in society.

There is no cause to deny the cogency of various justice-related arguments concerning how modern people should interact with isolated groups of people, and/or people whose culture is threatened, or who have suffered various kinds of historical injustices, or who are economically and socially marginalized. However, the fact that the group in question is indigenous, in the sense of having first occupied the land, is not relevant to these kinds of arguments. The focus of this section of the chapter is on the more problematic claim that indigenousness, in the sense of first occupancy, confers a right to territory.

The claim to territory which flows from indigenousness is primarily a claim to prior, rightful ownership, based on first occupancy. Since the indigenous people are rightful owners of the land, the later arrivals were engaged in 'theft'. This is the suggestion behind the title of a recent book on American history, *Stolen Continents: The 'New World' Through Indian Eyes*[30] and it has intuitive plausibility in so far as everyone can understand the idea that I have a right to evict unwelcome guests from my home, or to set the terms under which guests can stay.

The plausibility of this line of argument is mainly connected to the fact that it is morally significant that groups and individuals were defrauded and expropriated. In the case of aboriginal people throughout the Americas and in Australia and New Zealand, entire communities were robbed of their land, of their capacity to exercise self-government, many were killed, and their cultures were degraded. Victims of injustice often stress the importance of remembering what occurred, in part because the past injustice continues into the present—they are *still* without their land—but also because their own individual self-identity as members of the group is bound up with the kinds of things that happened to the group, and this is partly constitutive of the kind of group it is.[31]

---

[30] Ronald Wright, *Stolen Continents: The 'New World' Through Indian Eyes* (Harmondsworth: Penguin, 1992).

[31] For many aboriginal groups, the claim to be entitled to land through an argument based on indigeneity is primarily a way of questioning the jurisdictional authority of the state. In many cases, these groups lack legal entitlement because their claims and their holdings were not recognized by the conquering regime, which forcibly incorporated them. The claim to land is in part a rejection of the jurisdictional authority of the current regime. Although I do not discuss this issue here, this argument is still subject to the general problem that *restoring* their jurisdictional authority would create many unfairnesses and injustices. I take it that we should endeavour to rectify past injustices, but that this is often not possible because it can only be done by creating new kinds of injustices.

Notwithstanding the moral force of this argument, there is a number of problems with the argument that indigenousness confers superior entitlement to land. First, human migration is and has been extremely common, and it is difficult to argue for differential rights on the basis of descent; second, the actual history of migration is contested; third, the claim of indigenousness depends very much on which geographical context is taken as relevant; and, fourth, even if the argument from indigenousness is accepted, it is not clear that it is sufficient to overcome rival arguments based on equity or equal treatment. The first two arguments are related to evidentiary problems of claims to injustice that occurred a long time ago, and the contested nature of the historical record; but the first, third, and fourth arguments are connected to problems in restoring or making amends for past injustices. In many cases, the problems attached to fixing the historical record creates new problems of injustice, because people build a pattern of expectations and attachments to land and goods that they are in possession of. Restoring this land or these goods to the original owners may create new, equally serious kinds of injustices. This, Waldron has contended, is one of the main arguments for the view that injustice can be superseded with the passage of time.[32]

The first problem with the indigenous argument stems from the fact that human migration is and has been extremely common: many people are descended from people who came from somewhere else and it would be very difficult and problematic to assign (general) rights to people based on where they originated. Where people originated may not bear any relation to where or who they are now. Non-indigenous people may feel a strong attachment to the place where they were born and not to the place where their ancestors came from. An alternative approach would be to give some people rights based on where they originated (indigenous people) but diminished rights to those people whose ancestors at one time migrated. If we take the view that any principle or policy should be capable of being justified to the person or group who does *worst* under it, then, it is not at all clear that it is straightforward to justify an inferior right to people born in a place but descended from one line of people, whereas others, who are descended from a different line of people and who are therefore indigenous may have a superior right.

Moreover, in many cases, the actual history of migrations is more complicated than the assertion of indigenousness might suggest. For

---

[32] See here Jeremy Waldron, 'Superseding Historic Injustice', *Ethics*, 103 (October 1992), 4–28.

example, in Sri Lanka, the Sinhalese claim to be indigenous, but in fact the Vedda people are aboriginal people whose time of arrival in Sri Lanka long preceded that of the Sinhalese. Similarly, in Malaysia, the Malays regard themselves as indigenous people—their name for themselves is *Bumiputra* (sons of the soil), but in fact the Orang Asli people were in Malaysia long before the Malays. Indeed, many Chinese families have been in Malaysia longer than some 'Malaysian' families, who in fact arrived relatively recently from Indonesia and assimilated to the Malay identity.[33] Many Sri Lankan Tamils have been in Sri Lanka a thousand years and so are hardly recent immigrants, and sometimes claim to be indigenous to the north and eastern parts of Sri Lanka, whereas the Sinhalese take as their relevant political context the whole of the island.[34]

Differing conceptions of the relevant geographical context are important in many cases of claimed indigenousness. In Durban, South Africa, many Africans settled on Indian owned land after World War II. Although the Africans arrived later than the Indians, they regard themselves as indigenous and the Indians as the outsiders, because they took the whole continent of Africa as the relevant political context.[35] Similarly in Ireland, some scholars claim that the problem in Northern Ireland is settler-native in origin, and implicit in that conception is the view that the Gaelic-speaking Irish people are indigenous (native) to Ireland, and that the Ulster Protestants, who form a majority in the north-east part of the island, are 'settler' people, who dispossessed the native Irish and oppressed them. However, the relevant geographical context is extremely important to the argument. It is generally accepted that waterways were a main mode of transportation in the past, that settlement tended to occur along waterways, and there was constant movement of people across waterways.[36] This generally accepted fact is used to support the claim that the 'settlers' from Scotland in the seventeenth century actually originated in Ireland, and were returning 'home' to their native land in the seventeenth century.[37] Here, the geographical context is politicized, with some viewing the island as a whole as the relevant (and static) geographical context, and others with a much more fluid conception of context. In this case, as in many others, the claim to indigenousness is subject to pseudo-historical and myth-making processes.

[33] Horowitz, *Ethnic Groups in Conflict*, 203.   [34] Ibid.   [35] Ibid.
[36] This point is made in Akenson, *God's People*, 105–6 for the period prior to the eighteenth century.
[37] Ian Adamson, *Cruthin: The Ancient Kindred* (Newtownards: Nosmada Books, 1974).

Considerations of equity pose a further complicating factor to claims of entitlement to land. Suppose that one group has a culture based on slash-and-burn agriculture or nomadic herding, which requires thousands of acres to support a small group of people. There are, it would seem, at least two kinds of argument for this group's right to territory. The first is a straightforward argument from indigenousness: this group has lived on this land for hundreds, perhaps thousands of years, and therefore are rightful owners of this land. Another slightly more sophisticated argument would go like this: the group has a right to its distinctive culture and the culture requires access to and control over a large amount of territory. But even this argument, which in itself, might be valid, is subject to other considerations. Suppose, for example, that a non-indigenous group has been stripped of its territory, or its territory has become so degraded or is so resource-poor that it cannot support them, and the thousands of acres reserved for indigenous people is more than sufficient to feed and support all the people, especially if the land was used in a different way. This is not an argument from efficiency: the claim here is not a Lockean one that efficiency grants entitlement; it is merely suggesting that considerations of equity may override such land entitlement. This is particularly the case once the outsider-group has lived on the territory for many years, perhaps even many generations; in this case, it does not seem fair to grant some people superior rights and others inferior rights to the territory on the basis of the line of descent of the two groups.

In conclusion, then, while the claim to indigenousness does suggest a historical attachment to the land, it does not generate a superior right to a particular territory that can be used, unproblematically, as the basis for defining the jurisdictional unit in which self-determination takes place. Of course, in areas where the group occupies a majority, it may be possible to carve out an area in which it can exercise majority self-government. In this case, indigenousness, combined with present occupancy, is an overwhelming argument.

In assessing rights to territory based on indigenousness, much will depend on the length of time that has passed since the occupation of the settler group. If that occupation was recent—within living memory—then it would seem that some kind of restitution of territory, if not the *status quo ante*, might be appropriate. However, in cases where the settlers have long been on the land, and have no other homeland, the appeal to indigenousness is much more problematic, for the reasons outlined above. In this case, it may be possible for the indigenous group to form self-determining local government areas, or native self-governing regions, within the sovereign state, in those areas where the group occupies a local majority. In this case, however, it would be problematic to grant rights only to people descended from the original inhabitants, and deny rights to other people who are minorities locally.[38]

In short, the four difficulties outlined with this argument means that this appeal to indigenousness cannot justify denying the right of another (non-indigenous) group to self-determination, by denying them the territory within which self-determination can take place. Nevertheless, to achieve just conflict-resolution and to recognize their attachment to the land and their identity as indigenous people, local forms of self-government may be necessary, as well as other measures designed to address the fact that, in many cases, indigenous people are among the most disadvantaged.

Historical Claims to Territory

A fourth, and closely related form of justification for a right to territory is based on *historic* occupancy. This justificatory argument has some merit, although its most prominent version does not.

The most problematic kind of historic argument is based solely or exclusively on an historic claim to occupy the land, without any connection to present occupancy patterns or to the different ways in which groups can become attached to land. This type of historic argument was one of the justifications for Nazi Germany's *lebenstraum* policies: that is, it was claimed that Germans had a 'mission' to 'resettle' territories once occupied by ancient Germanic tribes.[39] This argument suggests some kind of entitlement to the land in question based on past occupancy. After World War II and the defeat of Germany, the Polish government argued that they were entitled not only to the area recently colonized by Germans since 1939, but also the provinces of Pomerania, Silesia, and East Prussia, all east of the Oder-Neisse line,

---

[38] This is a problem with the Nisga'a treaty negotiated with the government of British Columbia (Canada). The treaty allows for Nisga'a self-government within a sparsely populated area in the BC interior. However, full political rights (voting and leadership roles) are only held by the Nisga'a. This means that some people on the territory, who are non-Nisga'a, are denied full political rights. See Jon Kesselman, 'Civil Rights under Nisga'a: The Experience from Musqueam', *Vancouver Sun*, 14 August, 1998. This is a serious problem. I do not think territorial self-government is consistent with a conception of membership defined in non-territorial terms. Moreover, I do not see why the Nisga'a, who constitute a large majority within their area, cannot exercise self-government as a majority community, and still allow the non-Nisga'a, who after all are a small minority locally, political rights.

[39] Michael Burleigh and Wolfgang Wippermann, *The Racial State: Germany 1933–1945* (Cambridge: Cambridge University Press, 1991), 62.

on the grounds that these had originally been Slav lands prior to the thirteenth century.[40] Along a similar vein, some Jews maintain their right to '*eretz yisrael*'—the land of Israel, which is larger or more expansive than the pre-1967 State of Israel—on the grounds that their ancestors inhabited the territory two thousand years ago, although some also stress a continued Jewish presence in the area.[41]

One difficulty with this kind of justification for territory is that it is essentially contested, as is the claim to indigenousness, and subject to myth-making. However, the most serious problem is that it is impossible to develop an adequate principle or mechanism to adjudicate such rival claims to territory: it depends on where in history one starts, and whose history one accepts. Appealing to historical links can legitimize claims to vast areas and many different irredentist claims. In an absurd, but revealing, example, James A. Graff points out that 'one could press claim to all of the Levant, including the Holy Land and most of North Africa, in the name of the Greek Orthodox people, insisting on a "return" to territory that was the homeland for people of that faith community during centuries of Byzantine rule.'[42] Why should Germans or Poles or Jews or Greeks be given rights to territory they occupied several centuries ago, rather than those whose ancestors were there before them, or after them?

This is an issue of contemporary importance. The Greek nationalist claim to the mainly Slavic-speaking Macedonia in the former Yugoslavia, and the Serb occupation of the Kosovo region, which has a 90 per cent Albanian population, are both justified on historic grounds. Yet, on the view I've been arguing here, historic ties are insufficient to generate rights to control the territory. Historic monuments and national sites can, at best, legitimize a *prima facie* case in favour of rights of *access* but not to control over the territory—and therefore the people—in which these national sites are located. It could legitimize right to access, not simply as an extension of a principle of free movement, but also in consideration to the special attachments that people may have for these monuments, graveyards, historic sites, and so on.

There is, however, a better argument for historic rights, which links past history with *current* occupation patterns, and with people's sub-

---

[40] A. M. deZayas, *Nemesis At Potsdam: The Expulsion of the Germans from the East* (Lincoln, NB: University of Nebraska Press, 1989), 168–72. Quoted in John McGarry, 'Ethnic Cleansing: Forced Expulsion as a Method of Ethnic Conflict Regulation', Paper presented at the *Canadian Political Science Association*, June, 1996, 9.

[41] McGarry, 'Ethnic Cleansing', 9.

[42] James A. Graff, 'Human Rights, Peoples, and Self-determination', in Judith Baker (ed.), *Group Rights* (Toronto: University of Toronto Press, 1994), 211.

jective sense of attachment. This argument has been put forward by David Miller, who elaborates some of the grounds on which a group can legitimately claim, not only to be entitled to exercise jurisdictional authority (statehood), but also to exercise it over a particular piece of territory.

At first glance, Miller's argument seems in some respects analogous to Locke's argument that we can acquire rights to individual property holdings through mixing our labour with it. Miller suggests that a nation can come to have 'rights' to land by mixing its culture with it. He writes:

The people who inhabit a certain territory form a political community. Through custom and practice as well as by explicit political decision they create laws, establish individual or collective property rights, engage in public works, shape the physical appearance of the territory. Over time this takes on symbolic significance as they bury their dead in certain places, establish shrines or secular monuments and so forth. All of these activities give them an attachment to the land that cannot be matched by any rival claimants. This in turn justifies their claim to exercise continuing political authority *over that territory.* (David Miller, 'Secession and the Principle of Nationality', in Margaret Moore (ed.), *National Self-Determination and Secession*, 68. My emphasis.)

Miller's theory about how territorial claims are established draws a very plausible link between occupancy and attachment. Indeed, this element also partly explains the initial force of the indigenous argument: it is because a particular group has been in a place for a long time—or since time immemorial—that they have come to *care* about the land; their myths and behaviour patterns are bound up with the land, its seasons, its topography, and so on; and, through this, they have greater claim to it than any other group.

Miller's argument that culture becomes bound up with a particular land, and land becomes transformed through people acting on it (culture) tends to dovetail with my emphasis earlier on the importance of incorporating the role of a homeland and the bonds of attachment that people feel into a normative theory of nationalism.[43]

[43] This is not intended to imply, of course, that the sentiments of attachment can never be altered. We know, for example, that over time, borders have changed and conceptions of 'homeland' have accordingly changed. Following the Second World War, Stalin moved the borders of the Soviet Union to the West, and this was accepted by the Western powers as a partial response to the Soviet Union's contribution to victory over Germany. Simultaneously, Poland's borders were moved westward, placing land occupied by ethnic Germans within the Polish state. The basic acceptance of these border changes by the people involved can be partially explained by its completeness—there were no German minorities left in the previously ethnic German land, to rouse nationalist passion about their mistreatment. The point here is that, while identities can, and do, change, and while

The Occupancy Argument

One important feature of Miller's argument is that it brings together two separate conditions: the first is historical, and suggests an attachment developed through rootedness in a particular place over time; the second is present occupancy of the land to which the person feels attached. Like the indigenousness argument, the historical argument is most successful when these feelings or bonds coincide with present occupancy patterns. When they don't, as in the Serb attachment to Kosovo, they cannot justify control over the land—and the people who live there—although they may justify rights of *access* and perhaps some jurisdictional authority, perhaps of a power-sharing nature, over the actual historical monuments or religious sites of significance.

Occupancy is the most convincing argument for jurisdictional authority over territory. First, it is generalizable in the sense that it is, at least in principle, capable of being applied to a large number of groups. Unlike the other arguments, which tended to be aggrandizing in the sense that they support an expansive definition of territory within which the people are to determine themselves, and deny the rights of other—unchosen, non-indigenous, unhistoric—people to be self-determining, this argument is at least in principle open to any territorially concentrated national group that aspires to form a political community.

Second, the occupancy principle is consistent with the generally accepted moral view that people should not be forcibly removed from their homes and communities merely in order to secure control over territory. This principle is implicit in the moral repugnancy that typically accompanies policies of ethnic cleansing or forced transfers of population. It has the added merit of helping to indicate what is wrong with state-directed settlement policies. If ethnic cleansing is wrong as a means for an ethnic/national group to gain control over land, so is swamping the territory with settlers. The Chinese policy of moving Han Chinese to Uighur, Tibetan, and Mongolian areas of China is repugnant: the means are not the same, and arguably not as coercive as 'ethnic cleansing', but the end—control over territory—is the same.[44] This method denies the associational life of the minority groups and

---

the boundaries of the homeland with which one identifies can also change, especially over several generations, this does not negate the moral significance of these identities or these feelings. The fact that they may be altered in certain conditions is not an argument for state-directed policy aimed at altering people's feelings. Rather, the importance of land in shaping a people's culture and identity should be taken into account in any full account of the moral dimension of territory, and in assessing rival claims to the same territory.

[44] See 'China's Uighurs; a train of concern', *The Economist*, 12 February, 2000, 40.

their capacity to determine the context in which they live. These policies, it is safe to say, would not have been pursued if the Uighurs, Tibetans, or Mongolians were self-governing peoples, who had jurisdictional authority over their land, and were able to decide the basis on which people should be permitted entry.

Thirdly, and most importantly, the occupancy argument is convincing because it is the only one that follows directly from the understanding that rights to territory are implicit in the notion of democratic governance. Throughout these two chapters, I have argued that, in the modern world, special claims to territory are unnecessary, because territory simply applies to the area in which jurisdictional authority extends. Democratic government implies that the rules and the institutions of the state are generally acceptable to the people who live under them. In cases where the national group resides as an overwhelming majority on land which it claims or thinks of as its historic territory, there is no need for would-be secessionists to demonstrate a special claim to the seceding territory. Regulation of territory is implicit in the status of a self-determining, self-governing people.

Finally, the occupancy argument can be conjoined with the most plausible element of the historic argument to confer rights only when the occupied land is not acquired unjustly, at least within living memory. Similarly, it can be combined with the indigenousness argument, in cases where the indigenous group, which seeks to be self-governing, is territorially concentrated in a particular area.

Implications of the Argument

In the sections above, I have suggested that there are no unproblematic first-order claims to territory. Rather, the claim to territory is second-order in the sense that it is derived from the claims that national minorities make to institutional recognition of their own identity. If we accept that there is moral value in recognizing national identities, then it follows that territorial recognition, where it is possible, is justifiable and sometimes even desirable.

This provides an answer to the jurisdiction problem, raised initially by Jennings:[45] it means that self-determination should be permitted

---

[45] Ivor Jennings, *The Approach to Self-Government* (Cambridge: Cambridge University Press, 1956), 56. Jennings argued that the idea that we should let the people decide is 'ridiculous because the people cannot decide until somebody decides who are the people'. An additional problem still remains on my formulation, which I will discuss in the next chapter, that, in any referendum on the subject, there will need to be local ridings, or small administrative units in which national preference votes are counted.

for nationally-mobilized local majorities, and that they should only be able to exercise self-determination over territory that they actually occupy. In the case of indigenous people who are dispersed into small communities—often no larger than 200 or 300 people in many reserves in Canada, for example—it is not possible to confer full national self-government on them. Nevertheless, the attachment that they feel to the land, and their strong attachments to their own communities suggests that they should at least have some kind of local or indigenous self-government in their own communities. In the case of national minority groups, there should be provision for the exercise of self-government, either through devolved jurisdictional authority in areas where they form a majority within the state, or, where they seek full independence, they should be entitled to secede from the state and bring with them the territory that they occupy.

This does not mean, following the argument in Chapter 5, that secession should be permitted only along the lines of existing administrative boundaries. In some cases, administrative boundaries are drawn to give some self-government for national groups; but, in other cases, they are intended to deny it. We need to develop institutional mechanisms, which will be discussed in the next chapter, to determine, at the local level, the extent and degree of nationalist mobilization for the self-determination project, and to draw the boundaries accordingly.

This conclusion is not coterminous with choice theory. Although both seem to permit the boundaries of the state to be carved up, choice theory relies on an individualist autonomy argument, and so can justify the secession of neighbourhoods or cities or trailer parks from the state. My argument, in terms of the collective autonomy of nations, only grants self-determination to national groups on their historic territory. The justificatory argument for the collective autonomy of nations, in turn, is based on arguments presented in Part I of this book, centred on fair treatment, intrinsic value, and the goods that can be achieved when national communities are self-governing.

In this chapter, I have argued that the occupancy argument is the only rule that can serve as a general basis for territorial entitlements—when it is combined, of course, with the proviso that the territory, and subsequent occupation, was not acquired unjustly, within living memory.[46] It is, however, limited in a number of ways. It is limited, first, by the imperatives of securing peace and justice, especially in the face of

---

[46] Of course, most territory, if one goes back far enough, was probably acquired unjustly. This is why a statute of limitations is necessary.

nationally mobilized groups who have a strong emotional and symbolic attachment to a particular piece of land that they do not occupy, or do not exclusively occupy. Second, because it applies most easily when groups are united behind the self-determination project, and when they are territorially concentrated, it is of only limited guidance—but still does offer some guidance—in other cases.

The first set of limitations points to the fact that normative theorizing about rival claims to territory is not simply about the just or impartial treatment of groups or claims based on generalizable principles, but should take into account the symbolic and emotional meaning of the land for many national groups. In many cases, a nationally mobilized group does not view the territory as simply a means or area in which self-government can occur. Rather, the land itself is infused with emotional significance. According to Serbian nationalist mythology, Kosovo is the 'cradle' of their nation. In 1999, Serbs were prepared to fight for control over Kosovo, while, eight years previously, they had accepted the secession of the much more prosperous or objectively desirable territory of Slovenia which did not have the same kind of emotional or national resonance for Serbs. The revered status of Kosovo in Serbian nationalist mythology has nothing to do with the current occupancy patterns—even before the 1999 NATO intervention, Kosovo was over 90 per cent ethnic Albanian.

It is probably the case that a peaceful political solution to such rival claims will have to take into account these feelings within the limits of justice. Thus, the Serb attachment to Kosovo, and particularly to the monasteries and ancient battlefields and Orthodox churches there, should, as I've said, give the Serbs a right of *access* to these places of significance, or even some kind of jurisdictional authority, in a power-sharing arrangement, over these places of significance—but not the people who live in Kosovo.[47]

Jerusalem, too, has an important emotional and symbolic significance for Jews and Muslims, just as Kosovo does in Serbia nationalist mythology, which the occupancy argument does not capture. In the Jewish case, the religious and nationalist motifs are strongly interwoven. These symbolic and emotional attachments compete with other, more functional conceptions of the territory, and the security-driven concerns that states typically have, for pre-eminence in Israeli political life. By ignoring all this, the occupancy argument has ignored

[47] After all, in the Middle Ages, Christians felt the same way about Jerusalem, and fought for its inclusion in the Christian world, but eventually came to terms with the fact that Christianity—and, by analogy, Serbia—can survive and flourish without direct control over these areas of significance—and over the people who live there.

something of great significance: it has abstracted from the attachments that groups feel, which is precisely what I earlier criticized anti-nationalist accounts of doing.

Indeed, it is very unlikely that a final settlement in the Middle East, between Israelis and Palestinians, could be reached that failed to take into account how both groups feel about Jerusalem. These concerns are practical ones, about the likelihood of reaching agreement, but they are also normative, in the sense that peace and stability are both important moral goals, and in the sense that some kind of internationalization of Jerusalem, or joint power-sharing arrangement in Jerusalem, or other fair division of jurisdictional authority would reflect the salience of both the occupancy arguments, and the attachment that these groups feel. These arguments suggest that neither group should have exclusive control, for this would deny the legitimate rights and claims of the other.

The overlapping claims to Jerusalem, and the close proximity of the groups to each other there, suggest the second kind of limitation connected with the occupancy argument. The occupancy argument works best when the groups occupy discrete areas of land. However, in many cases, rival claims arise when there is considerable intermixing of rival populations groups, and territorial settlements are extremely difficult. In cases where rival groups are territorially intermingled and make rival claims to the same territory, they may be able to be accommodated through complex blurred (shared or joint or international) sovereignty arrangements. It would be very difficult to arrive at a solution to the Northern Ireland conflict without some recognition that the Irish nationalists regard the whole island of Ireland as the legitimate jurisdictional domain, and any attempt at partition does violence to this national aspiration. In this case, their claims are buttressed by the significant Irish nationalist (Catholic) minority living there, more than 40 per cent of the population, and the artificial nature of the original partition.

Similarly, while the current partition of Cyprus is clearly unjust—in which 38 per cent of the best land is controlled by Turkish occupying forces, when, in 1974, at the time of the Turkish invasion, Turkish Cypriots only constituted 18 per cent of the population[48]—this does not necessarily mean that re-partition into two independent states is the appropriate solution. Not only would it tend to legitimize the earlier forced movements of Greeks from the northern part of the island,

---

[48] Demographic details are found in Tozun Bahcheli, 'Missing the European Train? Turkish Cypriots, the European Union Option, and the Resolution of the Conflict in Cyprus', in Michael Keating and John McGarry (eds.), *Minority Nationalism and the Changing International Order* (Oxford: Oxford University Press, forthcoming).

but, more importantly, would be totally unacceptable to Greek Cypriots, who view the whole island of Cyprus as a single, indivisible entity. Any settlement to that impasse will have to take into account both Turkish-Cypriot feelings of insecurity and their desire for self-government, and Greek Cypriot attachment to the island as a whole, and the settlement, prior to the 1974 expulsion, of Greek Cypriots throughout the island.

An Objection Considered

There is, however, a serious objection to the argument advanced in this chapter, concerning the moral importance of ensuring the collective autonomy argument of national groups. This objection does not ultimately succeed, but it does indicate areas of genuine concern about national recognition, and the limits of national self-determination.

It might be claimed that, defending the collective autonomy of nations by appealing to the moral importance of national communities and national identities, seems to presuppose that nations are stable features of one's identity. It seems to suggest that there is a fixed number of identities and possible national communities, within which self-government can occur. Yet, as this deconstructionist criticism is anxious to emphasize, nations emerge in the context of modernity and are neither natural nor fixed. Indeed, nationalism itself may lead to a dynamic in which resistance to the nation-building project will foster minority antagonism, and lead to a domino effect in which minorities feel marginalized and alienated from the political community, and thereby engage in their own national mobilization project. If nations are constructed through historical contingency and political mobilization, is it not contradictory and self-defeating to treat them as though they are natural facts and fixed features of one's identity? Rogers Brubaker has argued, critiquing various misconceptions about national identities and national communities, that we should not regard nationhood 'as an unambiguous social fact; it is a contestable—and often contested—political claim.'[49] Treating nations as a fixed category ignores the 'fluidity and ambiguity that arise from mixed marriages, from bilingualism, from migration, . . . from intergenerational assimilation (in both directions), and from sheer indifference to the claims of ethno-cultural nationality.'[50]

---

[49] Rogers Brubaker, 'Myths and Misconceptions in the Study of Nationalism', in Margaret Moore (ed.), *National Self-Determination and Secession* (Oxford: Oxford University Press, 1998), 238.

[50] Brubaker, 'Myths and Misconceptions', 256.

The logic of this deconstructionist account is away from any kind of institutional solution to national antagonism or national conflict. Indeed, Brubaker is explicit that there are no institutional solutions, that 'national conflicts are in principle irresolvable'—although, revealingly, he admits that in certain contexts they become less important or no longer salient and may fade away![51]

The problem with the conclusion that this deconstructionist account seeks to draw, as I argued in Chapter 1, is that the mere fact that nations are constructed as a result of political mobilization in certain contexts does not mean that these identities are less real or morally salient, or that they are easy to deconstruct.

However, this critique does point to a legitimate concern about the fixity involved in defining areas of territorial jurisdiction. National groups aspire to form political communities, and for their political aspirations to be fulfilled, they require a jurisdictional domain (or territory) in which they can be self-governing. National groups, in other words, are not pure membership organizations, particularly in so far as they aspire to have some political and institutional reality; and self-government does not apply to members of the national group only, as is the case with voluntary associations or religious groups, but to everyone within a territory. As long as liberal democracy is organized in territorial terms, which will be the case as far into the future as we can realistically see, it requires not only that boundaries are sufficiently flexible to express people's aspirations, and not be a means to victimize minorities, but that they are also sufficiently stable that they are able to define membership in a political community.[52]

All this points to the evident fact that territorial jurisdiction, by its very nature, must be stable. If democratic decision-making procedures are to function effectively, they must provide a stable democratic order in which decisions can be made for the future, and in which membership is clearly defined. This does seem to freeze identities, and to negate overlapping and competitive identities.[53] However, this difficulty in expressing fluidity, ambiguity, and the contested nature of various overlapping identities, is not connected so much with what Brubaker calls 'groupness', but with the requirements of territorial self-government. There must be stability attached to membership in a territorially inclusive government. This stability requirement does

[51] Brubaker, 'Myths and Misconceptions', 240.
[52] This model is consistent with the one advocated by Bauböck in 'Self-determination and self-government', 21–2. He develops a formal model to illustrate the instability attached to what he calls 'the secession game'.
[53] This point is from Rainer Bauböck, 'Self-determination and self-government', 22.

pose a challenge to institutional recognition of national identities: it indicates that this recognition must take a form that does not lead to the destabilization of democratic polities or the very conditions of collective self-government.[54] But it also indicates a reply to the implicit critique of Brubaker's, which accuses attempts at recognition of national identity of failing to take into account this fluidity and of failing to recognize various kinds of ambiguity. The problem is not simply the institutional recognition of nationality, but a more general problem of artificial exclusiveness that attaches to self-government in the first place.

Conclusion

This chapter has examined two kinds of arguments in support of the view that groups or individuals within the state should be permitted to redraw state boundaries. The first argument, identified with choice theories of secession, is grounded in the exercise of individual autonomy. I argued that the transition from individual autonomy to collective self-government and control over territory was very problematic.

The collective autonomy argument avoids this problem by focusing, not on individual autonomy, but on the moral importance of respecting the collective autonomy of national groups. Implicit in this argument is a rejection of the civic integration model of undifferentiated equality and an acceptance of the normative merits of institutionally recognizing national identities.

However, the principle of national self-determination does not itself indicate a single principle, or unitary formulation, for assigning rights over territory. This chapter went on to examine different principles for demarcating boundaries in which self-determination can occur, and analysed the arguments that groups deploy to justify rights over, or control over, territory. Nationalists often appeal to different principles under the rubric of national self-determination: they appeal to the particular nation's history, or religion, or ethical conception to justify rights to territory, or jurisdictional authority over a particular territory; or to a democratic majority amongst people who see themselves as belonging to a particular nation, within administrative boundaries

---

[54] As Bauböck has argued, 'The existence of political boundaries is a necessary condition for self-government to flourish. But a right to change them so that all groups . . . can achieve a maximally exclusive and comprehensive form of self-government undermines this very condition and is therefore ultimately self-defeating'. Rainer Bauböck, 'Self-determination and self-government', 11.

designed to encapsulate that majority, if that group is territorially concentrated.

The special (non-occupancy) justifications are problematic in the sense that they are only acceptable to people who accept that particular version of history, or religion, or ethical value. For this reason, while these views and beliefs and attachments do have to be taken into account to achieve the resolution of conflict over territory, and while these sorts of arguments can generate some limited rights, they should not be used to deny the rights of other groups to exercise their right to self-determination.

The 'occupancy principle', which is usually institutionalized in terms of an appeal to a democratic majority in areas that the nation occupies, is less problematic, because it is, in principle, open to all nations. On this view, territory is a corollary of self-government. The idea that boundaries should be drawn *around* groups is based on an acceptance of the moral value of recognizing national identities. This is therefore consistent with the rest of the argument in this book, where I suggest that there are good normative and practical reasons for recognizing and giving institutional expression to group-based differences, and particularly those differences that involve diverse political aspirations. One aspect of this recognition—indeed, the chief or prime aspect—is the capacity to redraw boundaries to allow a group to be collectively self-governing.

Sometimes, of course, the claim that nations make on their own behalf will fall short of independent statehood: not all nations seek outright independence—especially in cases where the group members have ambivalent, or overlapping national identities—and, even for those who do, their claims cannot always be met, because doing so will compromise the (equally) good claims of another national group. But in the latter case, it is, at least in principle, open to everyone to recognize cases where the national group is not territorially concentrated, or there are disputes about territory, and more imaginative political forms are necessary to give the group control over its identity, and to give expression to its shared national identity.

One of the tricky elements in this institutional recognition, which is the subject of Chapter 8, is the difficulties in implementing the precise balance between flexibility and stability. I have suggested that there are problems attached to an inflexible regime where there are no mechanisms for changing boundaries, and in which boundaries can be used as means to deny group identity and prevent the group from enjoying its collective life. At the same time, democracy requires a certain amount of stability to make rules for the future and to define membership in territorially inclusive government. There is therefore a certain tension inherent in this justificatory argument, between the capacity to define and redefine borders and therefore membership, which is implicit in this understanding of the relationship of territory to democratic self-government, and the need for stability in democratic polities, particularly with regard to defining membership rules.

CHAPTER 8

Implications: The Ethics of Secession

Throughout this book, and particularly in Chapters 2, 3, and 4, I argued that there are good moral and practical reasons to recognize and accommodate national identities. If this is right, if national bonds of attachment and solidarity and identity have moral value, if it is unfair and hypocritical to give institutional recognition to majority nations but not to minority nations, then, we must consider the practices of our domestic states and the interstate order. One of the fundamental operating assumptions of this chapter is that it is wrong that in many cases minority nations can achieve recognition of their political aspirations only through bloodshed and violence. This chapter examines the kinds of procedures and rules that might bring the quest for self-determination under the rule of law and also examine the justifiable limit of the exercise of self-determination.

This chapter is concerned with the possibility of developing principles and procedural mechanisms to help us cope with groups that aspire to be collectively self-governing. The chapter will specify the type of (legal) right to secede that could be placed in the domestic constitutions of multinational states, or processes that could be spelled out in international law. It will argue that the procedural criteria that rights typically invoke are useful in addressing the substantive normative issues that arise in cases of mobilized national groups seeking to become self-determining. It will also discuss the role that international law currently plays and could play in helping to regulate self-determination claims. Finally, at the end of the chapter, I argue that in the changing global order there are emerging more opportunities to manage national conflict and accommodate rival national claims.

Institutional vs. Non-Institutional Approaches to the Ethics of Secession

An important methodological question that arises in debates on the ethics of secession is the purpose such a theory is intended to serve. Allen Buchanan has argued that the issue of secession should be regarded primarily as an issue of institutional morality, by which he means a theory about the design of morally progressive institutional responses to secession. In his view, the various permissive treatments of secession on offer possess cogency only because they are viewed in an institutional vacuum. His focus on the kind of right compatible with a just international law regime allows him to narrow the scope and kinds of considerations that are relevant to the issue of secession. A crucial move in Buchanan's argument is to distinguish between two kinds of normative questions about secession. They are as follows:

1. Under what conditions does a group have a moral right to secede, independently of any questions of institutional morality and in particular apart from any consideration of international legal institutions and their relationship to moral principles?
2. Under what conditions should a group be recognized as having a right to secede as a matter of international institutional morality, including a morally defensible system of international law?[1]

Without going into detail on the arguments that he advances in support both of the criteria and the application of the criteria to choice and just-cause theories of secession, it is clear that he thinks that the first question—the one most philosophers have tried to answer—is the wrong question because it abstracts from many considerations that are relevant to secession.

This distinction permits Buchanan to deploy four criteria to 'test' choice theories and just-cause theories of secession. These criteria are: minimal realism; consistency with morally progressive principles of international law; absence of perverse incentives; and moral accessibility.[2] These criteria enable Buchanan to focus on the kind of right compatible with a just international law regime, and he concludes, unsurprisingly, that a right to secede is restricted to groups that have just cause.

Buchanan is right to suggest that many of the philosophical treatments of the issue of secession display ignorance of the complexities of

[1] Allen Buchanan, 'Theories of Secession', *Philosophy & Public Affairs*, 26/1 (1997), 30–61, at 31–2.
[2] Buchanan, 'Theories of Secession', 42–4.

institutionalizing such a right. I agree that we should consider issues
of the ethics of secession within a larger context, and, by this, I mean
that we should not only consider the consequentialist implications of
developing a just international law regime, but also situate the ethics of
secession within the context of nationalist mobilization and national
conflict generally.

There are, however, good grounds for questioning Buchanan's
sharp distinction between the two questions. Underlying Buchanan's
formulation of the two questions is the view that the moral rights and
obligations that we have flow from the institutional structure of our
society. If the rights, obligations, and duties that we have are conceived
of as the products of our institutional structure, then, prudential and
consequentialist reasons enter at the theoretical ground floor, because
relevant to the design of the basic structure of society. This means that
determining whether or not we can be said to have a right involves, in
the first instance, an examination of the structure of just international
institutions.

There are two principal problems with Buchanan's general conception that rights, duties, and obligations are strongly linked to institutions. First, it seems counter-intuitive in the sense that we may want to
say, for example, that someone has a right, but that it would be impru-
dent to exercise the right. We may also want to describe the lack of
institutional recognition or the difficulties of institutionalizing the
right as suggestive of moral loss, and, in order to do this, we would
have to say that the person in question has a right. This suggests that
we can separate the moral question of whether the person has a moral
right from the legal or institutional question of whether the person
cannot or ought not to exercise the right.

The second problem with Buchanan's general conception of rights
and obligations flowing from the institutional structure of society is
that it seems to give too much credence to those who do not wish to
recognize the legitimate aspirations of groups in society. The four criteria, which are used to test both just-cause and choice theories, flow
directly from his institutional focus of his ethics of secession. Two of
the criteria—minimal realism, and moral accessibility and, even,
arguably, consistency with morally progressive principles of international law[3]—tend to point to the consequentialist arguments and

---

[3] I do not want to elaborate a full argument here, except to say that Buchanan uses this
criterion to focus on the principle of territorial integrity, which he then says should be
enjoyed by every state that avoids injustice. This is subject to the same objection outlined
in Chapter 7, namely, that it presupposes that the only moral principles at stake in any conception of justice are respect for individual human rights and democratic governance. It

objections of state actors and majority groups as reasons for denying an institutional right to secession. 'Minimal realism' is described by Buchanan as requiring that the principle or proposal has 'a significant prospect of eventually being adopted in the foreseeable future, through the processes by which international law is actually made.'[4] 'Moral accessibility' involves the idea that the 'justifications offered in support of the proposal should incorporate ethical principles and styles of argument that have broad, cross-cultural appeal and motivational power, and whose cogency is already acknowledged in the justifications given for well-established, morally sound principles of international law'.[5] In both cases, the denial of the right is based on the fact that power-holders are unlikely to grant the right or there is no international consensus that there is indeed such a right. But this flies in the face of the purpose of most rights-based arguments historically. Political rights for women, rights to liberty and personal integrity for slaves would have failed Buchanan's tests in the eighteenth and nineteenth centuries. There was no international consensus against slavery in the seventeenth and eighteenth centuries, and certainly no likelihood that a principle of liberty and equality for slaves would be adopted. But we may still want to say that slavery was wrong, that the enslaved had moral rights to freedom, and that these were being denied. Similarly, the arguments that women should have political rights, to vote or to hold high office had no 'widespread, cross-cultural appeal and motivation power', even as late as the early twentieth century, because the societies in question were ones in which female subordination was taken as normal and accepted, and politics assumed to be a masculine activity.

While I think we shouldn't adopt an institutional theory of secession in Buchanan's sense, he is right to suggest that one goal—although not necessarily the pre-eminent goal—in reasoning normatively about secession is to consider how to institutionalize a right to secede in a state or in international organizations. Indeed, many of the theories that Buchanan criticizes attempt to do just that.[6] Unlike Buchanan, however, they attempt to establish basic principles

---

fails to take seriously, from the very beginning, the validity of a broader conception of justice that incorporates fair treatment of national groups, or some form of ethno-national justice.

    [4] Buchanan, 'Theories of Secession', 42.   [5] Ibid., 44.

    [6] Philpott, for example, tries to suggest that there are various safeguards surrounding the institutionalizing of a right to secession, and that his theory does not have the dire consequences that Buchanan predicts. See Daniel Philpott, 'Self-Determination in Practice', in Margaret Moore (ed.), *National Self-Determination and Secession* (Oxford University Press, 1998), 79–102.

first, and then try to implement them in ways that will avoid the negative effects. They are not trying to develop 'a morality that is free of all institutional constraints', in Buchanan's phrase. Rather, they are trying to develop principles that should be incorporated (ideally) in international legal regimes or in domestic constitutions and are sensitive to these constraints when they apply the principles.

In short, Buchanan is right to draw attention to the problem of perverse results, but he is wrong to think that there is no place for moral reasoning about secession in abstraction—to some degree—from the existing interstate system. Part of the goal of moral reasoning is to allow one to assess the present institutions, processes and structure, and to challenge them, if they are deemed flawed or wanting.

A Right to Secession in Domestic Constitutions

The first problem with any attempt to constitutionalize a right of secession is the issue of boundaries. I argued earlier that the boundaries in which self-determination is to occur are often strongly contested, as different groups appeal to different principles in support of their claim, and I have tried to evaluate these claims to indicate that they are certainly not equally valid. In the previous chapter I argued that strongly mobilized national communities on their historic territory should have the right to determine their own political and institutional future, and the exercise of self-determination should include a right to secede from the state. I also argued that this right to self-determination may mean that current administrative boundaries have to be carved up.

An important merit of a constitutional right to self-determination, including a right to secede in a domestic constitution, is that it would introduce clarity into the debate on national self-determination, especially in the tense political atmosphere of a possible secession. This is especially true of the jurisdiction problem. Any right to secede would have to indicate the sorts of groups and areas to which the right applies, and who would have access to the outlined procedure. In a multinational state, the relevant units are typically federal republics, but there also should be some procedure for allowing a region to leave one subunit and form their own or join another.

Switzerland has procedures of this kind, which are termed 'rolling cantonization'. This process allows cantonal units to be partitioned if this is desired by the people living in it. In 1980, plebiscites were held commune by commune to produce a new commune—the Swiss Jura.

This was effectively internal secession from the Berne canton, operationalized through local plebiscites. Moreover, because Protestants in part of the Berne canton voted to stay in the Berne canton, it meant that the procedure permitted the carving up of the Berne administrative unit, in accordance with the preferences of the people living there.[7]

A procedure such as Switzerland's 'rolling cantonization' is related to the underlying principles of Swiss federalism, and could be easily adapted to the recognition of national communities. The cantonal units are drawn in accordance with the religious and linguistic diversity of Switzerland. Because they are roughly coterminous, the Swiss federal model allows maximal self-determination of linguistic groups within the Swiss federation. The process of 'rolling cantonization' is an attempt to ensure that the political institutions of the state express the full religious and linguistic diversity of Switzerland. If the principle of 'rolling cantonization' is applied to national groups, it would work quite differently from choice theory's attempt to give institutional expression to individual wishes and desires. Both theories could justify secessions within secession, but the principle of national self-determination is justified on a collective autonomy argument, and grants the right of collective self-determination to national groups, not individuals. Choice theory is based on an individual autonomy argument, and can justify the secession of individual neighbourhoods or cities or trailer parks. The argument for national self-determination advanced in this book limits the right to self-determination only to those groups who self-identify as a national group and are generally recognized by others as a national group, although this is a generally true description, not a necessary requirement; are situated on their historic territory; and have not acquired that territory unjustly—at least not within living memory.

In many cases, especially where national minorities are historic communities, the territory where the majority and minority national communities live is well known, and can be addressed at the constitutional level in the form of group rights to exercise self-determination or secede from the state.

---

[7] John McGarry and Brendan O'Leary (eds.), *The Politics of Ethnic Conflict Regulation* (London: Routledge, 1993), 31; Graham Smith, 'Mapping the Federal Condition: Ideology, Political Practice and Social Justice', in Graham Smith (ed.), *Federalism. The Multi-ethnic Challenge* (London and New York: Longman, 1995), 1–28, at 14–15; and C. Hughes, 'Cantonization: Federation or Confederation in the Golden Epoch of Switzerland', in Michael Burgess and Alain G. Gagnon (eds.), *Comparative Federalism and Federation* (London: Harvester, 1993), 154–67.

The above discussion suggests that there are problems attached to an inflexible regime where there are no mechanisms for changing boundaries, and where boundaries are used as a means to deny group identity and prevent the group from being collectively self-determining. This type of politics of denial raises serious concerns about fair treatment.

At the same time, democracy requires a certain amount of stability to make rules for the future and define membership in a territorially inclusive government. For this reason, it is necessary to put in place some procedural hurdles in the way of too easy a right of secession, such as a requirement of a clear or weighted majority, and a clear, negotiated (fair) question. These, I will argue, are justifiable, first, in terms of a concept of state legitimacy—or more precisely, state illegitimacy; second, in democratic terms; and, finally, in terms of not creating perverse incentives on the creation or formation of national identities in the first place.

Many of these procedural requirements have been specified as necessary by the Canadian Supreme Court in the reference case on Quebec secession, which I think should be viewed by normative theorists as a model of the kind of rights and procedures that should be incorporated in the constitutions of liberal-democratic states.[8] This case involved three questions referred by the federal government to the Supreme Court of Canada concerning the legality of unilateral secession.[9] The judgment was widely viewed as a political masterstroke. The Court negotiated a middle ground between Quebec's claim that it had a unilateral right to secession, and the federal government position that a 'clear' yes vote on secession in a referendum on a clear question could simply be ignored by the federal government. In the Court's opinion, there was no right of secession in either the Canadian constitution or in international law, but that a yes vote in a referendum on secession would put the federal government under a constitutional duty to negotiate the terms of separation in good faith.

---

[8] *Reference re Secession of Quebec*, S.C.C. no. 25506 (20 August, 1998). http://www.droit. umontreal.ca/doc/csc-scc/en/pub/1998scr2. Address correct as of September 2000.

[9] The three questions are: (1) Under the Constitution of Canada, can the National Assembly, legislature or government of Quebec effect the secession of Quebec from Canada unilaterally? (2) Does international law give the National Assembly, legislature or government of Quebec the right to effect the secession of Quebec from Canada unilaterally? In this regard, is there a right to self-determination under international law that would give the National Assembly, legislature or government of Quebec the right to effect the secession of Quebec from Canada unilaterally? (3) In the event of a conflict between domestic and international law on the right of the National Assembly, legislature or government of Quebec to effect the secession of Quebec from Canada unilaterally, which would take precedence in Canada?

Although the rules and procedures outlined by the Court are designed to help effect a peaceful transition from subunit to post-secessionist sovereign state, they do not exhaust the number of contested issues that arise in cases of secession. Many issues—such as the share of the federal debt, the terms of future economic relations, compensation for infrastructure and share of assets—will have to be subject to negotiation. On these matters, negotiations will likely be fraught with difficulty. There was some suggestion of this in the 1995 Quebec referendum, when Quebec's Premier Jacques Parizeau argued that if the post-referendum bargaining was not proceeding quickly, Quebec would withhold sending cheques to Ottawa for its share of the payment on the national debt—interest and principal, presumably.[10]

It is also useful to think about the kinds of institutional mechanisms necessary in a negotiation process. There have been some debates in Canada on the necessity to give authority to a body to negotiate the terms of secession on behalf of the remainder state (Rest of Canada).[11] The federal or central government is not qualified, because it may be comprised of representatives from the seceding region—in the case of Quebec during the 1995 referendum, the Prime Minister's seat was in Quebec.

While the Court left many issues unresolved—on the grounds that they are properly the subject of constitutional negotiations—it did provide some guiding principles to govern the process of Quebec secession. The Court argued that four norms underlie the Canadian constitution—federalism, democracy, the rule of law, and respect for minority rights—and these have to inform the procedure on secession. They also specified certain procedural principles that should govern the referendum process. Specifically, the Court argued that the question posed in a referendum on secession should be a 'clear question'

[10] Tu Thanh Ha, 'Canada will "beg" for talks: Bouchard', *Globe & Mail*, 28 September, 1995. The reaction in the Rest of Canada to perceived threats from Quebec was predictable.
[11] Wayne Norman, 'The Ethics of Secession as the Regulation of Secessionist Politics', in Margaret Moore (ed.), *National Self-Determination and Secession* (Oxford: Oxford University Press, 1998), 34–61, at 53; Alan Cairns, 'The Legacy of the Referendum: Who are We Now?', Paper prepared for the post-referendum panel organized by the Centre for Constitutional Studies, University of Alberta, Canada, November 1995, 6–7. This was dubbed by journalists as the federal government's notorious Plan B. Many journalists blamed the federal government for failing to consider these sorts of possibilities. Jeffrey Simpson, 'With no clear thinking, Canada was ill prepared for its dismemberment', *Globe & Mail*, 8 November 1995; Jeffrey Simpson, 'Not thinking the unthinkable left Canada ill prepared for Quebec', *Globe & Mail*, 23 November 1995; Keith Spicer, 'A clean start or a clean break: English Canada should prepare two options: a renewed federalism or a Canada without Quebec', *Montreal Gazette*, 24 January 1996.

and that a justified secession would require 'a clear majority' in favour of secession.

Of course, while the Canadian Court argued that there should be 'a clear majority', thus suggesting some kind of weighted majority, they did not say definitively what kind of weighted majority—60 per cent, two-thirds?—should be adopted. Moreover, there are other formulae, possibly more appropriate in other political cultures, for erecting a procedural hurdle that gives some empirical indication of the strength and extent of national feelings. Wayne Norman has pointed out a number of these mechanisms, such as requiring a majority of registered voters, or a series of affirmative votes over a period of two or three years, to take account of temporary distortions, caused by once-off political events. In the referendum on Scottish devolution, held in 1979, the Thatcher-led government specified that the rule had to pass by a simple (50% plus 1) majority, but that the voter turnout had to constitute at least 40 per cent of the electorate.[12] A requirement such as this could be justified in the context of a secession, especially since the argument for accommodation is at least partly based on the presumed strength of nationalist sentiments and feelings.

Legitimacy

Although the Court did not justify its rules in these terms, the procedural requirements suggested by the Canadian reference decision are both normatively justifiable and necessary. First, these procedural hurdles—and especially the requirement that secession is permissible when there is a clear majority on a clear question—enable us to retain some of the most persuasive points made in the ethics of secession literature. One of the central insights of choice theory, for example, is that it is important, in a democratic state, that people accept the institutional structure in which they live. This may not mean—*pace* Beran and Philpott—that all of them have to *consent* to the state. Almost no modern liberal democratic state could be described as legitimate on that criterion, and it is doubtful that any could get the consent of all their members to exercise authority over them. However, it is possible to distinguish between requiring consent for state legitimacy and viewing a state as illegitimate if it clearly and expressly lacks consent.

This move is similar to one made in some variants of justice theory. Brian Barry has argued that we may not be able to say what justice is—

---

[12] In this case, the Scottish nationalists succeeded in securing a simple majority, but were unable to meet the 40% voter turnout requirement.

because there are many competing conceptions, or there are problems with specifying any particular conception, or with showing that one particular principle of justice is uniquely 'rational'.[13] Nevertheless, we may able to identify what *injustice* is—torture, murder, genocide, slavery.

The distinction between requiring consent and requiring evidence of non-consent operates with the basic assumption that a state is legitimate if it fulfils certain functions, such as respecting basic human rights and upholding democratic governance. For most purposes, we have a teleological conception of legitimacy, that is, we assume that a state is legitimate if it fulfils certain functions that we assume are in the best interests of those who are subject to its rules. However, in cases of explicit non-consent—in cases where we have good reason to believe that most people or a particular group of people *don't* want to be ruled by the state—the legitimacy of the state is brought into question. This may not be because the state has failed to fulfil its functions, but because the assumed link between democratic governance and justice, on the one hand, and the assent of the people on whose behalf power is exercised, on the other, can no longer be made. This non-consent comes into play in cases where there is a strong, successful nationalist movement, which consistently wins elections on a platform supportive of secession or some other form of self-determination. It comes into play when the representatives of the people—or at least a significant portion of the people—and their counterparts in civil society question the legitimacy of the particular structure and institutions of the state.

In effect, a legitimate state is secured by two tests. The main one is the teleological legitimacy test: a state is legitimate if it upholds basic human rights and is governed democratically. In most cases, we can assume that the state that satisfies this 'test' is operating in the interest of the governed, and that its rules benefit those who are subject to them. In most cases, the teleological conception suffices, because we assume that such a state would be generally accepted by the people subject to its authority. However, when there is clear, strong empirical evidence of non-consent, we cannot assume that governance is in the best interests of the governed, or that the people subject to its rules accept the state's authority, and hence, the legitimacy of the state comes into question.

Although this general theory of the relationship between legitimacy and consent is not the one generally on offer from political philosophers,

---

[13] Brian Barry, *Justice as Impartiality* (Oxford: Clarendon Press, 1995), 168–9.

it is implicit in the behaviour of some multinational liberal-democratic states. In Canada, the Quebec reference case made it clear that it is part of the constitutional law of the country that a majority 'yes' vote for secession would precipitate a crisis of legitimacy and that there is, therefore, a constitutional requirement for the parties to negotiate.[14] There would be a crisis of legitimacy—not perhaps in many philosophers' sense, for philosophers have tended to reject a consent theory due to the problems outlined above with requiring express consent—but certainly in practice. In the United Kingdom, too, the government has said that, notwithstanding its efforts to uphold law and order, justice and democratic governance, if the majority of people in Northern Ireland no longer wished to be part of the United Kingdom, the UK would allow them to leave the political association.[15] The same principle has been affirmed by former British Prime Minister Major with respect to Scotland. Speaking in the context of Scottish constitutional demands in 1992, Major declared that 'no nation can be kept in a union against its will'.[16]

While the emphasis and foundational role played by autonomy and consent in choice theory is problematic, the core idea of choice theory—that state institutions and practices should be acceptable to the people who live under the authority of the state—is generally accepted, and indeed is at the heart of democratic governance. This core idea also applies to normatively acceptable nationalist politics. It is not sufficient for a nationalist to *claim* to be speaking for or on behalf of a national group: this claim should be subject to the test of free and fair elections. The moral importance of demonstrated electoral success and/or a free, fair referendum on secession flows, not from the simple application of a principle of autonomy, but from arguments about the normative force of nationalism. This book has not argued that nations in and of themselves are morally valuable but only in so far as members care about them and identify with them. It follows from this that, in a democratic society, where people's preferences, choices, beliefs and commitments *matter*, a successful nationalist politics will have some consequences for state practice and

[14] See Supreme Court of Canada (1998). *Reference re: Secession of Quebec*, Art. 101 and 103.
[15] Under the terms (Article One) of the Anglo-Irish Agreement of 1985, Northern Ireland has a 'right' to leave the United Kingdom in order to join Ireland, but not to become its own independent country.
[16] This reference is from Michael Keating, 'So many Nations, So Few States. Accommodating Nationalism in the Global Era', Paper presented to the *Conference in Search of Justice and Stability*, McGill University, Canada, March 1998, 10.

state institutions.

It is also implicit in this argument that the depth and extent of support for nationalist parties, and nationalist positions, are crucial to the moral argument that nationalist claims should be recognized. Nationalists like to claim that they are united behind the national self-determination project, and almost always speak in terms of the nation as a whole, with no hint of division or dissent within the national community, or the territory as a whole.

Of course, the reality may be quite different from the one portrayed by nationalist élites, particularly when those nationalists do not put those claims to the test of elections. Sometimes, there are serious divisions in the national community on the kind of political autonomy that is desirable. This is true of Quebec, where polls and other evidence suggest that there is serious division over whether some kind of renewed federalism should be sought or whether stronger forms of self-determination—independence or sovereignty within some kind of economic and loose political association—should be sought.[17]

Sometimes, there is evidence that the national group itself is internally divided by subnational identities, which, in the new context of a newly secessionist state, may threaten to pull the state apart. Horowitz argues that this tendency characterizes the Albanian national community, which is internally divided between Ghegs and Tosks.[18] Some have argued that this is also a problem for Kurds, who are not only divided by the experience of living in different states, but are also further divided into distinct tribes, with different leaders. Moreover these different tribes have somewhat different histories and traditions, and their dialect makes mutual comprehension somewhat difficult.[19]

In other cases, as with the Basque claim for self-determination, the claim applies to areas beyond the Basque stronghold, to the province

[17] Although polls fluctuate of course, 1991 survey data showed that approximately 40% of Quebec francophones identified primarily with Quebec, and most were sovereignists. About one third of francophones were divided in their loyalty between Quebec and Canada and were federalist. A further 25% were slightly more attached to Quebec than to Canada and tended to be equally divided between supporters of sovereignty and supporters of federalism, and answers here depended on whether the federal arrangement is conceived as 'renewed federalism' or whether sovereignty is conceived as exercised within some form of association with (the rest of) Canada. See Kenneth McRoberts, *Misconceiving Canada. The Struggle for National Unity* (Toronto: Oxford University Press, 1997), 222–3.

[18] See Donald L. Horowitz, 'Self-Determination: Politics, Philosophy, and Law', in Margaret Moore (ed.), *National Self-Determination and Secession* (Oxford: Oxford University Press, 1998), 181–214, at 183.

[19] See David McDowell, *The Kurds: A Nation Denied* (London: Minority Rights Publications, 1992), 11–23. These differences do not affect McDowell's assessment that they constitute one nation, however.

of Navarre in Spain, and to areas in France, where there is little support, not simply for the aims of ETA (Basque Homeland and Freedom), but very little identification with a Basque identity.[20] The requirement that nationalist support should be demonstrated convincingly, through elections and through a referendum on self-determination, with significant procedural hurdles, reveals these claims as largely bogus. If there is little or no support for the national self-determination in an area, the referendum on this issue will reveal the territorial limits of that support, in a way consistent with the occupancy principle advanced in the previous chapter.[21]

Democracy

This conception of the relationship between state legitimacy and democratic support for nationalist causes brings us directly to the issue of the relationship of a right to secession to democracy and the democratic institutions of the state. The previous section has already discussed the democratic imprimatur of procedures designed to regulate secessionist politics. There are two further related issues. The first is whether the right to self-determination, including a right to secession, should be *limited* to groups that are internally democratic. The second issue is the effect of the constitutional right on democratic governance itself.

On the first issue, the discussion above, on legitimacy, makes it clear that the rule of law, the claims of justice, and democratic governance are important criteria for legitimate governance. However, in this book, I have not based the right to national self-determination on either a democratic argument or a justice-based argument—in fact, I have explicitly rejected theories that proceed in this way—and I think it is inappropriate to limit the right to self-determination to those groups who are demonstrably committed to both. At the same time, I have also argued, in the section above, that the exercise of the right to self-determination should accord with the fundamental democratic ideal that the people should assent to, and have a say in the rules and institutions that they are subject to. These two positions are quite

---

[20] Michael Keating, 'Northern Ireland and the Basque Country', in John McGarry (ed.), *Northern Ireland and the Divided World* (Oxford: Oxford University Press, forthcoming), 9.

[21] This is not the end of the matter, however. As I argued in Chapter 7, there may have to be negotiations on the appropriate jurisdictional unit, and there may have to be some institutional recognition of (religious or historic) attachment to a particular territory, possibly in the form of rights of access, as part of any comprehensive national settlement.

compatible, as reflection on the example of East Timor reveals. In the view advanced here, it was important that, in 1999, a UN-supervised referendum was held on the status of East Timor, not only for democratic reasons, but to assess the strength and intensity of popular mobilization for self-determination. This does not require a further assessment of the likelihood that an independent East Timor will uphold democratic governance, although, obviously, the norms and practices of a progressive international system should facilitate this. While a normatively acceptable nationalism would be committed to the basic rules of procedural (legal) justice and respect for human rights, the exercise of self-determination does not hinge on a confident prediction that the minority nation (would-be secessionist unit) is committed to respecting human rights and the rule of law. Not only are such predictions somewhat speculative, and raise the question of the competence of judicial bodies or outside agencies to assess this— or indeed make any judgment of a predictive nature—but it is not justified by the argument for the moral status of national identity.

In many cases, minority nations have mobilized successfully partly because the group was treated unjustly by the majority: they were denied freedom of religion, or freedom of association, and were subject to forms of coercive assimilation. In these cases, their desire to be self-governing is more understandable, and their claims seem to be more urgent in so far as the state in which they live has failed to fulfil its basic obligations towards its citizens. In this respect, just-cause theory captures an intuitively plausible idea of the relationship between injustice and state legitimacy. However, it is also probably the case that such a group, with no experience of justice or democratic governance, is also less likely to practice justice or democracy within their own group. In many cases, just, democratic states will contain minorities that are already committed to justice and democracy; and unjust, undemocratic states will have minorities with no experience of either justice or democracy and so unlikely to practice it themselves.

The second issue is connected to the consequences of institutionalizing a right to secession on democracy. Modern liberal-democratic states are justified, in large part, by reference to the interests and will of the people who are subject to its rules, and this suggests that the basic institutional design of the state and its boundaries should also be subject to the will of the people. Yet, at the same time, I argued earlier that democratic governance presupposes stable political boundaries. It is important, therefore, that the right to secede is institutionalized in a way that does not undermine the democratic process itself.

This has been argued most persuasively by Allen Buchanan with reference to Hirschmann's categories of exit, voice, and loyalty.[22] Buchanan has argued that if the right to exit (secession) is very easy to exercise, it will undermine voice and loyalty (democratic institutions). If the process of exit is too easy, it would not be rational for individuals to invest their time and energy in political decision-making processes that generate decisions, since they have little confidence that they will be governed in the future by these processes, or subject to these decisions.[23] In this scenario, the very conditions that make it rational for individuals to invest in the practice of political deliberation and debate would be eroded.

The procedural hurdles argued for here are designed to strike the right balance between flexibility and stability, between responding to the democratic will of the people and ensuring that democracy itself is not destabilized. Further, a clear question is justifiable both in terms of democratic accountability and as a requirement of fairness. While the Court did not specify what counts as a clear question, it is possible to envision mechanisms to achieve a clear question, fair to both sides. One possibility is to give each side—the federal government and the Quebec government, in this case—mutual vetoes over the wording of the question. This has the disadvantage of inviting political posturing and polemics into the debate on the issue. A better strategy would be to set up a commission, charged with the task of formulating a clear, unbiased question, and perhaps even oversee other aspects of the referendum process. This commission might conceivably be comprised of a nominee from each of the federal government and the Quebec government, and a third person, agreed to by the first two. This does not preclude input from the respective governments and groups in civil society. Not only is this justifiable in terms of democratic values of transparency and representation, but it would prevent either of the parties from asking a question designed to obfuscate the object of the exercise and thereby secure the desired result.[24]

---

[22] Allen Buchanan, 'Democracy and Secession', in Margaret Moore (ed.), *National Self-Determination and Secession* (Oxford: Oxford University Press, 1998), 21–4.

[23] Ibid., 21.

[24] This was a serious problem in the October 30, 1995 referendum. The salient part of the referendum question asked: 'Do you agree that Quebec should become sovereign, after having made a formal offer to Canada for a new economic and political partnership . . . Yes or No'. Not only is this problematic because it introduced strategic decision-making, instead of basing decisions on first-order preferences, but there is a great deal of confusion about what being 'sovereign' actually involved. Polls in Quebec indicated that many more people were in favour of Quebec being 'sovereign' than Quebec becoming 'a sovereign country' and federalists in the Quebec legislature argued (unsuccessfully) for the latter formulation in the referendum question.

It is also normatively important, in this context, to examine the possible 'vote-pooling' effects of a clear or weighted majority requirement. In some cases, minorities have supported self-determination projects. Indeed, the peaceful breakup of the former Soviet Union has been partially attributed to the fact that many ethnic Russians in republics outside Russia supported it, particularly in referendums in Estonia, Latvia, and the Ukraine.[25] Their support did not rely on historic memories or shared bonds of attachment, and may therefore have been more conditional than the national majority, but evidently it was possible for them to feel not only that it would be economically advantageous, but that their ethnicity was no barrier to full citizenship and inclusion in the newly secessionist state.

To encourage this kind of scenario, Donald Horowitz in *Ethnic Groups in Conflict*, has analysed the dynamics between various ethnic groups in severely divided societies, and has suggested that it is important to design institutional mechanisms to encourage political élites to reach out to minority groups in their midst to address their concerns. Chapter 4 discussed Horowitz's proposal that, in ethnically and nationally divided societies, it is important that electoral systems are designed to have a 'distribution requirement' in addition to straightforward majoritarian rule, and the difficulties of implementing this as an electoral rule in divided societies such as Nigeria. In the context of a right to secession, however, there is no risk attached to failing to meet the requirement—it would just maintain the status quo. Moreover, the weighted majority requirement in a referendum on secession will, in many societies, serve exactly the same kind of 'vote-pooling' function. It does not deny the right of the majority group from exercising its own right to self-determination, its own capacity to determine the conditions of its existence, including the state in which they are to live. However, in certain contexts, such as when there is a significant minority population, it may prevent nationalist leaders from adopting ethnically exclusive, and therefore divisive, appeals, and instead encourage them to reach out to minority communities in their midst, to secure the 'clear majority' that is required.[26]

---

[25] Paul Kolstoe, *Russians in the Former Soviet Republics* (Bloomington, IN: Indiana University Press, 1995), 11, 186.

[26] Sometimes, a 'clear majority' can only be obtained in a much smaller jurisdictional area than nationalists would like. Another advantage of this rule is that it would have the consequence of preventing nationalist groups from maximizing the 'territory' to which they think they are entitled. If the local minority group is both territorially concentrated and strongly opposed to the (local majority's) self-determination project, they may have the option of exercising their own right to self-determination. This would permit both groups to be collectively self-governing.

Perverse Consequences

A positive consequence of adopting the procedural hurdles discussed here is that it may be helpful in preventing a proliferation of national self-determination projects and the deliberate fostering of ethnic or cultural identities into full-blown national ones. It is difficult to specify what ought to 'count' as a nation, particularly since this type of community may be constructed over time, and groups that were not nationally mobilized may become so, in certain conditions. We should be alert to the danger of erecting perverse incentives that encourage leaders to foster national resentments and nationalist mobilization.

The requirement that negotiated secessions are justified when there is support of a weighted majority in a fair and free referendum, subject to a clear question on secession, and hopefully preceded by electoral debate on the issues, would serve to deter what Norman calls 'vanity secessions'.[27] Here, he refers to the Northern League movement in Italy and the attempted secession in Western Australia in the 1930s. By 'vanity secessions', Norman means secessions that do not have just-cause. I don't think the issue is connected to justice at all. I think, however, that he is right that these hurdles would serve a deterrence function, and especially would deter nationalist élites from making nationalist claims that do not have widespread resonance in the population. These procedural hurdles address the criticism that a right to national self-determination would create a proliferation of secessions.

A constitutional right to self-determination, including a right to secession, is necessary because we do not want to trap minorities in states that they do not identify with or regard as legitimate. If their claims and identities are have any moral bearing at all—and this book has argued that they do—we should think about the process by which they can achieve institutional recognition of this identity within the rule of law. A right of exit, involving a duty to negotiate fair terms on outstanding issues on the part of the remainder state, and specifying some procedural hurdles that nationalists would have to overcome, would, I think, increase the power of minorities within the state for greater recognition of their identity. The best method for ensuring that would-be secessionists are unable to muster the requisite majority support in favour of seceding from the state is to accommodate their identity within the state. As is probably clear by now, I regard this increased power to minority nationalists as a positive outcome of constitutionalizing a right to secession. In some cases, minorities will be

[27] Norman, 'The Ethics of Secession as', 55, 57, note 12.

able to use these procedures to give institutional reality to their legitimate aspirations and identities.

The discussion in this section is admittedly speculative, and subject to an implementation problem. By this, I mean that I have not offered any reason why state actors would implement a constitutional right to self-determination. Indeed, in so far as they are largely representative of the state as a whole, their overriding interest would seem to be in preventing secession, either by making it extremely difficult to exercise such a right, or denying the right altogether. In many states likely to experience secessionist movements, the would-be secessionists and majority national (unionist) community are well-known. This is a problem, but it is not a decisive objection. First, it could be argued that a right to secession clause and the fair accommodation of national minorities within the state is the best guarantee that the aspirations of the minority nationalist community will be fulfiled within the existing state. The kind of accommodation that this book is concerned about, and which is implicit in the right to secede from the state, is in fact the best mechanism that the state could employ to ensure the territorial integrity of the state. Second, and more importantly, once we acknowledge that there are legitimate questions about the fair treatment of national groups—and this book attempts to be a contribution to that argument—people who are responsive to considerations of justice and fair treatment may find it hard to ignore the case for including these sorts of rights in the domestic constitution of their (just and democratic) state.

A Right of Secession in International Law

The previous section examined the type of domestic constitutional right to self-determination, including a right to secession, that would be appropriate. One obvious problem with institutionalizing such a right is that most states have no incentive to institutionalize such a right in the absence of a nationalist movement; and any attempt to institutionalize a right when there is a significant nationalist movement for self-determination is apt to be politicized inappropriately.[28] A right with stringent procedural hurdles will probably be viewed as an attempt to deny the right of the minority, or, alternatively, in the case of a permissive right to secede, viewed as a nationalist plot to

---

[28] There may, however, be a 'window' of opportunity when the kind of accommodation associated with a right to self-determination—a domestic secession clause—is precisely what is needed to hold the state together.

dismember the state.[29] In the rare cases where states do have such a right, as in the former Soviet Union, the right was farcical and existed alongside Soviet troops stationed on the territory of the right-holders—the republics—and tight Communist Party control of the republics' governments.

Moreover, those states most likely to adopt a constitutional provision for secession, and to respect such a provision—here Canada comes the closest—already accept the rule of law, liberal justice, and democratic governance. In many parts of the world, where national minorities are persecuted for their religion or language or culture or political aspirations or all of these, there is very little prospect that they would be granted a constitutional right to self-determination, or that such a right would be respected. In these circumstances, victimized minorities have little (non-violent) alternative but to appeal to the international community for external support to legitimize their struggle.

The appeal on the part of national minorities to the international community against the sovereign state in which they live is also testimony to a second, related, problem with institutionalizing a right to self-determination in domestic constitutions. Since the central government is supposed to operate in the interests of the state as a whole state, and of all the citizens in the state, viewed collectively, it is difficult to conceive the central government, or organs of the central government, as impartial arbiters, designing fair rules of the game. There is, therefore, a serious question, which applies to all states, concerning the capacity of the state to render judgements on this issue impartially.[30] This problem of the existing state's neutrality and impartiality on the issue of the rights of national minorities is raised even more acutely when, as is often the case, the central government is the main agent of their persecution. For this reason, institutionalizing a legal right to self-determination in international law would seem to be more promising than in domestic constitutions, because international actors

[29] These obstacles are acknowledged by Norman, 'The Ethics of Secession as', 55. The problem of politicization seemed, initially, to plague the federal government's reference to the Supreme Court in the case of Quebec secession. In this case, the respect that attached to the Court, and the political sagacity of the judgment that was issued—giving a little to both sides—helped to address this initial concern.

[30] There is a parallel problem with indigenous people's rights. Under the property rules of the states in which native peoples were forcibly incorporated, native people do not have clear entitlement to the land. This is so, even though they have occupied the land for millenia, they have an attachment to the land, and have utilized the land under their own cultural rules and structures of government, and have a strong interest in ensuring a continued link with the land. This point is made by Allen Buchanan, 'The Making and Unmaking of Boundaries: a Liberal View', in Allen Buchanan and Margaret Moore (eds.), *The Making and Unmaking of Boundaries* (Princeton, NJ: Princeton University Press, forthcoming).

and institutions have a greater capacity to act in a disinterested fashion. This is especially true if these rights take a procedural form, such as the one outlined in the previous section, involving a sequence of activities that could be verified by third parties.

There is, however, a number of problems attached to any proposal for institutionalizing a right to self-determination at the international level. The first problem is conceptual and connected to rival conceptions of international law and the appropriate relationship of morality to the law. The second problem is connected to the immaturity and neutrality of international institutions, and their capacity to champion a legal right to self-determination. In this regard, the lack of enforcement mechanisms is the most serious problem, but there are other problems with the legitimacy of international institutions. This section concludes by suggesting that, notwithstanding these limitations, there is a number of pressures on the international community for a clear and coherent institutional response to self-determination claims on the part of national minorities.

There are at least two rival conceptions of international law,[31] which have accordingly different views of the appropriate relationship between law and morals, and of the possibility and desirability of giving any kind of legal status to the principle of national self-determination.

The dominant conception of international law, stemming from the 1648 Peace of Westphalia settlement, which ended the Thirty Years War, is that of a system of minimal rules centred on the mutual recognition of state sovereignty.[32] This settlement is commonly viewed as a *modus vivendi* among the various parties to the Thirty Years War not to interfere in one another's territory, or internal matters.[33] There is a number of elements implicit in this view of international relations and the rules that should govern it. At the heart of this settlement is a principle of the absoluteness of state sovereignty. All the other rules that later developed into a system of international law are based on the acceptance of myriad state authorities and power relations. Many of

[31] Andrew Hurrell, 'The Making and Unmaking of Boundaries: International Law' in Buchanan and Margaret Moore (eds.), *The Making and Unmaking of Boundaries*. In this excellent article, Hurrell identifies three images of international law. I have adapted his typology. What he refers to as the 'pluralist statist' image, I call here the 'Westphalian' system.

[32] I am neutral on the issue of whether the 1648 Peace of Westphalia settlement constituted a dramatic break with the system in place or whether it merely consolidated a number of moves made over a period of time in international relations. For the latter view, see Charles Tilley, *Coercion, Capital, and European States, AD 990–1992* (Oxford: Basil Blackwell, 1990), 166–7.

[33] For a clear discussion of the importance of the Westphalian model in the development of international relations, see Daniel Philpott, 'Sovereignty: An Introduction and Brief History', *Journal of International Affairs*, 48/2 (winter 1995), 353–68.

the rules were attempts to elaborate how to determine precise boundaries—for boundaries are fundamental to the system; rules regulating authority over territory and the methods by which this could be altered—occupation, subjugation, cession, accession; as well as rules to promote security, such as the idea of a buffer zone, agreed-on spheres of influence, and the idea of defensible frontiers.[34] The ethical merits of this system rest on the claim that a system based on respecting state sovereignty is necessary to maintain order and stability. The guiding intuition here is that it is better to permit injustices and evils within domestic states than to allow domestic matters to serve as a pretext or justification for intervention, for there will then be no end to war and strife. This view presupposes two further kinds of claims. The first, empirical claim is that there is no consensus, or common ground, on more substantive issues. The most that can be hoped for is coexistence based on the allocation of jurisdictional authority. The second, related claim is that the system has the virtue of permitting many different kinds of societies to coexist. It is therefore a framework for liberty and pluralism.

This is, of course, a very limited conception of the relationship between law and morality. On this view, the law, including the international legal order, should be sharply distinguished from morality, and international law is concerned with the law as it is, not as it ought to be. This view of the relationship between law and morals leaves very little room for moral arguments of the kind put forward in this book, or for the view that particular (moral) rights ought to be institutionalized in international law.

The minimalist rules vision of international law implicit in the Westphalian system has increasingly been challenged by a more solidarist conception of international law, which has been on the ascendant throughout the twentieth century. This rival, solidarist view is characterized by an emphasis on substantive norms and values to govern international society, rather than mere coexistence. Sometimes these solidarist values have been pursued by states acting together; sometimes, they have been pursued through international institutions, such as the World Court. In either case, there have been attempts to cultivate common values, such as the promotion of human rights or democratic governance; but, in other areas too, broader understandings and increased co-operation have been viewed as necessary to deal with common (global) interests—to manage the global economy, to deal with environmental problems, or international crime.

[34] This discussion is taken from Hurrell, 'The Making and Unmaking of Boundaries', 4.

This solidarist vision is a direct challenge to the view associated with the Westphalian system and especially the primacy of territorial integrity and sovereignty of the state. In a number of cases, which are typically viewed as evidence of this increasing push to a solidarist vision of international law and international society, the UN has intervened in domestic affairs of states—in Somalia, Bosnia, Rwanda, Haiti, Iraqi Kurdistan, Kosovo, East Timor, and other places. Intervention has not been applied generally, and has not always been entirely successful, but in these cases, the intervention was not solely motivated by the self-interest of the most powerful states, but was at least partly aimed at either preventing a humanitarian disaster or grave injustices; and these humanitarian aims were viewed, at least in these cases, as outweighing the norm of the absolute sovereignty of the states concerned.

There are three reasons why pressure to alter the norms of international law is likely to continue. The first reason is connected to the process by which international law is made and international norms become recognized and institutionalized. This process is dominated, not by overt power, but by discussion. In many cases, international norms emerge from a broad consensus among state actors—no doubt of course this consensus is disproportionately affected by the more powerful states—but it is still a consensus forged through discussion and reason, not overt threats and coercion. The process by which international law is made—and especially the space that it provides for discussion and debate—means that it will always be a site of contestation. It will be a political space in which different moral and self-interested visions compete with one another to shape the institutional structure of international society.

Moreover, the sharp distinction between law and norms that is implicit in the Westphalian model is extremely problematic, both in theory and in practice. International law is not something independent of norms, but institutionalizes the norms of the international system. It empowers some international actors, while disempowering others. For example, the principle of absolute state sovereignty is itself a norm, which privileges state actors and marginalizes non-state actors, such as national communities and non-governmental agencies, and so on. Because international law is itself a system of institutionalized norms—indeed, it is the *only* set of global institutionalized norms—there is hope on the part of national minorities that international law can be brought to bear on oppressive states.

It is not only the *process* by which international law is made, and the *context* of international law, that fuels the pressure by minorities for changes in the international legal regime, but also its *content*. Specifically, international law is riddled with ethical contradictions and incoherences, many of which are the result of compromises between principles and political practice, or between the two rival conceptions of international law canvassed here. These contradictions create space to challenge the current norms, or to use some norms of international law to challenge others.

The contradictions are of course embedded in the United Nations Charter itself, which states its commitment both to human rights and the sovereignty of states.[35] The contradictions with respect to the principle of self-determination in international law and political practice since 1945 have been extensively documented,[36] but, like a commitment to any other substantive norm, it runs directly up against the commitment to the absolute sovereignty of states. The right to 'self-determination of peoples' is endorsed in Article 1, par. 2 and Article 55 of the United Nations Charter. This principle has of course potentially far-reaching consequences, and so, in qualified by numerous other articles in the UN Charter affirming the sanctity of the principle of the territorial integrity of states and denying the right of the UN or its member states to intervene in the internal affairs of recognized states.[37] For example, the 1970 UN Declaration regarding the right of secession makes it clear that the UN condemns 'any action aimed at the partial or total disruption of the national unity and territorial integrity of any other state or country'.[38] In 1970, UN Secretary General U Thant argued that the recognition of a state by the international community and its acceptance into the UN implied acceptance of its territorial integrity and sovereignty. He added, 'the United Nations' attitude is unequivocable. As an international organization, the United Nations has never accepted and does not accept and I do not believe it will ever accept the principle of secession of a part of its Member State.'[39]

---

[35] Marianne Heiberg, *Subduing sovereignty: Sovereignty and the Rights to Intervene* (London: Pinter, 1994), 9.

[36] See Rupert Emerson, 'Self-determination', *American Journal of International Law*, 65 (1971), 459–76, at 464–6; Rosemary Higgings, *Problems and Progress: International Law and How We Use It* (Oxford: Clarendon Press, 1994); Alexis Heraclides, 'Secession, self-determination and non-intervention: in quest of a normative symbiosis', *Journal of International Affairs*, 45 (1992), 399–420; Brendan O'Leary, 'Determining Our Selves: on the norm of national self-determination', Paper presented to the *International Political Science Association*, Berlin, Germany (August, 1994).

[37] See Emerson, 'Self-determination', 463.

[38] Quoted in Alexis Heraclides, *The Self-determination of Minorities in International Politics* (London: Frank Cass, 1991), 21.

[39] This was in the context of the attempted secession by Biafra of Nigeria. Quoted in Emerson, 'Self-determination', 464.

The main strategy adopted by the member states and the United Nations to limit the potentially destablizing scope of the principle of self-determination is to narrowly define the right-holders. Thus, the right to self-determination has been qualified by a whole series of resolutions passed by sovereign states, concerned about the potentially destructive effects for them of this principle. The main effect of this is to make it clear that the 'peoples' in question are not national groups, but rather, peoples within territorial states; and that the right to self-determination could only be invoked by people under Colonial rule or people living under alien or racist regimes— Palestinians under Israeli occupation, blacks under apartheid in South Africa, respectively.[40]

The strategy of narrowing the right to self-determination to certain classes of right-holders is both unconvincing and ethically problematic. It is difficult to justify why the right to self-determination of peoples living under colonial rule can only be exercised *once* to restore sovereignty to the people, who had been illegitimately deprived of it by the colonial power, but can never be used again.[41] This makes sense in terms of the political interests of sovereign states who are concerned about their territorial integrity, but certainly not to unhappy national groups inside these states who question the legitimacy of the states.

The moral idea justifying both democracy and decolonization is surely that political power should be in the hands of the people over whom it is exercised. This provides some basis for condemning states dominated by a particular national group that exercised power and control over another national group. It might be 'politically correct' to describe only Western powers controlling overseas territories as imperialists, but it is not factually correct: the term 'imperialism' can be coherently and persuasively applied to any attempt by one people to dominate politically another people, especially if the latter perceive the rule to be hostile to their national identity.[42]

---

[40] Anna Michalska, 'Rights of Peoples to Self-determination in International Law' in William Twining (ed.), *Issues of Self-determination* (Aberdeen: Aberdeen University Press, 1991); Donald Horowitz, 'Self-Determination: Politics, Philosophy, and Law' in Margaret Moore (ed.), *National Self-Determination and Secession* (Oxford: Oxford University Press, 1998), 181–214, at 200–3.

[41] This point is made by O'Leary, 'Determining Our Selves', 3.

[42] Most theories of imperialism are Marxist and are linked by Marxists to capitalism. However, many people have called the Soviet rule over non-Russian nationalities 'Russian imperialism' and have emphasized the continuity between Tsarist and Communist nationalities policies. See Hugh Seton-Watson, *Nations and States: an Enquiry into the Origins of Nations and the Politics of Nationalism* (London: Methuen, 1977), 77–87, 188–91.

Other inconsistencies flow from this very narrow interpretation of the principle of self-determination of peoples.[43] Why, for example, should a *majority* suffering racist discrimination—blacks in South Africa under apartheid—be entitled to self-determination but not *minorities* in a state who are suffering under racist or discriminatory policies—a much more common phenomenon? And why are Palestinians the only people living under 'alien' rule when there are many national groups who perceive the state as alien to them and hostile to their national identity?

The dissolution of the former Soviet Union and former Yugoslavia, in particular, has given new urgency to the need to consider the appropriate relation of national identity to the state and international state system. The inconsistencies and ethical shortcomings of international law are not merely a theoretical or conceptual problem, but a pressing practical issue. In the former Soviet Union, the West—most notably, former US President Bush in his famous 'Chicken Kiev' speech—supported Gorbachev, who had no democratic legitimacy, and very little popular support, against popular democratically-elected national leaders, until it was apparent, on the ground, that the Soviet Union had collapsed. Similarly, the response of the international community to the dissolution of the former Yugoslavia was first to try to hold Yugoslavia together, thereby wasting valuable time in which it could have searched for a just settlement of these rival claims to national self-determination.

Faced with the collapse of these federations, the (belated) response of the international community—the UN and the EU, in particular—was to recognize the self-determination of peoples, defined in territorial terms, as members of specific republics, but not as national groups. Federations could disintegrate along the lines of their constituent units, but there was to be no reconsideration of borders, 'no secessions from secessions'.[44] This was so, even though it was evident that many people living within the republican borders of the former Yugoslavia did not share this view. Once secession was inevitable, or had occurred *de facto*, the international community reluctantly accepted it, but attempted to limit its 'damage' by applying a territorial understanding of 'peoples'. Indeed, the Badinter Arbitration Committee specifically mentioned concern about the 'stability of frontiers', even in a case— the former Yugoslavia—where the *external* frontier of the former

---

[43] These arguments are also found in O'Leary, 'Determining Our Selves', 1–3; and Horowitz, 'Self-determination', 200–2.

[44] A. Pellet, 'The opinions of the Badinter Arbitration Committee: a second breath for the self-determination of peoples', *European Journal of International Law*, 3 (1992), 184.

Yugoslavia was not being disputed; and it justified its decision in terms of the principle of 'territorial integrity', which it described as 'this great principle of peace, indispensable to international stability'.[45]

Whatever one might think of the merits of this and related legal decisions, it is now widely accepted that the international community's response in Bosnia was profoundly inadequate, and provided for neither stability nor peace. The idea of national self-determination has profound resonance across the globe, and it is necessary to elaborate ways of dealing with the national dimension of these conflicts, so that a peaceful solution can be achieved.

What, then, are the prospects for institutionalizing a right to (national) self-determination and specifying the process by which the right can be accorded? First, international law is relevant principally because it is a set of institutional norms; and if the norm of (national) self-determination becomes accepted and recognized as legitimate, this will influence the actions of individual states. The main tool that external individual states have concerning a right to self-determination is the prerogative of recognition: when a state dissolves, the issue of being recognized by other states arises, and this carries with it not only the conferral of legitimacy but also implied diplomatic or even military support. There are two main problems with recognition as an instrument for advancing a right. The first problem is that it is a very limited form of support. The second problem is that recognition is currently viewed as the prerogative of individual states—not based on shared norms—and, like other foreign policy issues, is subject to the vagaries of domestic politics, self-interest, and other factors.

The Security Council, while potentially more disinterested than single states, is also not wholly impartial, comprised as it is by the most powerful countries, who often make decisions based on their own interests. In a number of cases—Somalia, Bosnia, Rwanda—where the UN has intervened in the affairs of sovereign countries, it has acted on humanitarian grounds, and not merely as an extension of power politics.[46] Nevertheless, these interventions have depended to an uncomfortable extent on the diplomatic and military support of the United States.

The most impartial international institution that could conceivably oversee a secessionist process is a world court.[47] This would require,

---

[45] Ibid., 180.

[46] This argument is from Daniel Philpott, 'Self-Determination in Practice', in Margaret Moore (ed.), *National Self-Determination and Secession* (Oxford: Oxford University Press, 1998), 79–102, at 86–7.

[47] Ibid.

not merely the establishment of a judicial body to assess the merits of a national self-determination case, but also an executive to enforce its decisions. A true court of international justice, and enforcement mechanisms to ensure compliance with it, is probably ideal from the standpoint of institutionalizing a moral right to self-determination, but is not likely to be realized in the near (foreseeable) future. Even without the institutional developments that would be necessary—a full judicial body, with enforcement mechanisms—individual state recognition and practice based on the norm of national self-determination would be an important step forward.

This would represent an advance, particularly for the kind of right to self-determination argued for in this book, which requires only that various procedural criteria are met. A just-cause theory, by contrast, would require a judicial or quasi-judicial body, like a world court, to consider whether standards have been violated, and whether intervention is sanctioned. A procedural right, on the other hand, only requires outside observers, of the kind often used to monitor the fairness of elections, and may be partially institutionalized if the norm becomes generally recognized, as part of international law, and state action. A policy of respecting the rights of one's own minorities, including their right to self-determination, and a recognition policy that is governed by those norms, could be effective, even without (or prior to) a full-fledged world court body with enforcement mechanisms.

Current international law and practice is far too confining, and a right such as the kind proposed here would be useful in reaching a more just and stable resolution of national conflicts. Consider the failed response, consistent with international law, of the international community to the situation in Kosovo, which, as this book goes to the press, means that Kosovo is *de facto* an independent entity, but the international community cannot recognize Kosovo as a *de jure* state— because, to do so would violate the principle of territorial integrity. Even after the massive forced transfer of population by the Yugoslav government, the international community was unwilling to fully come to terms with the fact that the Kosovars should not be forced to live within a Yugoslavian state, even symbolically, and unwilling also to recognize that the Serb minority would be vulnerable in a Kosovar Albanian-dominated state. The international force in Kosovo cannot, in these circumstances, properly protect the Serb national minority there.

Consider, by contrast, the implications for international law of the arguments advanced in this book. In Chapters 6 and 7, I argued against the inviolability of administrative boundaries, against the approach of the Badinter Commission, and in favour of the occupancy principle. It is obvious from this argument that minorities should have the right to opt out of a state-wide (or territory-wide) vote on secession. These principles, applied to Kosovo, would permit the mainly Kosovar Albanian population to secede from Yugoslavia, either to form its own state or join, by mutual consent, the Albanian state. I also argued that there should be some provision, along the lines of the Swiss principle of 'rolling cantonization', to partition administrative units if there were two rival national communities, and this facilitated their respective self-determination projects. This implies a right of the Serb minority in Kosovo, in areas where they constitute a majority, and that are contiguous with the border, to remain within Yugoslavia, if they choose. Minorities outside this area should be able to exercise local self-government, and should have their linguistic and religious rights protected. This does not address all the problems, of course: there will still be issues of compensation and of Serb access to historical or religious sites, as discussed in Chapter 7. However, just as Serbia/ Yugoslavia should not be able to deny the self-governing aspirations of Kosovo, so the Kosovars should not be able to deny the national identities and aspirations that Serbians feel for their own collective self-government. It is a different (non-moral) issue, of course, if groups are so dispersed that they are unable to exercise full territorial self-government.

The issue of flexibility of international law to achieve the resolution of national conflict is an important issue, in itself, of course, but also important to the international community. Third-party intervention by the international community is increasingly concerned with finding macro-political institutional responses to the conflicts, rather than just (permanently) separating the parties to the conflict through armed force.

There are several limitations to the formula advanced in the book, which are related to the context or situation of the group and the requirements of collective self-government. Groups that are not territorially concentrated—or who lack territory—cannot exercise political self-government, but can only have individual rights and cultural recognition within the political community. A second kind of limitation to the general application of this formula is posed by the fact that most groups, while territorially concentrated to some degree, do not have 'hard' borders, but are often demographically intermingled. The next section discusses the kinds of collective recognition that may be appropriate in these situations, and the emerging possibilities for more complex institutional designs.

Minority Nationalism and Globalization, or: Is Nationalism Still Relevant?

There are some who may object to the argument of this book, and especially to the view presented here that nationalism is a powerful source of identity in the modern world that we should accommodate, or, at the minimum, find institutional mechanisms and procedures to cope with. There are different aspects of this basic position—some, more flimsy than others—but two powerful sources of this argument are the views that these identities are not based on 'real' differences and that they are being eroded by globalization; and that the nation-state model is based on a nineteenth century, anachronistic view of sovereignty.

We can dispense with the first claim quite quickly. The view that nations are eroded by globalization is based on the empirical claim that various elements of the global economy—increased migration, travel, communications technology, economic integration—have an important cultural dimension. Specifically, they are leading to the creation of a global culture, which, it is claimed, will erode more particularist (minority nationalist) forms of identity.

One problem with this, as I argued in Chapter 3, is that this view presupposes a false view of the relationship between cultures and nations. In fact, even if cultural differences become less significant, this does not necessarily lead to the erosion of national identities. This view also seems to falsely suggest that the fact that national identities are socially constructed means that they are easy to deconstruct—that minorities can be assimilated or these identities can be replaced by non-territorial forms of allegiances, based on gender, sexual orientation or function. As I argued in Chapter 1, this doesn't follow. Indeed, the evidence suggests that national identities are highly resistant to assimilation—and especially public policies designed to facilitate it—and that minority nationalism is quite resilient and contextual: it is a form of political mobilization that can be adapted to new contexts. There is very little empirical evidence of the erosion of minority nationalism in the new, global context. There is some evidence that conglomerate identities, such as the British and Swiss identities, have been weakened, but most of the empirical evidence suggests growth in support for minority nationalism. The processes associated with globalization have coincided with the emergence of significant nationalist movements in the Basque Country, Catalonia, Scotland, Quebec, and elsewhere. The evidence suggests that globalization has had a transformative effect on nationalism—in Quebec, for example, a conservative religious (Catholic) rural traditional nationalism was replaced or remobilized into a strong secular and more secessionist nationalism— but not that nationalism in general is likely to wither away.

The second source of the view that nationalism is no longer relevant points to the rapid changes in the inter-state order, and the erosion of the traditional (nineteenth century) nation-state model, both by regional and supranational institutions. Many proponents of cosmopolitanism, and critics of minority nationalism, have argued that minority nations are a romantic and conservative reaction or resistance to global economic forces, which make no sense in the global economy. What is needed, it is suggested, is increased international co-operation to cope with the global reality of the economy, not the proliferation of smaller and smaller units, claiming sovereignty over smaller and smaller pieces of territory.

This view frequently draws on the work of historians of nationalism, such as Hobsbawm, who have pointed out that the nation-state is a modern construction, and was a functional political form in the nineteenth century, with the modernization of the economy, and the bureaucratization of the state. Nationalism, or the modern nation-state, it is suggested, no longer makes sense. Supranational political institutions are necessary to cope with the interdependent nature of the global economy. Minority nationalism, by which is meant the assertion of small nationalities within larger states, is an attempt to copy the nation-state model, which is, itself, outdated, and should be dismissed as a doomed romanticism.

There is some truth in this argument. It is true that absolute sovereignty on the Westphalian model makes less and less sense in the global economic era. Practice has, to some extent, overtaken theory. First, as I argued earlier in this chapter, the Westphalian ideal of absolute sovereignty has been challenged by the view of international law and the international community acting in defence of certain norms or a certain conception of state legitimacy. On this newer view, the international community has some obligations toward individual members of other states. It is difficult to pinpoint the origins of this view, or even to claim that it is now the dominant one, for it is certainly not consistently applied or universally accepted, but, by the 1970s, there was certainly a strong view that *legitimate* states have to meet minimal standards of human rights towards their (individual) members. This was the basic insight behind the anti-apartheid movement, which sought to isolate South Africa from the rest of the international community, and also underlay the 1975 Helsinki Accords, and the Copenhagen Agreement of 1990, which superseded the earlier

Helsinki Accords.[48] It is also, arguably, the fundamental idea behind the earlier decolonization movement. More recently, as I mentioned earlier, there have been several cases of international intervention in the 'domestic affairs' of states, which suggests that the era of the individual nation-state is being transformed and that any nation that is seeking national independence or national sovereignty in the traditional sense is probably revering an ideal whose time is passing.

Moreover, the traditional nation-state model, developed in the nineteenth century, viewed the economic sphere in national terms, as subject to national regulations and controls. Historically, states were instrumental in breaking down the barriers erected by the medieval charters of towns and corporations, as well as instituting a common currency and a common system of weights and measures.[49] Central to eighteenth- and nineteenth century nation-building policies was the promotion of national economic policy. This frequently involved various forms of protectionism, in addition to internal liberalization and the development of infrastructure to facilitate capitalist development.

This traditional nation-state model is challenged by the globalization of the economy, and especially the mobility of capital markets. These have reduced the ability of the state to pursue national economic policies. States have had to respond to this new situation by restructuring the economy, with various forms of regional mobilizations, such as NAFTA, ASEAN, the EU, Mercosur. These have further limited the sovereignty of individual member states by constraining them to abide by the rules and procedures—and, in the case of the EU, the law—of the association.

In this context, the idea of absolute sovereignty and autarkic economic policies for small nations make very little sense. In fact, it made very little sense prior to this erosion of state sovereignty. For example, in 1945, Alfred Cobban, in his book *National Self-Determination*, criticized President Woodrow Wilson's principle of national self-determination on the grounds that economic autarky on the part of smaller states would not work, that these minority nations could not be viable states in the sense of pursuing their own independent

---

[48] Allen Buchanan also makes the link between political legitimacy and the anti-apartheid movement. Allen Buchanan, 'Democracy and Secession', in Margaret Moore (ed.), *National Self-Determination and Secession* (Oxford: Oxford University Press, 198), 14–33. See also Thomas M. Franck, 'The Emerging Right to Democratic Governance', *American Journal of International Law*, 86 (1992), 46–91.

[49] Michael Keating, *Nations Against the State. The New Politics of Nationalism in Quebec, Catalonia and Scotland* (London: MacMillan, 1996), 30–3; Eugene Weber, *Peasants into Frenchmen: The Modernization of Rural France, 1870–1914* (London: Routledge & Kegan Paul, 1979).

national economic policy.[50] In the era in which he wrote, where the international state system presupposed national economies, Cobban was right.

However, many contemporary minority nations, operating in the context of regional economic associations and the erosion of absolute sovereignty, do not aspire to this form of control over their economy. Most minority nationalists do not seek to resurrect the traditional sovereign nation-state on an even smaller scale, with complete national control over their economy. Many minority nationalists in Quebec and Western Europe—Catalonia, Flanders, Scotland—are liberal-democrats: they support access to a global economy and favour the regional associations that make this possible, as well as traditional liberal and democratic rights and the rule of law. They have supported liberalization of the economy, although with a concern that this is consistent with the reproduction of their culture and identity.

It is wrong, therefore, to associate minority nationalism with a backward-looking quest to realize the Westphalian sovereignty system. This is to saddle minority nationalists with the charge of being anachronistic and romantic, in the pejorative sense, which is quite against the evidence. Rather, minority nationalism can convincingly be seen as a particular response to the global restructuring of the economy. In some cases, nations which could not be viable under the traditional nation-state model, described by Cobban, have a role to play in the context of regional economic associations and military defence pacts.

While critics have argued that the changing context has affected the sovereignty and independence of states, and so made the very idea of state sovereignty questionable, one could claim, on the contrary, that the new context has opened up a new political space in which minority nations can co-operate and have changed the criteria of viability—after all, in what sense is Luxembourg 'viable'? Minority nations are no longer as dependent on their host multinational or binational state, and are more dependent on international and continental regimes, like NAFTA or the EU, and the IMF. Sovereignty is, indeed, being transformed into something quite different, but this does not mean the demise of minority nationalism. Rather, these developments have redefined national autonomy as a space in which nations, and especially small nations, can play off their various forms of dependency against one another.[51] Moreover, while transnational institutions have

---

[50] Alfred Cobban, *National Self-Determination* (Oxford: Oxford University Press, 1945), 157–66.

[51] Keating, *Nations Against the State*, 62–4.

diminished sovereignty, having a state within one of those institutions matters. Consider the cases of Ireland and Scotland. Both are similar in size, but Ireland has more clout within the EU because it is a state. This is a point made repeatedly by the Scottish Nationalist Party in Scotland.[52]

Moreover, there is a plausible case, put forward by Michael Keating in his book *Nations Against the State*, that, in this increasingly global economy, smaller units like nations have advantages over larger nation-states.[53] This is partly because they have a higher degree of interaction and mutual trust, and this social consensus helps to manage change. Even more importantly, small nations, in part because of this high degree of social interaction, can adapt more quickly to changes in their environment, and are better positioned to promote local skills and resources, which is crucial to adapting to changes in the global environment.

In short, the challenges posed by the global economy do not seem to lead in the direction of breaking down these forms of identity, or rendering them irrelevant. There is little empirical support for the general view that minority national identities are being eroded by the forces associated with globalization. Indeed, there is strong evidence that in fact the global economy will facilitate the emergence of new nationalism, because in this context minority nationalism is more viable.

The processes associated with globalization are particularly relevant for the ethics of secession, not only because, as I've argued, there may well be more of them, but because this new interdependent world raises more opportunities for conflict-regulation and conflict-management. There are clearly cases where permitting secession, or allowing the separation of two groups, makes sense. The previous chapter discussed the growing consensus that partition would be an appropriate way to resolve the Israeli-Palestinian conflict, given that the two groups are largely segregated from each other and that each of them is overwhelmingly wedded to ethnic self-determination—although this is not simply a question of separation because more complex institutional arrangements are appropriate to deal with the special status of Jerusalem to both groups, and to allow access to and control over sites of special historic and religious significance. A reasonable argument

[52] James Mitchell and Michael Cavanagh, 'Context and Contingency: Constitutional Nationalists and Europe', in Michael Keating and John McGarry (eds.), *Minority Nationalism and the Changing International Order* (Oxford: Oxford University Press, forthcoming).
[53] Keating, *Nations Against the State*, 52–8.

could be made that partition in 1974 was the correct response to the Cypriot conflict, given that many people were killed in the fighting that preceded partition, and that hardly any have been killed since—although the precise lines of partition are clearly unfair. However, even in this case, any partitionist solution should be accompanied by some overarching institutional arrangement that recognizes Greek Cypriot attachment to the island as a whole. There is a good argument that the Allies should have carved up the Austro-Hungarian Empire in a way that respected self-determination rather than punished losers and rewarded victors, for this might have prevented many of the minority problems that contributed to the Second World War. In other areas, also, where peaceful coexistence seems out of the question, as in Chechnya, or Nagorno-Karabakh, a strong case could be made for methods of conflict management that rely on separating the groups in question—as secession does.

However, as has been emphasized at various times in the previous two chapters, secession should not be viewed as a general model of solving ethnic conflict, for it is only appropriate in certain contexts. The first problem with secessionist solutions is that in some conflict zones, national groups are interspersed in such a way that secession is not a practical option, at least not without massive ethnic cleansing. This is the case in Northern Ireland, for example. Any redrawing of the boundary to bring a larger number of Catholics into the Republic of Ireland would still leave a significant number of Catholics within a truncated Northern Ireland. While partition might address the concerns of Magyars living close to the Romanian border with Hungary, it is difficult to see it as a solution for their co-ethnics who live in the Romanian interior.

Finally, secessionist solutions to national conflicts are not generally sensitive to the kind of national identity that the group evinces. Many members of minority nations have overlapping or nested identities. Thus, large numbers of Quebec Francophones feel both Québécois *and* Canadian; large numbers of Scots consider themselves to be both Scottish and British; and many Catalans see no incompatibility between their Catalan and Spanish identities. In all of these cases, and many others, secession would satisfy one part of an individual's identity at the expense of the other.

In these cases, more imaginative constitutional changes are necessary. There is some evidence of the positive effects of globalization on this front. Specifically, while globalization has not eliminated particularist identities, especially minority nationalist ones, it has created new political space that facilitates the management of national conflict.

There are three areas which suggest the positive effects of globalization.

First, there has been a trend toward third-party intervention, mainly limited to securing quite specific humanitarian goals, such as delivering food aid and medical supplies, but also designed to achieve more permanent peace. In this context, external agencies have been involved in designing the political and institutional structures to achieve peace and justice, which generally involve provision for some kinds of group rights or limited forms of autonomy.

Another positive result is that it is more difficult for governments to repress minorities without bearing some of the costs of this repression. The spread of democratic and human rights norms, combined with the proliferation of non-governmental and intergovernmental agencies that expose these transgressions, means that governments are not given a completely free hand with respect to their minorities, but have to contend with international pressure. This should not be exaggerated: minority–majority relations are still rarely based on mutual respect and co-operation, and in some places, such as Rwanda and Iraq, are characterized by overt brutality, murder, and repression. Nevertheless, these international norms have signalled an improvement in minority treatment, especially when the state in question tends to care about international principles and international approbation. Indeed, in some cases, direct pressure has been applied to countries to accord rights to their minorities: some of the harsher 'nation-building' policies, which tended to have a discriminatory effect on Russian minorities in the Baltics, were rescinded, following pressure from the EU and the Organization for Security and Co-operation in Europe (OSCE).[54]

Finally, the trend toward sovereignty pooling in mutual defence associations and regional economic associations—which, at one level, can be viewed as a response to globalization because it represents an attempt by states to position themselves in the global economic marketplace—opens up possibilities for more imaginative institutional arrangements, which could have a conflict-management dimension. It suggests the possibility of moving beyond the nation-state model, which recognizes only one national identity within a particular territory, to more complex institutional arrangements, which require deepened intergovernmental co-operation and sovereignty pooling. These types of arrangements may permit the recognition of different

[54] Details can be found in Julie Bernier, 'Nationalism in Transition: Nationalizing Impulses and International Counterweights in Latvia and Estonia', in Michael Keating and John McGarry, *Minority Nationalism and the Changing International Order*.

national identities. This is normatively important in cases where the identities in question are nested in particular ways, or in cases where the group in question is so territorially intermingled that this represents the only fair method to give institutional recognition to these identities.

Acceptance of the principle, argued for in this book, of (non-aggrandizing) national self-determination has important practical and moral policy implications. In Bosnia, for example, prior to the forced expulsion of large numbers of people during the war, there was no way of drawing boundaries that would have 'solved' the nationalities problem by separating antagonistic groups. According to the 1991 census, Bosnia-Hercegovina comprised 44 per cent Slav Muslim, 31 per cent Serb, 17 per cent Croat, and 5 per cent Yugoslav—in practice, people in, or children of, mixed marriages. It had no dominant national group and no neat dividing line along which to fragment, because, with the exception of Croat-populated Hercegovina, the different national groups were thoroughly mixed.[55] Nevertheless, recognition of the importance and legitimacy of national ties, combined with the view that administrative boundaries (internal borders) are not inviolable, but must have demonstrated democratic legitimacy, in fair plebiscites or referenda, would have led the international community to develop a different policy with regard to Bosnia. The West would not have been eager to extend international recognition to a *civic* Bosnian state, in which all people have rights as *individuals*. The obvious route, following from acceptance of these two principles, would have been negotiations with all national groups to arrive at a solution which recognizes the *equal* right of all nationalities.

Moreover, a fair referendum, or number of referenda, on a clear question would have enabled the international community to identify whether or not a secessionist solution was appropriate. Any application of the principle of recursive secession—secession from a secession—in Bosnia-Hercegovina would not have resulted in a satisfactory settlement, but would have involved a patchwork of enclaves or pockets of sovereign units throughout the republic. Where the communities are intermingled in this way, and the domino threat is genuine, different mechanisms for realizing the fundamental principle of giving equal recognition to national identities are necessary. At the same time, a unitary, civic Bosnian state would be exposed as clearly inadequate, because unacceptable to some of the national groups that make up the

[55] Christopher Bennett, *Yugoslavia's Bloody Collapse; Causes, Course and Consequences* (New York, NY: New York University Press, 1995), 53.

country. One possible arrangement, among others, would have been a loose federation, in which the constituent elements were subject to a unifying treaty for certain purposes, but retained their individual sovereignty and international identity for other purposes.[56] This would have enabled the Serb and Croat national groups to develop links with their co-nationals in Serbia and Croatia, without violating the equal right of the Bosnian Muslims to determine their own group's future. This would also represent an attempt to move beyond the Westphalian nation-state model, not only through devolved sovereignty, into relatively autonomous constituent units, but also by developing shared sovereignty arrangements where groups in the society wish this.

Similarly, in Northern Ireland, a partitionist settlement is not optimal, because the existence of both communities in enclaves throughout the province, but particularly in Belfast, means that there is no way to solve the fundamental problem of majority and minority through boundary-drawing (separation). Giving importance to national self-determination without domination requires imaginative solutions, which go beyond a purely 'internal' settlement. The Anglo-Irish Agreement of 1985 represented the first step in a more imaginative move beyond the Westphalian model, for it pointed the way towards an internal power-sharing government combined with a joint role for the British and Irish governments in governing Northern Ireland. The fundamental idea behind this Agreement was the recognition of two distinct, national identities. The equal recognition of national identities has been deepened by the Good Friday Agreement of 1998, which provides for mechanisms to realize a power-sharing executive within Northern Ireland between the two—Protestant/British and Catholic/Irish—communities over some areas of jurisdiction, while some areas of jurisdictional authority are governed by an all-Ireland body, and others by the United Kingdom. Settlements such as this underline the fact that in nationally divided communities, the best hope of achieving lasting peace is through institutions that are based on recognizing distinct national identities. In many cases, equal recognition cannot be realized by the creation of two nation-states, but only through complex institutional arrangements involving sovereignty sharing, and the creation of multiple political spaces to recognize and accommodate identities.

It is not clear, of course, to what extent these sorts of arrangements can be duplicated in other conflict-zones. In Northern Ireland, these

[56] For a discussion of these options, see Daniel Elazar, *Federalism and the Way to Peace* (Kingston: Queen's University Institute of Intergovernmental Affairs, 1994).

sorts of arrangements were facilitated, first, by the fact that the two external actors—Britain and Ireland—have good relations, and, second, because they are partners of relatively equal stature. This was not so historically, for Ireland was clearly the junior partner, but the relationship has equalized, in part, by the recent economic success of Ireland, and by the structure of the European Union and continued co-operation in that context.[57]

In addition, the ceding of sovereignty to the European Union may set a precedent for the decentralization of power to national minorities within the state, which make this kind of step politically possible. Regional economic associations can also be designed in ways that allow for some recognition of national minorities, short of secession, such as the EU's Committee of the Regions. Within the EU, regions within states are beginning to co-operate even across state frontiers, and regions of states are included in the policy-making process of the European Commission. These developments, still admittedly in their infancy, at least open up the possibility of different channels of access to Brussels and the international community. These types of institutional structures could be developed and enhanced to allow for greater international recognition of those regions that represent minority national identities. This could help to manage national conflicts, not only by making secession less attractive, but by creating political space in which more than one national identity can be given institutional recognition.

It remains an open question whether these more imaginative arrangements will be extended beyond the limited attempts seen so far, and, even more so, whether this phenomenon, which has progressed the farthest in Europe, will be repeated in other parts of the world. Of course, even if the conditions for giving fair institutional recognition of minorities are not universally present, this does not impugn the principle of national self-determination, which ultimately justifies these institutional arrangements.

Conclusion

Throughout this book, I have argued in favour of the institutional recognition of national identities, and in this chapter, I have outlined the kind of procedural right that should be institutionalized either in

[57] John McGarry, 'Globalization, European Integration and the Northern Ireland Conflict', in Michael Keating and John McGarry (eds.), *Minority Nationalism and the Changing International Order* (Oxford: Oxford University Press, forthcoming).

domestic constitutions or in international law, or both. To some extent, the discussion in this chapter has been somewhat speculative, because there is little likelihood that domestic states or international law will be transformed in the right direction, at least in the short term. It is not surprising that the rights and norms outlined in domestic constitutions and international law, which have been created by states, run strongly in favour of maintaining the territorial integrity of existing states, and that these states are very reluctant to change these norms. However, this does not itself bring into question the moral right that minority nations have to self-determination; rather, it brings into question the legitimacy of current procedures and practices.

The last third of this chapter has argued that we may be moving beyond the traditional Westphalian nation-state. International and continental regimes have replaced some of the functions of the traditional sovereign state. But this does not mean that minority nationalism is harking back to an ideal whose time has passed. Rather, this new context has opened up opportunities that may permit new forms of nationalism to flourish. Globalization has helped to give rise to a new context of both international regimes and international co-operation in a global economy, and local and regional forms of social solidarity to cope with these changes. At the same time, there are new opportunities for recognition of different national identities, and effort should be expended on encouraging these developments. I've argued throughout this book that the strongest claim that national minorities make is a claim to fair treatment. If we can create structures and institutions that treat these groups fairly, we will be closer to realizing a more just world.

SELECT BIBLIOGRAPHY

Adamson, I. (1974), *Cruthin: The Ancient Kindred* (Newtownards: Nos-mada Books).

Akenson, D. H. (1991), *God's Peoples: Covenant and Land in South Africa, Israel, and Ulster* (Montreal and Kingston: McGill-Queen's University Press).

Anderson, B. (1993), *Imagined Communities: Reflections on the Origin and Spread of Nationalism* (London and New York, NY: Verso).

Appiah, K. A. (1996), 'Cosmopolitan Patriots', in J. Cohen (ed.), *For Love of Country* (Boston, MA: Beacon Press).

Arend, A. C. and Beck, R. (1993), *International Law and the Use of Force: Beyond the U.N. Charter* (New York, NY: Routledge).

Armitage, A. (1995), *Comparing the Policy of Aboriginal Assimilation: Australia, Canada, New Zealand* (Vancouver: University of British Columbia Press).

Armstrong, J. (1982), *Nations Before Nationalism* (Chapel Hill, NC: University of North Carolina Press).

Attanasio, J. B. (1991), 'The Rights of Ethnic Minorities: The Emerging Mosaic', *Notre Dame Law Review*, 66: 1205–8.

Bahcheli, T. (forthcoming), 'Missing the European Train? Turkish Cypriots, the European Union Option, and the Resolution of the Conflict in Cyprus', in M. Keating and J. McGarry (eds.), *Minority Nationalism and the Changing International Order* (Oxford: Oxford University Press).

Barry, B. (1991), 'Self-Government Revisited', in *Democracy and Power, Essays in Political Theory I* (Oxford: Clarendon Press).

——(1995), *Justice as Impartiality* (Oxford: Clarendon Press).

Bauböck, R. (1998), 'Differentiating Citizenship', Paper for the 'Conference Citizenship and Cosmopolitanism', University of Wisconsin, Madison, Wisconsin, November 6–8, 1998.

——(2000), 'Why Stay Together? A Pluralist Approach to Secession and Federation', in W. Kymlicka and W. Norman, (eds.), *Citizenship in Diverse Societies: Theory and Practice* (Oxford: Oxford University Press).

——(unpublished), 'Self-determination and self-government', March 1999 version of manuscript.

Bauer, O. (1996), 'The Nation', in G. Balakrishnan (ed.), *Mapping the Nation* (London and New York, NY: Verso).

Bayart, J-F., Ellis, S. and Hibou, B. (1999), *The Criminalisation of the State in Africa* (Bloomington, IN: Indiana University Press).

Beiner, R. (1999), 'Nationalism's Challenge to Political Philosophy', in R. Beiner (ed.), *Theorizing Nationalism* (Albany, NY: State University of New York Press), 1–25.

Beitz, C. (1989), *Political Equality* (Princeton, NJ: Princeton University Press).

Bell, D. V. J. (1992), *The Roots of Disunity: a Study of Canadian Political Culture* (Toronto: Oxford University Press).

Benner, E. (1995), *Really Existing Nationalisms: A Post-Communist View from Marx and Engels* (Oxford: Clarendon Press).

Bennett, C. (1995), *Yugoslavia's Bloody Collapse: Causes, Course and Consequences* (New York, NY: New York University Press).

Beran, H. (1984), 'A Liberal Theory of Secession', *Political Studies*, 32: 21–31.

Bernier, J. (forthcoming), 'Nationalism in Transition: Nationalizing Impulses and International Counterweights in Latvia and Estonia', in M. Keating and J. McGarry (eds.), *Minority Nationalism and the Changing International Order* (Oxford: Oxford University Press).

Birch, A. H. (1984), 'Another Liberal Theory of Secession', *Political Studies*, 32: 596–602.

Brighouse, H. (1996), 'Against Nationalism', in J. Couture, K. Nielsen, and M. Seymour (eds.), *Rethinking Nationalism, Canadian Journal of Philosophy* Supplementary Volume, 22: 375–405.

Brilmayer, L. (1991), 'Secession and Self-Determination: A Territorial Interpretation', *Yale Journal of International Law*, 16: 177–202.

Brubaker, R. (1992), *Citizenship and Nationhood in France and Germany* (Cambridge, MA: Harvard University Press).

——(1995), 'Aftermaths of Empire and the Unmixing of Peoples: Historical and Comparative Perspectives', *Ethnic and Racial Studies*, 18/2: 189–218.

——(1998), 'Myths and Misconceptions in the Study of Nationalism', in M. Moore (ed.), *National Self-Determination and Secession* (Oxford: Oxford University Press).

Buchanan, A. (1991), *Secession: The Morality of Political Divorce from Fort Sumter to Lithuania and Quebec* (Boulder, CO: Westview Press).

——(1995), 'The Morality of Secession', in W. Kymlicka (ed.), *The Rights of Minority Cultures* (Oxford: Oxford University Press).

——(1996), 'What's So Special About Nations?', in J. Couture, K. Nielsen, and M. Seymour (eds.), *Rethinking Nationalism, Canadian Journal of Philosophy* Supplementary Volume 22.

——(1997), 'Theories of Secession', *Philosophy & Public Affairs*, 26/1: 30–61.

——(1998), 'Democracy and Secession', in M. Moore (ed.), *National Self-Determination and Secession* (Oxford: Oxford University Press).

——(forthcoming), 'The Making and Unmaking of Boundaries; a Liberal View', in A. Buchanan and M. Moore (eds.), *The Making and Unmaking of Boundaries* (Princeton, NJ: Princeton University Press).

Cairns, A. (1991), 'Constitutional change and the three equalities', in R. Watts and D. Brown (eds.), *Options for a New Canada* (Toronto: University of Toronto Press).

——(1991), *Disruptions: Constitutional Struggles from the Charter to Meech Lake* (Toronto: McClelland & Stewart).

——(1995), 'The Legacy of the Referendum: Who are We Now?', paper prepared for the post-referendum panel organized by the Centre for Constitutional Studies, University of Alberta.

Calhoun, C. (1991), 'The Problem of Identity in Collective Action', in J. Huber (ed.), *Macro-Micro Linkages in Sociology* (Newbury Park, CA: Sage).

——(1997), *Nationalism* (Buckingham: Open University Press).

Callan, E. (1997), *Creating Citizens: Political Education and Liberal Democracy* (Oxford: Clarendon Press).

Caney, S., George, D., and Jones, P. (1996), (eds.), *National Rights, International Obligations* (Boulder, CO: Westview Press).

Canovan, M. (1996), *Nationhood and Political Theory* (Cheltenham: Edward Elgar).

Cassese, A. (1995), *Self-Determination of Peoples. A Legal Reappraisal* (Cambridge: Cambridge University Press).

Chabal, P. and Daloz, J-P. (1999), *Africa Works: Disorder as Political Instrument* (Bloomington, IN: Indiana University Press).

Christiano, T. (1993), 'Social Choice and Democracy', in D. Copp, J. Hampton, and J. E. Roemer (eds.), *The Idea of Democracy* (Cambridge: Cambridge University Press).

Cobban, A. (1945), *National Self-Determination* (Oxford: Oxford University Press).

Colley, L. (1992), *Britons: Forging the Nation 1707–1837* (London: Pimlico).

Connor, W. (1984), *The National Question in Marxist Leninist Theory and Strategy* (Princeton, NJ: Princeton University Press).

——(1994), *Ethnonationalism. The Quest for Understanding* (Princeton, NJ: Princeton University Press).

Conquest, R. (1970), *The Nation Killers: The Soviet Deportation of Nationalities* (London: MacMillan).

Crnobrnja, M. (1994), *The Yugoslav Drama* (Montreal and Kingston: McGill-Queen's University Press).

Davies, W. D. (1991), *The Territorial Dimension of Judaism* (Minneapolis, MN: Fortress Press).

de Tocqueville, A. (1961), *Democratie en Amerique* (Paris: Gallimard).

de Zayas, A. M. (1986), *A Terrible Revenge: The Ethnic Cleansing of the East European Germans, 1944–50* (New York, NY: St. Martin's Press).

——(1989), *Nemesis At Potsdam: The Expulsion of the Germans from the East* (Lincoln, NB: University of Nebraska Press).

Dworkin, R. (1971), 'Lord Devlin and the Enforcement of Morals', in R. Wasserstrom (ed.), *Morality and the Law* (Belmont: Wadsworth Publishing Company).

Elazar, D. (1994), *Federalism and the Way to Peace* (Queen's University, Kingston: Institute of Intergovernmental Affairs).

Emerson, R. (1960), *From Empire to Nation* (Cambridge, MA: Harvard University Press).

Emerson, R. (1971), 'Self-Determination', *American Journal of International Law*, 65/3: 464.

Eriksen, T. H. (1993), *Ethnicity and Nationalism: Anthropological Perspectives* (London: Pluto Press).

Etzioni, A. (1992–3), 'The Evils of Self-Determination', *Foreign Policy*, 89: 21–35.

Fearon, J. D. and Laitin, D. (1996), 'Explaining Interethnic Cooperation', *American Political Science Review*, 90/4: 715–35.

————(1999) 'Violence and the Social Construction of Ethnic Identities', unpublished manuscript, 22 January 1999 version.

Foucault, M. (1977), *Power/Knowledge: Selected Interviews and Other Writings, 1972–77* (New York, NY: Pantheon).

Franck, T. M. (1992), 'The Emerging Right to Democratic Governance', *American Journal of International Law*, 86: 46–91.

Fraser, N. (1995), 'Recognition or Redistribution? A Critical Reading of Iris Young's Justice and the Politics of Difference', *Journal of Political Philosophy*, 3/2: 168–70.

Galston, W. (1991), *Liberal purposes: Goods, virtues and diversity in the liberal state* (New York, NY: Cambridge University Press).

Gauthier, D. (1994), 'Breaking Up: An Essay on Secession', *Canadian Journal of Philosophy*, 24: 357–72.

Geertz, C. (1994), 'Primordial and Civic Ties', in J. Hutchinson and A. Smith (eds.), *Nationalism* (Oxford: Oxford University Press).

Gellner, E. (1964), *Thought and Change* (London: Weidenfeld and Nicholson).

————(1983), *Nations and Nationalism* (Ithaca, NY: Cornell University Press).

Gomberg, P. (1990), 'Patriotism Is Like Racism', *Ethics*, 101/1: 144–50.

Goodin, R. (1988), 'What Is So Special about our Fellow Countrymen?', *Ethics*, 98: 3–86.

Graff, J. A. (1994), 'Human Rights, Peoples, and Self-Determination', in J. Baker (ed.), *Group Rights* (Toronto: University of Toronto Press).

Grand Council of the Crees (1995), *Sovereign Injustice: Forcible Inclusion of the James Bay Cree and Cree Territory Into a Sovereign Quebec* (Grand Council of the Crees).

Greenfeld, L. (1992), *Nationalism. Five Roads to Modernity* (Cambridge, MA: Harvard University Press).

Gross, L. (1948), 'The Peace of Westphalia', *American Journal of International Law*, 42: 20–41.

Halberstam, M. (1989), 'Self-Determination in the Arab-Israeli Conflict: Meaning, Myth and Politics', *New York University Journal of International Law and Politics*, 21: 465–87.

Hall, J. A. (1994), *Coercion and Consent: Studies on the Modern State* (Cambridge: Polity Press).

Hannum, H. (1990), *Autonomy, Sovereignty, and Self-Determination: The Accommodation of Conflicting Rights* (Philadelphia, PA: University of Pennsylvania Press).

Harris, R. (1972), *Prejudice and Tolerance in Ulster* (Manchester: Manchester University Press).

Heiberg, M. (1994), *Subduing Sovereignty: Sovereignty and the Rights to Intervene* (London: Pinter).

Heraclides, A. (1991), *The Self-determination of Minorities in International Politics* (London: Frank Cass).

——(1992), 'Secession, Self-Determination and Non-intervention: In Quest of a Normative Symbiosis', *Journal of International Affairs*, 45: 399–420.

Higgins, R. (1963), *The Development of International Law through the Political Organs of the United Nations* (Oxford: Oxford University Press).

——(1994), *Problems and Progress: International Law and How We Use It* (Oxford: Clarendon Press).

Hobsbawm, E. J. (1990), *Nations and Nationalism Since 1780* (Cambridge: Cambridge University Press).

Hoffman, M. (1992), 'Third party mediation and conflict resolution in the post-cold war world', in J. Baylis and N. Rengger (eds.), *Dilemmas in World Politics* (Oxford: Oxford University Press).

Holmes, S. (1993), 'Tocqueville and Democracy', in D. Copp, J. Hampton, and J. E. Roemer (eds.), *The Idea of Democracy* (Cambridge: Cambridge University Press).

Horowitz, D. L. (1985), *Ethnic Groups in Conflict* (Berkeley, CA: University of California).

——(1991), 'Irredentas and Secessions: Adjacent Phenomena, Neglected Connections', in N. Chazan (ed.), *Irredentism and International Politics* (Boulder, CO: Lynne Rienner).

——(1991), *A Democratic South Africa? Constitutional Engineering in a Divided Society* (Berkeley, CA: University of California Press).

——(1998), 'Self-Determination: Politics, Philosophy, and Law', in M. Moore (ed.), *National Self-Determination and Secession* (Oxford: Oxford University Press).

Human Rights Watch/Helsinki (1994), *Denying Ethnic Identity: The Macedonians of Greece* (New York, NY: Human Rights Watch/Helsinki).

Huntington, S. P. (1996), 'Democracy for the Short Haul', *Journal of Democracy*, 7/2: 1–13.

Hurka, T. (1997), 'The Justification of National Partiality', in R. McKim and J. McMahan (eds.), *The Morality of Nationalism* (New York, NY: Oxford University Press).

Hurrell, A. (forthcoming), 'The Making and Unmaking of Boundaries: International Law', in A. Buchanan and M. Moore (eds.), *The Making and Unmaking of Boundaries: Diverse Ethical Perspectives* (Princeton, NJ: Princeton University Press).

Hutchinson, J. and Smith, A. D. (1994), *Nationalism* (Oxford: Oxford University Press).

Ignatieff, M. (1995), 'Nationalism and the Narcissism of Minor Differences', *Queen's Quarterly*, 102/1: 13–25.

Jennings, I. (1956), *The Approach to Self-Government* (Cambridge: Cambridge University Press).

Keating, M. (1996), *Nations Against the State: The New Politics of Nationalism in Quebec, Catalonia and Scotland* (Basingstoke: MacMillan).

——(1998), 'So many Nations, So Few States: Accommodating Nationalism in the Global Era', paper presented to a Conference on 'In Search of Justice and Stability', McGill University, Montreal, Quebec, March 1998.

——(forthcoming), 'Northern Ireland and the Basque Country', in J. McGarry (ed.), *Northern Ireland and the Divided World* (Oxford: Oxford University Press).

Kingsbury, B. (1992), 'Claims by Non-State Groups in International Law', *Cornell International Law Journal*, 25: 481–530.

Kolstoe, P. (1995), *Russians in the Former Soviet Republics* (Bloomington, IN: Indiana University Press)

Kukathas, C. (1995), 'Are there Any Cultural Rights?', in W. Kymlicka (ed.), *The Rights of Minority Cultures* (Oxford: Oxford University Press).

——(1997), 'Cultural Toleration', in W. Kymlicka and I. Shapiro (eds.), *Nomos XXXIX: Ethnicity and Group Rights* (New York, NY: New York University Press).

Kymlicka, W. (1989), *Liberalism, Community and Culture* (Oxford: Oxford University Press).

——(1990), *Contemporary Political Philosophy* (Oxford: Clarendon Press).

——(1995), *Multicultural Citizenship: A Liberal Theory of Minority Rights* (Oxford: Oxford University Press).

——(1998), *Finding Our Way* (Toronto: Oxford University Press).

Laitin, D. (1998), *Identity in Formation; The Russian-Speaking Populations in the Near Abroad* (Ithaca, NY: Cornell University Press).

Laponce, J. (1987), *Languages and their Territories* (Toronto: University of Toronto Press).

Levine, A. (1996), 'Just Nationalism: The Future of an Illusion', in J. Couture, K. Nielsen, and M. Seymour (eds.), *Rethinking Nationalism*, *Canadian Journal of Philosophy* Supplementary Volume 22: 345–63.

Levinson, S. (1995), 'Is Liberal Nationalism an Oxymoron?', *Ethics*, 105: 626–45.

Lichtenberg, J. (1981), 'National Boundaries and Moral Boundaries: A Cosmopolitan View', in P. Brown and H. Shue (eds.), *Boundaries: National Autonomy and Its Limits* (Totowa, NJ: Rowman and Littlefield).

Lijphart, A. (1977), *Democracy in Plural Societies: A Comparative Exploration* (New Haven, CT: Yale University Press).

Lind, M. (1994), 'In Defense of Liberal Nationalism', *Foreign Affairs*, 23: 87–99.

Lipset, S. M. (1960), *Political Man: The Social Bases of Politics* (Baltimore, MD: Johns Hopkins University Press).

Lorberbaum, M. (forthcoming), 'Making and Unmaking the Boundaries of the Holy Land', in A. Buchanan and M. Moore (eds.), *Making and Unmaking Boundaries* (Princeton, NJ: Princeton University Press).

Lustick, I. S. (1993), *Unsettled States, Disputed Lands: Britain and Ireland,*

France and Algeria, Israel and the West Bank-Gaza (Ithaca, NY: Cornell University Press).

——(1995), 'What Gives a People Rights to a Land?', *Queen's Quarterly*, 102/4: 53–68.

MacCormick, N. (1981), 'Is Nationalism Philosophically Credible?', in W. Twining (ed.), *Issues of Self-Determination* (Aberdeen: Aberdeen University Press).

——(1982), *Legal Rights and Social Democracy* (Oxford: Oxford University Press).

Macedo, S. (1990), *Liberal Virtues: Citizenship, Virtue, and Community in Liberal Constitutionalism* (Oxford: Oxford University Press).

Malcolm, N. (1994), *Bosnia: A Short History* (New York, NY: New York University Press).

Mansbridge, J. (1997), 'What Does a Representative Do? Descriptive Representation in Communicative Settings of Distrust, Uncrystallized Interests, and Historically Denigrated Status', paper prepared for the Conference on 'Citizenship in Diverse Societies: Theory and Practice', Toronto, Canada, 4–5 October 1997.

Margalit, A. and Raz, J. (1990), 'National Self-Determination', *Journal of Philosophy*, 87: 439–61.

————(1994), 'On National Self-Determination', in J. Raz (ed.), *Ethics in the Public Domain* (Oxford: Clarendon Press).

Masalha, N. (1992), *Expulsion of the Palestinians: The Concept of 'Transfer' in Zionist Political Thought 1882–1948* (Washington, DC: Institute for Palestine Studies).

McDowell, D. (1992), *The Kurds: A Nation Denied* (London: Minority Rights Publications).

McGarry, J. (1996), 'Ethnic Cleansing: Forced Expulsion as a Method of Ethnic Conflict Regulation', paper presented at the Canadian Political Science Association, June 1996.

——(1998), 'Orphans of Secession', in M. Moore (ed.), *National Self-Determination and Secession* (Oxford: Oxford University Press).

——(1998) 'Demographic Engineering: The State-Directed Movement of Ethnic Groups as a Technique of Conflict Regulation', *Ethnic and Racial Studies*, 21/4: 613–38.

——and O'Leary, B. (1993) (eds.), *The Politics of Ethnic Conflict Regulation* (London: Routledge).

————(1995), *Explaining Northern Ireland* (Oxford: Blackwell).

McKim, R. and McMahan, J. (1997), (eds.), *The Morality of Nationalism* (New York, NY: Oxford University Press).

McMahan, J. (1997), 'The Limits of National Partiality', in R. McKim and J. McMahan (eds.), *The Morality of Nationalism* (New York, NY: Oxford University Press).

McRoberts, K. (1997), *Misconceiving Canada. The Struggle for National Unity* (Toronto: Oxford University Press).

Michalska, A. (1991), 'Rights of Peoples to Self-determination in International Law', in W. Twining (ed.), *Issues of Self-determination* (Aberdeen: Aberdeen University Press).

Mill, J. S. (1993) *On Liberty, Utilitarianism, On Representative Government* (London: J. M. Dent).

Miller, D. (1993), 'In Defence of Nationality', *Journal of Applied Philosophy*, 10: 3–16.

——(1995), *On Nationality* (Oxford: Oxford University Press).

——(1996), 'On Nationality', *Nations and Nationalism*, 2/3: 409–21.

——(1998), 'The Limits of Cosmopolitan Justice', in D. R. Mapel and T. Nardin (eds.), *The Constitution of International Society: Diverse Ethical Perspectives* (Princeton, NJ: Princeton University Press).

——(1998), 'Secession and the Principle of Nationality', in M. Moore (ed.), *National Self-Determination and Secession* (Oxford: Oxford University Press).

Mitchell, P. (forthcoming), 'Transcending an Ethnic Party System? The Impact of Consociational Governance on Electoral Dynamics and the Party System', in R. Wilford (ed.), *Aspects of the Belfast Agreement* (Oxford: Oxford University Press).

Mojzes, P. (1995), *Yugoslavian Inferno* (New York, NY: Continuum Press).

Moore, M. (1998) (ed.), *National Self-Determination and Secession* (Oxford: Oxford University Press)

——(1999), 'Nationalist Arguments, Ambivalent Conclusions', *The Monist*, 82/3: 469–90.

Nielsen, K. (1993), 'Secession: The Case of Quebec', *Journal of Applied Philosophy*, 10: 29–43.

——(1998), 'Liberal Nationalism and Secession', in M. Moore (ed.), *National Self-Determination and Secession* (Oxford: Oxford University Press).

Noel, S. J. R. (1971), 'Consociational Democracy and Canadian Federalism', *Canadian Journal of Political Science*, 4/1: 1–22.

Nootens, G. (1996), 'Liberal Restrictions on Public Arguments', in J. Couture, K. Nielsen, and M. Seymour (eds.), *Rethinking Nationalism*, *Canadian Journal of Philosophy*, Supplementary Volume 22.

Norman, W. (1997), 'Prelude to a Liberal Morality of Nationalism', in S. Brennan, T. Isaacs, and M. Milde (eds.), *A Question of Values: New Canadian Perspectives in Ethics and Political Philosophy* (Atlanta, GA: Rodopi).

——(1998), 'The Ethics of Secession as the Regulation of Secessionist Politics', in M. Moore (ed.), *National Self-Determination and Secession* (Oxford: Oxford University Press).

Nussbaum, M. (1996), 'Patriotism and Cosmopolitanism', in J. Cohen (ed.), *For Love of Country* (Boston, MA: Beacon Press), 3–17.

O'Leary, B. (1994), 'Determining Our Selves: On the Norm of National Self-Determination', paper presented to the *International Political Science Association*, Berlin, Germany, August 1994.

——(1997), 'On the Nature of Nationalism: An Appraisal of Ernest Gellner's Writings on Nationalism', *British Journal of Political Science*, 27: 191–222.

——(1998), 'The Elements of a General Theory of Right-Sizing the State', paper presented to the SSRC 'Right-Sizing the State: The Politics of Moving Borders' Conference, New York, 17–18 May 1998.

Pagden, A. (1986), *The Fall of Natural Man: the American Indian and the Origins of Comparative Ethnology* (Cambridge: Cambridge University Press).

——(forthcoming), 'The Christian Tradition', in A. Buchanan and M. Moore (eds.), *The Making and Unmaking of Boundaries* (Princeton, NJ: Princeton University Press).

Parekh, B. (1994), 'Discourses on National Identity', *Political Studies*, 42: 492–504.

——(1995), 'Ethnocentricity of the Nationalist Discourse', *Nations and Nationalism*, 1/1: 25–52.

——(1997), 'Dilemmas of A Multicultural Theory of Citizenship', *Constellations*, 4/1: 54–62.

Parfit, D. (1986), *Reasons and Persons* (Oxford: Oxford University Press).

Patten, A. (1999), 'The Autonomy Argument for Liberal Nationalism', *Nations and Nationalism*, 5/1, 1–17.

——(1999), 'Democracy and Secession', paper presented to the Conference 'On Secession and the Quebec Reference Case', University of Western Ontario, London, April 1999.

Pellet, A. (1992), 'The Opinions of the Badinter Arbitration Committee: A Second Breath for the Self-Determination of Peoples', *European Journal of International Law*, 3: 178–85.

Pflanze, O, (1966), 'Characteristics of Nationalism in Europe: 1848–1871', *Review of Politics*, 28: 129–43.

Philpott, D. (1995), 'In Defence of Self-Determination', *Ethics*, 105/2: 352–85.

——(1995), 'Sovereignty: An Introduction and Brief History', *Journal of International Affairs*, 48/2: 353–68.

——(1998), 'Self-determination In Practice', in M. Moore (ed.), *National Self-Determination and Secession* (Oxford: Oxford University Press).

Pogge, T. (1992), 'Cosmopolitanism and Sovereignty', *Ethics*, 103: 48–75.

——(1997), 'Group Rights and Ethnicity', in I. Shapiro and W. Kymlicka (eds.), *Ethnicity and Group Rights* (New York, NY: New York University Press), 187–222.

Poole, R. (1996–7), 'Freedom, Citizenship and National Identity', *Philosophical Forum*, 28/1–2: 125–48.

Premdass, R. (1986), 'Ethnic conflict Management: a government of national unity in Fiji', in B. Lal (ed.), *Politics in Fiji* (London: Allen & Unwin).

Rawls, J. (1993), 'The Law of Peoples', in S. Shute and S. Hurley (eds.), *On Human Rights. The Oxford Amnesty Lectures 1993* (New York, NY: Basic Books), 41–82.

Raz, J. (1994), 'Multiculturalism', in J. Raz (ed.), *Ethics in the Public Domain* (Oxford: Clarendon Press).

Rée, J. (1996–97), 'Cosmopolitanism and the Experience of Nationality', *Philosophical Forum*, 28/1–2: 18–22.

Renan, E. (1939), 'What is a Nation?', in A. Zimmern (ed.), *Modern Political Doctrines* (London: Oxford University Press).

Resnick, P. (1994), 'Toward a multination federalism', in L. Seidle (ed.), *Seeking a New Canadian Partnership: Asymmetrical and Confederal Options* (Montreal: Institute for Research on Public Policy).

Rose, R. (1971), *Governing Without Consensus: An Irish Perspective* (London: Faber).

Rousseau, J.-J. (1973), *The Social Contract and Discourses*, G. D. H. Cole, J. H. Brumfitt, J. C. Hall (eds.), (London: Everyman).

Said, E. W. and Hitchens, C. (1988) (eds.), *Blaming the Victims* (London: Verso).

Sandel, M. (1982), *Liberalism and the Limits of Justice* (Cambridge: Cambridge University Press).

Schlesinger, Jr., A. M. (1992), *The Disuniting of America. Reflections on a Multicultural Society* (New York, NY: W.W. Norton & Co.).

Schopflin, G. (1997), 'Civil Society, Ethnicity and the State', paper presented at the 'Conference for Civil Society in Austria', Vienna, Austria, 20–1 June.

Seton-Watson, H. (1977), *Nations and States: an Enquiry into the Origins of Nations and the Politics of Nationalism* (London: Methuen).

Seymour, M. (1998), 'Une conception sociopolitique de la nation', *Dialogue*, 37/3.

——Couture, J., and Nielsen, K. (1996), 'Introduction: Questioning the Ethnic/Civic Dichotomy', in J. Couture, K. Nielsen, and M. Seymour (eds.), *Rethinking Nationalism*, *Canadian Journal of Philosophy*, Supplementary volume 22.

Shachar, A. (1998), 'Group Identity and Women's Rights in Family Law: The Perils of Multicultural Accommodation', *Journal of Political Philosophy*, 6/3: 285–305.

Smith, A. D. (1983), *The Ethnic Origins of Nations* (Oxford: Basil Blackwell).

——(1991), *National Identity* (Harmondsworth: Penguin).

Spinner-Halev, J. (1996), 'The Religious Challenge to Diversity and Equality', paper delivered to the Annual Meeting of the American Political Science Association in San Francisco, September.

——(1999), 'Cultural Pluralism and Partial Citizenship', in C. Joppke and S. Lukes (eds.), *Multicultural Questions* (Oxford: Oxford University Press).

——(2000), 'Land, Culture and Justice: A Framework for Group Rights and Recognition', *Journal of Political Philosophy*, 8/3, 319–42.

——(2000), *Surviving Diversity: Religion and Democratic Citizenship* (Baltimore, MD: Johns Hopkins University Press).

Stannard, D. E. (1992), *American Holocaust; Columbus and the conquest of the New World* (New York, NY: Oxford University Press).

Steiner, H. (1996), 'Territorial Justice', in S. Caney, D. George, and P. Jones (eds.), *National Rights, International Obligations* (Boulder, CO: Westview Press).

Stevenson, G. (1995), 'Federalism and Inter-Governmental Relations', in M. S. Whittington and G. Williams (eds.), *Canadian Politics in the 1990s* (Toronto: Nelson).

Sunstein, C. (1991), 'Constitutionalism and Secession', *University of Chicago Law Review*, 58/2: 633–70.

Supreme Court of Canada *(1998), Reference re Secession of Quebec*, SCC no. 25506 (20 August).

Tamir, Y. (1993), *Liberal Nationalism* (Princeton, NJ: Princeton University Press).

——(1995), 'The Enigma of Nationalism', *World Politics*, 47: 418–40.

Taylor, C. (1992), *Multiculturalism and the Politics of Recognition*, in A. Gutmann (ed.), (Princeton, NJ: Princeton University Press).

——(1999), 'Nationalism and Modernity', in R. Beiner (ed.), *Theorizing Nationalism* (Albany, NY: State University of New York Press).

Tilly, C. (1990), *Coercion, Capital, and European States, AD 990–1992* (Oxford: Basil Blackwell).

United Nations (1993), *Declaration on the Rights of Persons Belonging to National or Ethnic, Religious and Linguistic Minorities*, United Nations General Assembly, A/RES/47/135, 3 February, 1993 (adopted 18 Dec., 1992).

Waldron, J. (1992), 'Superseding Historic Injustice', *Ethics*, 103: 4–28.

——(1992), 'Minority Cultures and the Cosmopolitan Option', *University of Michigan Law Reform*, 25: 751–93.

——(1993), 'Special Ties and Natural Duties', *Philosophy & Public Affairs*, 22/1: 3–30.

Walker, B. (1996), 'Social Movements as Nationalisms or, On the Very Idea of a Queer Nation', in J. Couture, K. Nielsen, and M. Seymour (eds.), *Rethinking Nationalism, Canadian Journal of Philosophy* Supplementary Volume 22: 505–47.

Walzer, M. (1992), 'The New Tribalism', *Dissent* (Spring): 164–71.

Weber, E. (1979), *Peasants into Frenchmen: The Modernization of Rural France, 1870–1914* (London: Routledge & Kegan Paul).

Weinstock, D. M. (1996), 'Is there a Moral Case for Nationalism?', *Journal of Applied Philosophy*, 13/1: 87–100.

Wellman, C. H. (1995), 'A Defence of Secession and Political Self-Determination', *Philosophy & Public Affairs*, 24/2: 142–71.

Williams, M. S. (1997), 'Impartiality, Deliberative Democracy, and the Challenge of Difference', paper prepared for the 'Conference on Citizenship in Diverse Societies: Theory and Practice', Toronto, Canada, 4–5 October.

Winthrop, J. (1964), 'Reasons to be Considered, and Objections with Answers', reprinted in E. S. Morgan (ed.), *The Founding of Massachusetts: Historians and the Sources* (Indianapolis, IN: Bobbs-Merrill).

Woodward, S. (1995), *Balkan Tragedy* (Washington, DC: Brookings Institute).

Wright, R. (1993), *Stolen Continents: The 'New World' Through Indian Eyes* (Harmondsworth: Penguin).

Yack, B. (1995), 'Reconciling Liberalism and Nationalism', *Political Theory*, 23/1: 166–82.

——(1996), 'The Myth of the Civic Nation', *Critical Review*, 10/2: 193–211.

Young, I. M. (1990), *Justice and the Politics of Difference* (Princeton, NJ: Princeton University Press).

INDEX